Malice In Wonderland

"Malice in Wonderland is a totally engrossing inside
look at one of the murder cases that made Los
Angeles a place of endless fascination. If you want to
know the truth about a case you go to the detectives
who worked it. That's what you get here."

—MICHAEL CONNELLY

Malice In Wonderland

The Inside Story of the Police Investigation of The Laurel Canyon Murders

Tom Lange and Robert Souza

Cover and artistry by Teresa Pratt

Copyright 2018 Tom Lange and Robert Souza
LVM Books
Printed in the United States

First Edition (paperback)
LVM Books

ISBN-13: 9780692973615
ISBN-10: 0692973613

This book is dedicated to homicide cops everywhere, past and present. In any homicide investigation, you alone are charged with the daunting task of meeting challenge with courage, rejection with resolution, falsehoods with facts, and indifference with integrity.

Tom Lange and Robert Souza
September 2017

Contents

In order to write about life, first you must live it.

—Ernest Hemingway

Preface

Unlike the familiar sounding title of the Lewis Carroll children's story *Alice in Wonderland*, *Malice in Wonderland* is no fairy tale. This is a firsthand account of what *really* occurred from the two primary detectives who handled the Laurel Canyon quadruple murders. Two other detectives were directly involved over the twenty-year life span of the case. One retired shortly after the original incident occurred, and a second became involved after the retirement of Bob Souza, following some six years of involvement in the investigation. This story is from our perspective alone.

The facts of this investigation as depicted by the two of us are taken from personal journals amassed over many years. These journals encompass hundreds of fact-filled pages, eyewitness statements, and anecdotal stories. Why keep journals? This will eventually become apparent to the reader. When this case became personal to us in so many ways, it became increasingly important to document every facet of our work.

There are no fictionalized narratives between characters and no supposition unless needed for context. There has never been a book attempted or written or a motion picture made that has captured what truly occurred. The few documentaries made years ago barely scratch the surface of reality. This is a story for a new generation. An older generation was offered a comic book version of what could have occurred. This story relates fact, not frivolity. There is no conjecture. It is for people who want to know what really happened in the investigation of one of the bloodiest mass murders in the history of Los Angeles.

This is a story of murder, thieving drug dealers, organized crime, corruption, favoritism, betrayal, and a bunch of very nasty human beings.

This is also a story about a period of time when Los Angeles could have been referred to as a city under siege. From the late 1960s into the 1990s, LA experienced a record number of killings. Several of these high-profile cases are highlighted in this book.

Between us, we have been involved in more than three hundred homicide investigations while employed by the Los Angeles Police Department. We are also both licensed private investigators in the state of California with extensive criminal investigative experience in the private sector. For the two of us, this was by far the lengthiest, most mentally challenging, and most confounding investigation we had ever been associated with. If there was one substantive facet of criminal investigation that was not covered in this monstrosity of a case, we are both unaware of it.

For all our combined fifty-plus years with the LAPD, we not only enjoyed what we did for the most part, but we also respected what we did. We empathized with those we worked with and those we worked for. That doesn't mean we didn't have questions and opinions. We also were fortunate enough to have worked with some of the finest men and women who ever called themselves police officers.

However, all police departments are still bureaucracies. Some are run by people who have forgotten what it's like to wear a badge and to actually get their hands dirty doing honest police work. They have forgotten or simply dismissed the fact that life can be messy and that sometimes there are no easy answers. Some things are not covered in law enforcement manuals, such as how to make a life-changing decision in a matter of seconds. Other agencies, driven by political correctness or concerns about image, cannot fathom that cops are recruited from members of the human race. They are not manufactured to some sociologist's specifications for a perfect society.

In October of 2016, Tom Lange was invited to participate in a program regarding the O. J. Simpson double murder case with the National Law Enforcement Memorial and Museum in Washington, DC. On the day before the program commenced, Lange was given an impromptu tour of the law enforcement museum.

At the entrance to the temporary glass-enclosed facility (a new museum is currently under construction) stands the original Robocop costume from the movie of the same name, which was donated to the museum. It had to be seven feet tall and appeared indestructible and certainly bulletproof. Lange mentioned to the guide, and later to the director of the facility, that they should put a sign just above Robocop when the new museum opens to the public that reads "This Is Not a Real Cop!" It would be gratifying if certain people today would realize that cops are still human beings with all the same frailties and faults as anyone else. The only difference is that they are expected to put their personal feelings and attitudes aside once they put on a badge.

The time will always come when law enforcement has to rise above doing business for appearance's sake or what's socially acceptable or trendy and get down to the real vocation that is police work, regardless of the circumstances.

We have always remembered what the mission of the Los Angeles Police Department was when we came through the police academy some fifty years ago: "The apprehension of criminals and the prevention of crime." Neither of us can recall when we heard that last.

Tom Lange and Robert Souza
Los Angeles
September 2017

One

Monday, June 29, 1981. Midmorning.

Panicked and half out of his mind with pain and sheer fear, Ed Nash could barely breathe as Ron Launius forcefully jammed the barrel of his revolver into Nash's mouth and down his throat as he squirmed on his living room floor. Gagging and choking, Nash pleaded for his life. He knew that even if he screamed, he would not be heard. The sanctity of his home, once considered his refuge, had now been violated. The single-story house sat on a hill at the end of a cul-de-sac on Dona Lola Place in the upscale area of Studio City in Los Angeles's San Fernando Valley.

Then a gunshot! But it wasn't meant for Nash. An accidental discharge from the gun of David Lind grazed Nash's three-hundred-pound bodyguard Gregory Diles in the side. The wound was superficial, but Diles went down to the floor screaming anyway. Standing frozen, Lind, with the rear end of his ragged pants torn out, had that "Oh, shit!" look on his face as Launius derisively yelled at him. At that point both Nash and Diles realized these guys, whoever they were, looked out of control, and they meant business. Nash was yanked to his feet and forced into his bedroom, then led to his closet and a floor safe. It now dawned on him that he had been compromised. Very few people were aware of the concealed safe, yet this bunch knew exactly where to go. A third armed accomplice, Billy Deverell, forced Nash to the floor and demanded he open the safe. Fearing for his life, Nash complied. The safe was emptied of some $100,000 in cash, jewelry (the good stuff), cocaine, heroin, and a handgun. Two antique rifles were taken from the closet. Several other small items were also grabbed up and wrapped in a confiscated shower curtain that had been ripped from the shower stall in Nash's bathroom.

After more slapping around, humiliation, and threats from the robbers, Nash and Diles were handcuffed before the trio searched the rest of the home. Deverell went into his pocket and whipped out a large pocketknife, opening it with an obviously practiced hand. Viewing this, Nash wanted to piss in his pants. But it was not for him. Deverell then went about his preplanned task of cutting all existing telephone lines.

With their search of the house complete, the grubby-looking bandits removed the handcuffs from their hostages and taped their ankles and wrists. The two men were told not to remove the tape until their attackers were long gone. There was no reason to warn Nash about calling the cops. That would be the very last thought a gangster like Nash would have had under the circumstances. And the robbers knew it.

Note: In a subsequent interview with David Lind, he stated that at the time of the robbery, Launius had wanted to kill Nash and Diles, as well as a young woman, Jamie McGuan, who had been at the home. McGuan was dependent on Nash to support her drug habit. She had been passed out for much of the rough-housing. It took a few tense moments for Lind and Deverell to talk Launius out of this, and eventually saner (albeit drug-addled) minds prevailed.

The three assailants made their way out the front door, dropping some smaller items from the shower curtain as they fled toward a 1975 Ford Granada parked at the curb facing downhill. Tracy Ray McCourt sat behind the wheel of the older sedan, nervously looking about as he awaited his three comrades and their newly acquired loot. At this point Tracy wanted only two things—to get out of there quick and a fix.

The stolen goods were tossed into the car, and the robbers quickly followed. Deverell yelled at McCourt to start moving. McCourt put the car into drive and realized the gas gauge was on empty. McCourt had never been considered the brains of the operation, but forgetting to put gas in the getaway car was beyond careless.

The raffish robbers were, however, able to coast down the hill that is Dona Lola Place and out onto Laurel Canyon Boulevard, turn south, and return to 8763 Wonderland Avenue on fumes.

Note: Lange and Souza had often thought about what would have occurred that morning had a lone cop stopped that car for some reason or another and been confronted with the likes of its occupants. Things would have gone sideways in a heartbeat and put the cop smack in the middle of a very bad situation.

Upon their return to Wonderland, the trio was met by well-known porn actor John Holmes. Also present was Joy Miller, forty-six, the girlfriend of Deverell. It was Joy's name that was on the rental agreement for the Wonderland house. Susie Launius had recently arrived to be with her husband, Ron. Their marriage had been in trouble for some time, driven by the violent criminal escapades and antics of the sociopathic Launius. Susie had been residing with her parents in Northern California. She had decided to give the relationship another chance. She, too, had her own unfortunate problems with addiction, as did all the residents of 8763 Wonderland. Barbara Richardson, at just twenty-two and several years younger than her boyfriend, David Lind, was present as well.

John Curtis Holmes was born on August 8, 1944, in rural Ohio. His parents divorced when he was young, and he, his mother, and his three siblings, moved to a housing project in Columbus. His mother later remarried, and the family moved to Pataskala, Ohio. A bad relationship with his stepfather had Holmes leaving home, joining the US Army, and serving in Germany for three years. Upon his discharge, Holmes ended up in New York, where he had his first taste of the porn industry. Apparently, it was the cold weather that drove him to the much warmer climes of Los Angeles. Shortly after his arrival in LA, Holmes met and married a nurse by the name of Sharon Gebenini. The porn business in Southern California was booming, and it took very little time for John to immerse himself in it. He would eventually come to be called the King of Porn.

For some time John Holmes had been totally dependent on cocaine or any other narcotic he could get his hands on. He had funded much of his habit through the theft and sale of other people's property. Some of these thefts involved luggage from the conveyer belts at the Los Angeles International Airport. Holmes had two sources who supplied his dope habit: the Wonderland bunch and Ed Nash.

Eddie Nash, also known as Adel Nasrallah, had arrived in the United States in the mid-1950s from Lebanon. He started small with a hot dog stand in Hollywood and then lived the American dream—that is, with several exceptions. The American dream was never meant to include living the life of a sociopathic, drug-addled mobster and being one of the biggest narcotics dealers and organized crime figures in the history of Los Angeles.

Nash owned several nightclubs in the Hollywood area, including the Seven Seas, the Odyssey, the Starwood, Ali Baba's, Soul'd Out and the Kit Kat Club, a well-known strip joint. There was a style of club for every taste and every fancy, whether it was gay, straight, a combination thereof, black entertainment, rock, or Polynesian. No one ever accused Ed Nash of not being an informed and successful businessman. He was an equal opportunity employer but a vile and brutal one. Watered-down alcoholic drinks and food were not the only things on the menu at Ed's spots. The clubs were to a greater or lesser extent used for illicit drug sales and to further support the Nash criminal empire. It was also well known that Nash had great influence with many people of prominence in Los Angeles. This certainly served to insulate him and his numerous business interests at any given time. Nash was also known to reciprocate in kind to benefactors.

———

Back at the Wonderland house, Billy Deverell, forty-two, divvied up the drugs and cash. Holmes and Tracy McCourt were given what turned out to be less than a half share of what the others received. Holmes was upset and complained to Launius. This went nowhere since Holmes was terrified of Launius and chose not to press the issue.

Holmes was miffed because, after all, he had set up the Nash robbery and left a rear sliding-glass bedroom door open and unlocked for the Wonderland bunch to enter just before he left Nash's home earlier. This facilitated the robbery. But Holmes knew Launius was no one to challenge. The spiteful Launius had a reputation for being fearless and was known to have committed some despicable crimes, including murder for hire.

Meanwhile, it was party time at Wonderland, but Holmes split early. He was still fuming after being slighted on his take, but he knew there was not a thing he could do about it. Holmes was staying at a local low-dollar motel in the San Fernando Valley with his girlfriend, Dawn Schiller. Still legally married, Holmes occasionally stayed with wife, Sharon, in Glendale; however, he had been spending more and more of his free time with Dawn.

Holmes, perhaps the most well-known male porn actor of his time, was between gigs. Blue movie parts were becoming more and more difficult for him to find and keep, mainly due to his drug usage. Holmes had fallen on hard times. His cocaine habit had caught up with him and would become the liability that could one day cost him not only his career, but his life as well.

Tuesday, June 30, 1981. Morning.

Perhaps John Holmes thought that by returning to Dona Lola Place the morning after the robbery at Nash's home, he would not be suspected of being complicit in the crime, or perhaps he wasn't thinking at all—probably the latter. In any event, when he arrived, he was escorted in by Greg Diles. Thoughts of scoring or having a beer with Nash and discussing the day's social calendar were quickly dashed.

Ed Nash was no fool. He'd had nearly a full day to figure things out. In his mind, it had to be Holmes who rolled him and set up the robbery. Even if it wasn't Holmes, there would be no harm in applying a little pressure anyway. Nash could do anything he desired with Holmes. He had used Holmes innumerable times in the past to lure young girls into his lair of ignominy.

Note: The following is the Holmes version of what occurred upon his arrival.

No sooner had Holmes entered when he was set upon by Greg Diles and thrown into a chair. He was then tied to the chair and given a couple of softening-up blows by Diles. Nash was still furious, and Holmes would be receiving the wrath of that fury.

According to Holmes, Nash took his address book from him and opened it up. Nash then pointed to the names and addresses of persons in the book, including family members of Holmes, and threatened to kill them if Holmes failed to tell Nash who had robbed him. Holmes then laid out the Wonderland gang.

There was, of course, the question of just how Nash would have gotten hold of Holmes's address book in the first place. What would Holmes be doing bringing his address book into Nash's home? Was this just another phony story from Holmes to cover himself for rolling over on the victims at Wonderland?

Note: Later, during a casual conversation with Holmes, unrecorded and in a confidential setting, he told the cops, "Nash did it!" when asked point-blank if Nash had been involved in the murders. Of course, it is easy to lay someone out for murder in private, but it is another thing to testify to that statement in open court. The detectives never got that from Holmes.

The real specifics of what occurred during this particular encounter will never be known. However, what is known is that it was during this time that Nash no doubt set his plans for the future of the Wonderland gang once Holmes rolled over. He wanted his dope back. He wanted his money back. He wanted his jewelry, his guns, and everything else the robbers took returned. But more than all that he wanted revenge. He wanted to send a message: no one screws with Ed Nash!

Nash set the plan. Once the location was nailed down, Holmes would return to the Wonderland home that very night and hang out with the occupants. In the early morning hours of the following day, July 1, he would be there to open the front door of the residence and allow Nash's people to enter. It was surmised that during the wee hours of the morning, all the occupants would be either asleep or in a drug-induced stupor. This would make the work at hand much easier. Once inside, the early morning visitors would deliver Ed Nash's brutal, deadly "message."

———

Meanwhile, back at Wonderland, forty-year-old David Lind was preparing to leave for a scheduled court appearance in the Sacramento area. For Lind this was business as usual. Some years back, he had been associated with an outlaw motorcycle club in the Bay Area and had accrued numerous felony convictions. He had spent more of his adult life in prison than out on the street. While away, he would leave his girlfriend, Barbara Richardson, at the Wonderland residence where she would surely be safe with his friends. Perhaps there was not a lot of critical thinking there either.

Wonderland had been a known drug house for some time and, ironically, had been under surveillance by the Los Angeles County Sheriff's Narcotics Division earlier on the night of June 30, 1981. No suspicious or criminal activity had been observed.

As Lind said goodbye to his girlfriend and his brothers-in-crime, he didn't realize that he would never see any of them again. At 3315 Dona Lola Place, some two miles to the north, Ed Nash and a few of his thugs were preparing to commit one of the bloodiest crimes in the history of Los Angeles. Meanwhile, John Holmes lurked about at Wonderland.

Tuesday, June 30, 1981. Late afternoon.

Tom Lange and Bob Souza walked from their third-floor office at Parker Center in downtown Los Angeles to their assigned police cars in the subterranean garage. They were partnered up that week, which included the Fourth of July holiday weekend. Lange's regular partner, Frank Tomlinson, was on vacation for the next few weeks.

Souza had been working solo since his partner received a promotion and moved on. The two detectives would be on call for essentially any homicide that might occur in the city; however, any so-called routine murder was normally handled by one of the LAPD's eighteen geographical homicide units. Souza and Lange's unit, the Homicide Special Section, had citywide jurisdiction and would get the call when a particular division was inundated with cases or wound up with a high-profile situation. Typical of cases handled by their unit would be serial killers or cases involving extensive investigation and travel. During their tenures at Robbery/Homicide Division, the detectives and their unit were involved in some twenty serial killer investigations involving dozens of suspects and hundreds of victims.

Lange and Souza were both on the backside of thirty and well into their careers. Souza stood six feet four inches and weighed in at around 240. Lange was a few inches shorter and stocky. Their appearance together led street people to believe the pair could aptly handle themselves and whatever came their way.

Before they split up for the day, Souza was looking forward to a relaxing weekend in his pool, but he knew the odds of their catching a case were good. With his wry sense of humor always intact, he told Lange, "With our luck we'll probably catch a triple ax murder in the Hollywood Hills or something." The team headed for home realizing the probability of a callout, taking them yet again to another bloody crime scene. Souza's little wisecrack got a laugh out of Lange, at least at the time.

Two

Murder's an Ugly Business

Wednesday, July 1, 1981. 4:00 a.m.

The lock on the electronic gate that blocked the narrow stairway leading up to the front entrance of the Wonderland house had been disengaged. A small group of men wielding lengths of metal pipe walked through the unlocked gate to the front door where one of them tapped lightly. The door opened. The mayhem-minded thugs entered

Susan Launius was in bed with her husband, Ron. Both were in a deep sleep. Two other women in the home were also well into a night of slumber, a fifth occupant was upstairs and "on the nod" watching television. There had been plenty of heroin to go around the night before, and all had taken full advantage of Ed Nash's purloined stash.

Susie was dreaming. She heard a knock at the door. Her hand was outstretched to open it. She felt the bedspread. She heard another knock. She felt herself being moved by a strong hand. The knocking got louder. It sounded metallic. She saw a cloud of red mist erupting. The metal knocking became clearer. Stark, piercing pain shot through her entire body. Everything was wrong! She never felt pain when she was on heroin. The red cloud cleared, and she saw the metallic object in the hand of a vague, large human shape.

There was a noise on the stairs going up. There were rapid footsteps. A TV was on somewhere. Someone hollered, "Ronnie! Ronnie, is that you?" She tried to call out to her husband, but no sound came from her mouth. She experienced the salty, metallic taste of blood.

An unmistakable, yet muffled voice, from upstairs: "Where's your friend with the beard?" There was the sound of furniture crashing into walls. Sounds like drum beats, something getting hit over and over again.

Once more, she tried to call for Ron, but she was choking on her own blood. She rolled over, and every part of her body ached in a dull sort of way. She vomited blood she had ingested and panted for breath. She passed out again. She imagined that the man who had struck her in the head had left her and was striking Ronnie's head.

She heard a clanging noise and a smashing sound with each blow. She could do nothing. She heard "Again! Hit him again!" She opened an eye and saw the shape of the man striking Ron. In an instant, she drifted off again.

Again she heard voices, furtive voices. They interrupted her dream. Then there was sunlight in the room. She wanted to talk but could only moan. She drifted off. Later she heard a different voice. Then she heard the voice say something to the effect of "Oh, man. The bitch is gonna die anyway. Grab the shit and get outta here!" Then it was back into unconsciousness.

So goes the only eyewitness testimony to one of the most brutal mass murders ever investigated in Southern California.

Note: Because of her unconsciousness and the severity of her wounds, the above information was gleaned from Susan Launius over a period of weeks. These were her recollections while in and out of consciousness. It is believed the last quote is from one of two groups of Wonderland cohorts who visited the scene after the attack and helped themselves to whatever they could carry out. This bunch paid attention to everything in the house except the victims. One of the intruders later admitted to stepping over Susie and hearing a moan and seeing slight movement, but he then went on about the business of looting the crime scene, believing that she would die anyway.

The killers moved independently throughout the home as they went about the gory business of crushing the skulls of anyone they found. Their weapons were as crude as their mode of attack—pipes. It was unknown if John Holmes directed any of them to any particular victim, but he certainly knew the layout of the house and where everyone slept. At some point Holmes left his partial left palm print on the upper left portion of the ornate metal bed railing just above the pulverized skull of Ron Launius. The latent print was left in such a manner as to suggest that Holmes had positioned and steadied himself, assisted by the bed railing, and beaten down on Launius's skull with the murder weapon.

Note: All information obtained regarding the Holmes/Launius relationship suggested that Launius reviled Holmes, and Holmes was deathly afraid of him. Launius would never have allowed Holmes to enter his bedroom under any circumstances. There is the possibility the killers forced Holmes to strike Launius as he lay in his bed to further implicate him in the murders. The detectives believed that Holmes was coerced and threatened with becoming victim number six if he did not comply. Or this could have been voluntary on the part of Holmes. The detectives would never know, but it is certainly believable that Holmes was a willing principal, at least when it came to the brutal beating attack on Launius.

Barbara Richardson was sound asleep, lying on the sofa in the front living room area. She was set upon quickly and beaten in the head so viciously that she was knocked from the sofa to the ground where her attackers continued to bash her limp, lifeless body. No defensive wounds were apparent on Richardson's hands or arms, indicating she had no chance to defend herself from the viciousness of the attack.

The killers thundered up the narrow staircase and into the bedroom occupied by Billy Deverell and Joy Miller. Both had been dozing and watching television. Hearing all the commotion downstairs, Deverell had leaped from their bed.

Joy had gotten no farther than the edge of the bed when she was set upon and beaten in the head over and over, so severely that she was not recognizable.

Billy, always known as a scrapper, was up and swinging at his attackers even through the overhand pipe barrage that was being delivered. He would not go down without a fight, but he did go down, and it was ugly. Deverell had several defensive wounds on his hands and arms, indicating he had put up a fight right to the end.

With all five victims either dead or certainly near death, the intruders ransacked the entire home. They were looking for items that had been taken from the Nash residence by the Wonderland bunch two days earlier. Of course, any other loose items lying around, such as handguns, money, or narcotics, would be fair game also.

The killers headed for the front door, their metal pipes still dripping with blood. As they filed out and stormed down the stairs, they passed Evie, Wonderland's pet pit bull. Evie was for show only and more interested in getting fed on time than protecting the premises. She cowered in a corner as they passed.

John Holmes was alone again. Human blood soaked the front of his clothing. He headed for the front door, then quickly descended the stairs and in minutes was heading down Wonderland Avenue on his way to Glendale. Sharon was there, and Holmes was thinking, "She will understand. She always understands."

Wednesday, July 1, 1981. Midday.

Melvin "Whitey" Hull needed to visit Wonderland. So did some other folks with him. No one was answering the phone there, so Whitey decided to take the short trip over and drop in with a couple of pals.

As he ascended the steps, he sensed that something was wrong. The gate, which was normally kept locked, was open. He walked past the gate and found the front door slightly ajar. He pushed the door open and was greeted by the stench of death. A quick check of the premises revealed the untimely end to his dope connection. He discussed the predicament with his cohorts. It didn't take long. They were all in agreement. Why waste a perfectly great opportunity to score? No one was going to get hurt. They were all dead anyway. The intruders fanned out and helped themselves to anything they could carry on their way out the door.

Whitey entered the Launius bedroom. He saw Ron Launius covered with blood, clearly dead in his bed with his skull in pieces. A young woman was lying on the floor, also apparently dead. Whitey stepped over her, and as he did, he heard her moan softly. Thinking things through in his muddled mind and certainly devoid of any compassion, Whitey stated to a companion, "She'll die anyway. Leave her. Let's get moving." And they did.

Note: Information regarding the above was subsequently gleaned from Whitey Hull during a jailhouse interview.

Whitey Hull later alluded to being at the Wonderland location to police but came up a bit short in admitting to any malfeasance. David Lind later stated that a second group also showed up and sifted through the crime scene, helping themselves to anything that was left over. This is somewhat corroborated by the extensive ransacking of the entire premises. Because the trashing of the scene had to take some time, it is doubtful that the killers would have stuck around long after their initial assignment was completed to look any deeper than they felt they had to.

As is apt to occur under the circumstances related above, word of one's misfortune spreads rapidly in the less-than-honorable community of dope-addled thieves. Throughout the day, the Wonderland crime scene was visited by all manner of human jackals. No one even considered calling the cops or anyone else for help, not even anonymously.

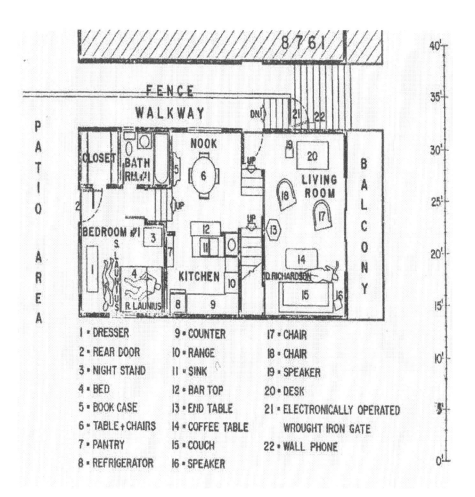

First level of Wonderland house with victims depicted. (H. Huckman)

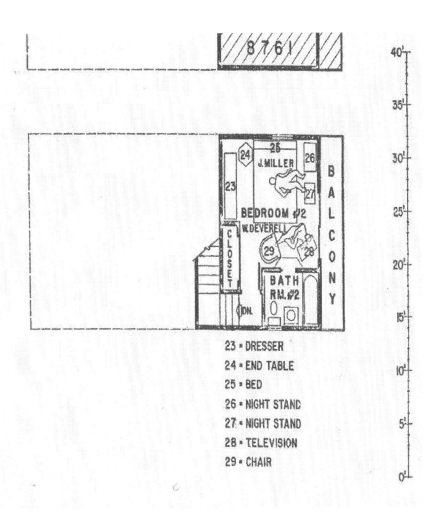

23 = DRESSER
24 = END TABLE
25 = BED
26 = NIGHT STAND
27 = NIGHT STAND
28 = TELEVISION
29 = CHAIR

Second level of Wonderland house with victims depicted. (H. Huckman)

Three

Buckets of Blood

Wednesday, July 1, 1981. Late afternoon.

The neighbors at 8761 Wonderland Avenue, just to the east, had had enough of the folks at 8763. The renters were moving out because their peace was constantly being disturbed by all-night parties and questionable-looking visitors moving in and out at all hours. Whether it was just good sense or plain fear that was causing the exodus, no one really knew. Friends of the tenants had arrived to assist them with the move.

The two homes shared a common staircase from the street level going up for eight steps to a point where the stairs were divided by a narrow brick wall. The entrances faced each other just a few feet apart. As the movers went about their work, one believed he had heard some type of moaning, at times barely discernable, coming from inside the home at 8763. Just before 4:00 p.m., "two or three men" exited through the front door. As they moved down the stairs toward the street, one man shouted to the movers, "There're dead bodies in there!" Then, more than a little curious, one of the movers walked over to 8763, pushed the open door slightly, and peered inside. One look and he was on the phone to an emergency operator.

It was just after 4:20 p.m. when the first police responders from the LAPD's Hollywood Division arrived. After checking with the original caller, the two uniformed officers entered the premises at 8763 Wonderland Avenue and observed the carnage.

The person who reported his observations of the gruesome scene to the police, Bruce Fisher, stood on the sidewalk in handcuffs. Clearly miffed, Fisher, a black man, stated "I'm the only brother here, and I'm the only one in cuffs!"

Note: After observing the bloody scene, the arriving officers, following departmental policy and good common sense, secured the scene and handcuffed the only person present, Fisher. He was subsequently transported to the Hollywood station, interviewed, and released.

Additionally, the "two or three men" observed leaving 8763 Wonderland by the movers were no doubt some of the same lowlifes who rifled the crime scene and stepped over Susan Launius, who was still breathing, but barely. The description of this group given by the moving party was scant at best.

Wednesday, July 1, 1981. Evening.

It was nearing 5:00 p.m. on July 1 when Lange's phone rang at home. His wife, Linda, answered. It was Lieutenant Ron Lewis, the officer in charge of the Homicide Special Section of the Robbery/Homicide Division. In other words, he was Lange and Souza's boss. Lewis told her he needed Tom to respond to a "multi-five" murder scene in the Hollywood Hills. Linda told Lewis she would attempt to reach her husband by phone and have him respond. Lewis also mentioned he was having a problem contacting Tom's partner, Bob Souza. After getting all the basic info, she hung up and called Lange at a friend's home.

Note: There were no cell phones in 1981, so when detectives were on call, it was always a good practice to stay near a phone. Although homicide cops had pagers, they were not always reliable, especially at great distances and in remote areas.

Lange was in one of those remote areas in Agua Dulce, a small rural area several miles northeast of Los Angeles, visiting a friend and former partner. They had been out horseback riding and just might have shared a beer or two. As they approached the friend's place, his wife came running out of the house. She told Lange that his wife was on the phone, and it was urgent. He dismounted and went inside.

Linda Lange told her husband she had just spoken with Ron Lewis, and he needed to respond to a multi-five murder in the Hollywood Hills. Lange was thinking his wife wanted him to get home fairly early for a change, so she had thrown a little tongue-in-cheek BS his way to get him motivated. Tom gave a little chuckle and told her he'd be home soon. She turned serious and gave him the details from Lewis. She also mentioned that Lewis couldn't find Souza. Tom told her he could reach his partner, and they would both respond. Lange then told his wife of two years what he had said so many times before: "I'll see you…whenever."

Lange had Souza's secret number, given out to a very few, and gave him a call. Souza was in his pool on his favorite floatation device with a six-pack on ice and a cordless phone. His wife, Sharon, and their two sons were out of town visiting family. Souza answered right away, knowing only those close to him had his private number. Tom shared the callout information with his partner and got some more wry humor: "Hey, partner. I'll try to work it into my busy schedule. See ya there." Souza's jest about catching a triple ax murder in the Hollywood hills the day before had proved prophetic. The only major difference was that they apparently had a quintuple instead of a triple murder.

Ron Lewis was a straight shooter. He was known for his natty western garb and a penchant for cowboy boots. Certainly not what one would call short, Lewis, at five feet eight inches, was also in excellent physical condition. He was, however, still the butt of pranks for his stature, as well as for the wearing of his boots. They did tend to make him appear taller.

Ron was a good man and took the ribbing in stride. This was demonstrated when he came to work one morning, sat at his desk, and then realized he was seated considerably lower than normal and unable to reach the top of the desk comfortably. It was as if a small child were trying to sit at a desk meant for an adult. After the guffawing died down, he discovered that all four legs of the desk were on blocks.

———

I t was about half past six in the evening, and the sun was beginning to recede behind the Mulholland hills. Moving west from Laurel Canyon Boulevard, Lange wound his way up several narrow streets toward the scene while Souza was still fighting holiday getaway traffic on the Ventura Freeway forty-five minutes out. While the Laurel Canyon area was still a high-dollar section of Los Angeles, the homes were older, and the narrow streets were congested with parked cars. Houses were all crammed close together on smallish residential lots, and the parking was practically nonexistent since driveways and garages were at a premium.

Lange spotted the trucks as he neared the Wonderland location. There were large television units and even larger vehicles with lighting equipment. The media had come prepared after monitoring the police radio frequencies and learning something big was going on. They were ready to make a night of it. The seemingly ever-present media had all the streets near the scene and in the surrounding area completely blocked. At first, there appeared to be no way in or out. Lange parked two blocks down the street, grabbed his briefcase, and began the trek up the hill to 8763 Wonderland Avenue.

As he approached the front of the location, a "newsy" spotted him and ran over. Barely out of his car, Lange had some innocuous question thrown at him before he was besieged by a dozen or more other reporters. One yelled in his direction, "That's not fair! You need to talk to all of us." Ignoring them, Lange walked to the officer standing by the yellow tape securing the scene and checked in. As he did, he was approached by a detective from the Hollywood homicide unit. The detective explained that his supervisor, Detective Russ Kuster, was on vacation, and he was filling in. Lange was a bit disappointed. He had hoped that Russ, who had been his first training officer in the Hollywood division, would be there. Russ was a no-nonsense homicide cop who knew how to get things done. Kuster's assistance would have been invaluable.

Note: Tragically, Russ Kuster was murdered in 1990 in a violent shoot-out with a crazed ex-con, who also succumbed as a result of Russ's accuracy with his weapon after he had been shot. Cops citywide mourned Russ's death, but it was consoling to know that he solved his own murder and in the process sent the suspect straight to hell.

The Hollywood homicide cop gave Lange the short version of what he had already observed. The upcoming walk-through would familiarize him with the actual crime scene up close and personal. He looked Tom straight in the eyes and stated, "Lange, it looks like someone walked through that house with buckets of blood and sloshed it everywhere!" The Hollywood detective led Lange up the stairs and to the front door. Lange figured he had seen it all and was prepared for the worst. And it was.

Souza was driving like a madman now, fighting commuter traffic up a heavily congested Laurel Canyon Boulevard. It was a warm, humid summer evening, and the air-conditioning unit in his 1976 Ford Torino police car had been on the fritz for a week. Souza had the windows down and could hear the whirring of a low-flying helicopter. He knew instinctively it was a police airship circling the Wonderland location where he was headed. He listened to the tactical frequencies on his radio. A Hollywood Division supervisor was requesting additional night watch units to relieve the day watch units still at the scene. Winding up Wonderland Avenue, he saw the media circus of lights, trucks, and cameras. Reporters were milling around the location outside the crime scene tape, anxiously awaiting a press release.

Souza double-parked close to the death house where a black-and-white police cruiser had the street blocked. He immediately spotted his partner holding his ever-present clipboard. His sleeves were rolled up, and he was huddled with a group of detectives on the sidewalk. Souza grabbed his notebook and a flashlight and climbed from his car. Reporters recognized him from other crime scenes and called him by name, throwing out questions he had no intention of answering. A uniformed officer greeted him at the yellow police tape barrier and lifted it for him to walk under.

Lange was outside inhaling some fresh air after his walk-through with the Hollywood detective. Souza trudged up the hill a short distance toward him. As Souza approached, the wry sense of humor was still present. "This isn't going to fuck up my Fourth of July weekend, is it?"

Lange didn't even manage a grin. Judging from Lange's reaction, Souza picked up on the vibe and put on his game face. Lange told his partner, "My head is still spinning from what I just saw inside. It's gonna be a very long night, Souz. I'll brief you as we go. Get your galoshes on; we're going in."

Note: This was the first high-profile case Lange and Souza worked together. There would be several more. From the outset the two detectives clicked and always seemed to be on the same page. Their thought processes aligned better than they had with other partners they'd worked with in the past. Their tactics weren't always conventional, but they were effective. This was a tremendous asset for partners to have, and it worked well for them over the years.

Lange led Souza up the stairs and through an older-looking security gate that had some type of locking device, no doubt controlled from the inside. Lange knew the route to take, and they entered through the front door and moved left into the living room area. Souza's senses were firing on all cylinders, and he knew being observant was the key to a good crime scene investigation.

Lange moved slowly, pointing out everything he had already seen. Souza was taking in everything in his path as Lange directed the walk-through, avoiding blood that had pooled up on the floor. Both detectives were already making mental notes and evaluating the scene, knowing they would soon be guiding their boss, Lieutenant Lewis, as well as several crime lab techs, through the grisly scene. At that time the documentation would begin in earnest.

Barbara Richardson was lying face down alongside a floral-designed sofa. A previously hanging potted plant was lying on the floor alongside her body, an apparent unintended target of some type of a swinging weapon meant for the young woman's head.

She was lying atop her outstretched right arm. Blood had pooled and soaked into the fabric of the sofa where her head had apparently been at the time she was first set upon. She was then either pulled from the sofa or rolled over and onto the floor instinctively during the beating. The blood castoff (splatter from the weapon) "tailed" up the wall and was evident even on the ceiling. The blood splatter didn't only indicate the ferocity of the attack, it also told the detectives that the victim had been continually beaten when down on the floor with overhand blows from a blunt instrument.

Note: The tailing of blood splatter refers to the elongation and direction of a blood droplet as it strikes a solid surface after being flung from the source. In this case, the source appeared to be some type of a blunt instrument. The so-called tail of the droplet is actually the frontal portion(s) of the drop, moving away from the contact point where the droplet initially strikes a surface.

On the wall off to the left, a faint swipe-type blood transfer had been left on the electric light touch plate. It appeared that a suspect with blood on his hand may have attempted to manipulate the switch to the on or off position. The light was off.

Note: Lange figured there was an insufficient amount of blood on the touch plate to type however, there was a strong possibility it was Richardson's. In 1981, DNA was only three letters in the alphabet and not a part of law enforcement lexicon.

Several other technicians from the LAPD's scientific investigation division were busy throughout the downstairs portion of the split-level home under the direction of the detectives. As Lange and Souza walked toward the narrow staircase, criminalist Jason Wasserman summoned them. He had found something interesting in the wall adjacent to the stairs in the stairwell.

They moved about halfway up the staircase, and Wasserman pointed out what appeared to be a small striation pattern indented in the wall. It was located in the drywall about two feet above the stairs. The marks appeared to be fresh. The pattern and the area surrounding it were eventually excised from the wall by the criminalist. There also appeared to be very small areas of blood spatter on the wall in the area of the indentation.

Note: It was later determined that the indentation pattern was made after the threaded portion of an apparent metal pipe came in contact with the wall. This finding was in keeping with the detectives' theory regarding the suspects running up and then down the stairs (relative to the upstairs attacks), swinging their pipes to and fro within the confined space of the stairwell as they ran.

Earlier, a critically injured Susan Launius had been removed from the floor of the rear bedroom that was still occupied by the shattered remains of Ron Launius. She was transported to Cedars-Sinai Hospital. She was not expected to survive. She was found on the floor in the northwest corner of the room, an area drenched with blood.

Note: It was later determined that she had lost something in excess of four pints of blood. The average human body holds approximately ten pints.

The walls, the carpet, and the bedding in the room were all soaked in bloody crimson. Souza commented, "How in the hell did she survive? That's a lot of blood, man."

Lange replied, "She was probably lying there for several hours before the paramedics got here."

Lange continued his guided tour of the Launius bedroom. Additional bloody castoff from a murder weapon was noted up the walls and on the ceiling. The entire room was a pile of overturned furniture and clothing. Much of the contents of the closet had been removed and dumped out into the center of the room, no doubt the work of the loathsome after-action thieves. The water was still running from the faucet into the sink in a small bathroom adjacent to the bedroom. It was apparent someone had used the sink in an attempt to clean up. The sink basin was splattered with blood. The overhead bathroom light was on.

The pulverized head of Ron Launius was lying on a soiled pillow soaked with his own blood. A pellet gun was hanging upside down on the wall near the bed. A hypodermic needle was located in the drawer of a small nightstand alongside the bed. On a nearby ransacked dresser, a narcotics injection kit, also known as a fit, was resting alongside an open pack of unfiltered Pall Malls. Souza remarked, "Pall Malls. Tells me this guy was an ex-con; he's a hype for sure." Lange nodded in agreement.

Note: Of the five victims, Ron Launius was the only one not to have his original position altered during the attack. He died instantaneously as he lay in bed and was repeatedly beaten in the head.

As alluded to earlier, John Holmes's partial left palm print was lifted from the ornate bed railing above Ron Launius. Numerous other prints were lifted as well throughout the crime scene. Dozens of empty aluminum soda cans were found in the open garage beneath the house, near the vehicle of Joy Miller. They were also dusted for prints. Several lifts were obtained and eventually made to the victims; however, many more remained unidentified. Not an overly unusual situation in this instance.

As Lange and Souza ascended the stairs to the third level, sounds from a television set could be heard coming from the bedroom of Billy Deverell and Joy Miller. Lange announced, "It gets worse." The television set was resting on a small TV cart and displayed a pattern of "snow" only. The selector dial was set to channel 3. Leaning against the lower half of the cart was the bloodied and beaten body of Deverell. He was dressed in white painter pants and wearing shoes. He was shirtless.

From the position of the body, it appeared Deverell had been roused from his bed just before being set upon. Due in part to that positioning, it also appeared as though he had fought back against his attackers before succumbing. Lange said, "Looks like this guy put up a fight. Bad guys won this one."

Souza stood taking in the room with his hands in his pockets. "What a fucking mess. This is worse than that Hollywood Thai blood bath at the Jack in the Box." Deverell's head was extensively traumatized. It and his upper body were lathered in blood. Lange continued the tour.

Blood was evident behind the TV cart and throughout the entire bedroom. The floor was soaked with the blood of the two victims, and some footwear impressions were evident in the blood, superimposed over one another, making any type of a match extremely difficult if not impossible. A stereo/radio set was also on, set to an FM station. The reception was poor with plenty of static. Numerous flies were annoyingly buzzing about the room.

Half on and half off the bed, lay the battered corpse of Joy Miller. It appeared she was partially out of the bed when attacked. Her skull was beaten in and crushed so severely from her eyebrows back that it was flat, and she was unrecognizable. She was lying in a pool of her own blood. Dresser drawers had been removed, ransacked, and thrown on top of her body. Drug paraphernalia was evident throughout. The entire bedroom was a shambles. Still-lit lamps and other small items had been thrown around as though tossed about in a storm.

After their walk-through, Lange and Souza exited the house and huddled away from the crowd outside. Souza spoke first. "Looks like those people pissed somebody off. Dope rip-off?"

Lange was contemplating. "A real overkill, looks like revenge to me." The detectives formed a game plan. Lange would walk Lieutenant Lewis through the crime scene and start the interior investigation while Bob Souza took over outside.

Souza marshaled a team of uniformed cops and detectives and began a thorough canvass of the area immediately outside the house and throughout the entire neighborhood in a search for any witnesses or evidence. He instructed his group to document everything in writing and have it photographed if and when it was deemed necessary. Experienced detectives always took the position that there would be someone who heard or saw something that could prove valuable at some point in the future.

Many people tend to disappear when the cops come around asking questions at a crime scene. If the cops can get to these folks in a timely manner, they will be more successful. Wasted time is wasted evidence.

As part of the canvass, the officers also checked out parked vehicles and noted license numbers. The contents of all garbage cans and any apparent spots where evidence from the crime scene might have been tossed were checked, searched, and documented. They searched for any type of evidence, including bloody clothing, weapons, and other personal property.

Note: This commonsense search approach had been used very successfully in the past. Unlike in the movies, most times crooks are not all that smart. They may need to dump an item of evidence in a hurry. The detectives had worked murder cases in which the suspects had actually left their vehicles at or near crime scenes for one reason or another. On one occasion, another suspect even misplaced his wallet containing his identification. It was later found at the crime scene under the bed.

Meanwhile, Lange hooked up with Lieutenant Lewis and discussed what Ron would release to the press. Then, with Lewis in tow, he began work on the inside with the crime scene technicians. The group included latent print experts, photographers, and criminalists. A videographer had also shown up. The video man reminded Lange that he had a shoulder-mounted video camera in the lab truck, and it was good to go. There were clumsy cables and a light to lug around, but the tech thought it might work. Lange decided on the spot and later told Souza they were going to shoot the entire crime scene starting from the outside and then moving to the inside. Souza was in agreement that footage of the victims in relationship to the evidence could be very valuable later.

As they moved through the crime scene, Lange did the narration, and the technicians commented if appropriate along the way. Aside from wrestling with the uncooperative cable and the lighting having a mind of its own, everything fell in place. In just over two hours, the entire crime scene, with the bludgeoned bodies in place, was captured on videotape not only for investigative purposes, but also to perhaps be used in court. The camera captured the incredible violence brought against the victims and in stark reality showed the relationship between those victims and much of the other evidence.

As it turned out, this was a ground-breaking coup. It would be the first time a videotape of a murder scene was admitted in court as evidence in the state of California. Of course, this was not the sum and substance of the crime scene investigation. The overall investigation continued throughout the night and into the next day.

Well into the night, the detectives received word that victim number five, Susan Launius, was still alive and unconscious although her chances of survival were anyone's guess. She had undergone extensive surgery at Cedars-Sinai Hospital in West Los Angeles. Cedars-Sinai was considered a world-class medical institution. Helping Susie's chances of survival immensely was renowned board-certified neurosurgeon Dr. Miles Saunders. Launius was under guard twenty-four seven by the LAPD's elite Metro Division officers.

Note: The detectives later heard from Dr. Saunders that, ironically, if it had not have been for the very severity of Susie's head wounds, she would not have survived. Fragments from her crushed skull had actually served to stem her cranial bleeding by their positioning after the beating, preventing her from bleeding out.

———

Thursday, July 2, 1981. Midmorning.

Night had turned to day, and Lange and Souza hardly realized it. They had been working nonstop for hours. It was important to identify absolutely every bit of evidence and every bit of possible evidence from this incredible monster of a crime scene. All items needed to be photographed and measured in place.

Also removed from the cluttered closet in Launius's bedroom were two antique long rifles. They appeared to be authentic and were booked into evidence.

Note: These antique weapons were originally taken in a residential robbery by Ron Launius and an accomplice. They were later pawned off to Ed Nash by John Holmes. They had been taken back by the Wonderland gang during the Nash robbery.

Everything the detectives observed was documented in writing, even the bizarre. A strange-looking wad of a brown substance was observed stuck to the outside of a kitchen cabinet. It appeared out of place and could not be identified. It was later found to be dog feces, no doubt belonging to Evie. What was it doing on the kitchen cabinet? It apparently didn't play an important evidentiary role in the investigation, and the detectives never figured out why it was there. It was booked anyway. Days later Souza, fearing that the pit bull would wind up in the dog pound or be euthanized, gave her secretly to a responsible neighbor near the Wonderland house who had asked for her.

Note: Whether it is the media, detractors in general (who will always marginalize the cops and their work), or the defense team itself, there are always some who go after the most inconsequential and mundane items or circumstances at a crime scene. They will question why various items were not documented and booked or followed up on, even if those items have no evidentiary value or relevance of any kind. Why? Simple! In the minds of these people or a defense team in particular, it may tend to show that cops miss things or are sloppy in their investigations. Hash tag - Cops on Trial. It was always what cops didn't do that they were challenged on. Ergo...book it all.

———•——

In March of 1991, Lange and his partner at the time handled the murder investigation of one Ronald Kowall. Mr. Kowall had a very interesting occupation. He was the curator of all memorabilia for Batjac Productions. Batjac had been founded many years earlier by the late actor John Wayne. His oldest son, Michael Wayne (a big supporter of the LAPD who was never afraid to voice his support), was now president of the company and had employed Mr. Kowall. Kowall's Studio City home was filled with hundreds of pieces of memorabilia from Wayne's westerns. This included more than 140 rifles and handguns.

Early one morning, after not being able to reach their son by phone, Kowall's parents keyed themselves into his home and discovered his lifeless body on the living room floor in a pool of his own blood. He had been shot in the back of the head with one of the commemorative handguns. Many of the items alluded to were taken by the killer, and the crime scene had been "staged." Staging occurs when a suspect intentionally alters a crime scene and evidence to misdirect the tenor of an investigation.

Lange and his partner solved the case, and during the trial, Lange testified to recovering some 126 firearms that had been taken by the suspect. Per LAPD department policy, when firearms are confiscated and booked, they are always examined forensically for latent finger or palm prints to either incriminate or perhaps exculpate possible suspects. Here, due to the sheer number of weapons and time involved in printing them, the print technician had only processed twenty weapons, referring to them as "representative samples." The defense had a field day. Of course, if the police had printed all the weapons, they would have identified the "real" killer! Aris Karimalis was convicted anyway. He's doing life without the possibility of parole.

Four

By early afternoon on July 2 Lange and Souza were thrashed. While the temperature outside continued to rise, inside the death house, it had climbed to over one hundred degrees. All the windows were closed. There was no central air and no fans in play. Nothing could be altered from its original state until the crime scene investigation was concluded. The detectives had cleared an area in the living room to make their lengthy stay at the crime scene bearable. They were seated in chairs from the kitchen nook that had been cleared, contemplating their next move. Several of the Scientific Investigation Division people were still moving about, and all the victims' bodies were still in place. None of the victims were to be moved until all evidence was documented, and the coroner's investigators had completed their independent scene investigation. Once the coroner's investigators were satisfied with their preliminary work, they would remove the victims.

The blowflies, known in homicide lingo as DB (dead body) flies, were also buzzing about downstairs, seemingly drawn to the stench of the decaying human bodies. Decomposing human remains reeked of an odor no one could possibly adjust to. Nose plugs helped…a little. In 1981 the white "play gel" the police use under their nostrils in cop movies had yet to be invented. Detectives learned that whatever you smell, you also taste, and that is a very unpleasant experience. In the Wonderland house, the decomposition process of the bodies moved along rapidly, driven by the oppressive heat.

Lieutenant Ron Lewis walked inside after dodging the paparazzi, still growing in numbers. He was as beaten up as the rest of the crew. The media outside would not go anywhere until someone talked to them and fielded their questions. Once they exhausted all efforts to corner the cops in the know, they would hang out for their final shots of the bodies coming out on gurneys and the brown coroner's wagons pulling away from the scene. The media always loved this as a grabber for their late-night television audience.

Lewis said he was going to drive home, shower and shave, change clothes, and return to take them on. As he exited through the front door and moved down the stairs, dozens of media folks, some roused from napping, leaped to their feet and ran toward him. Ron ignored their screaming questions and blurted, "No comment at this time. I will give a press release later." He strode briskly to his police ride and jumped in, and much to the disappointment of the press, he was gone.

Meanwhile, inside, the phone rang. It could have been a customer or an associate of the victims. Lange and Souza quickly decided to answer it and play things out, not knowing what kind of info they might obtain.

Souza picked up the freshly "dusted" phone. He casually stated, "Yeah, talk to me."

A hesitant voice on the other end asked, "Ronnie there?"

Souza: "Ronnie's a little busy right now, man. What do ya need?"

Caller: "Who is this?"

Souza: "Robert, man. Who the fuck is this?"

Caller: "OK, that's cool. It's Cherokee. Hey, tell Ronnie and Billy I got nailed for GTA [grand theft auto] in Kingman."

Souza: "What the fuck is a Kingman?"

Caller: "Arizona, man! I got bail last night. Tell him I'll be there tonight."

Souza: "OK. Where you stayin' when you get here?"

Caller: "Hell, it's Cherokee. Just tell 'em I'll be there tonight…Who's this again?"

Souza: "Robert, man. I live up the street. I'm down here feeding the fuckin' dogs."

Caller: "Uh, OK."

The caller hung up. Souza made a note of the date and time and the name "Cherokee."

Between records and identification checks and the dozens of notifications required on a homicide case, Souza handled several other incoming calls throughout the day. He jotted down small tidbits of information, anything he could glean from the likes of "Curly," "Popeye," and "Jimmy D." One thing was for sure: they could certainly have used a phone receptionist around there during the day. Wonderland was a damn busy place.

Two hours later, Lieutenant Lewis rolled up. He could now park a little closer to the Wonderland house since the street cops had a much better grip on perimeter security. As he exited his vehicle, he was set upon by the media once again. Like starving dogs going for the last pork chop, they confronted Ron in his fresh change of clothes. The detective's lieutenant looked like he had just stepped out of a men's suit commercial, smartly tailored and shaved, his silvery gray hair perfectly coiffed and blown dry.

The questions came fast and furious, but Ron was a pro and adept at answering questions without giving much information. The media really couldn't be blamed for their aggression since they had not been formally addressed since their arrival late the previous day. They were hungry for anything thrown their way because of the tremendous amount of interest already building.

Lieutenant Ron Lewis had the demeanor of a losing NFL coach trying to keep his job at an after-game press conference as he tap-danced around the details, much the way he had so many times in the past. After answering a few general questions, Lewis proceeded to deliver a short, terse statement lacking any details or color. He stated that while the five victims had been identified, he could not release their names before notifying next of kin. He told his inquisitive group that one victim was still alive in critical condition and was being treated at Cedars-Sinai Hospital. She had survived surgery. He also explained he could not share any evidentiary details that could "jeopardize the investigation."

Note: Rule number one when dealing with the media in a murder case: always tell them something…never give them anything.

Most in the assemblage of reporters already knew this was coming, but it did not stem their ire at being snubbed, at least in their minds. Of course, the folks in the gaggle already knew there was one survivor and had identified at least one or two of the victims through their own sources. They probably had more info on the neighborhood than the detectives had at that time. There were many situations in which the media had more resources than the police, and they were adept at using them.

Note: In any high-profile investigation, there is always a race between the cops handling a particular case and the reporters assigned to that case to get to any potential witness first. If the media gets to a witness first, it usually taints that person's statement in one way or another. For whatever reason, potential witnesses usually talked differently on camera to the news folks than they did to the cops. Perhaps it's just human nature, but it's real.

It was late afternoon. Because of the multiple victims, four coroner's investigators from the Los Angeles County Coroner's Office had arrived in two vans. The media folks cherished this arrival. Four murder victims being rolled out of a crime scene on gurneys was big news.

The coroner's people entered the residence and began the grisly business of inspecting and photographing each dead body up close and in the presence of the two assigned detectives. It was always a solemn scene with no frivolity when the stone-faced coroner's reps went to work. As part of the procedure, the business end of a thermometer was inserted directly into the decedent's abdominal area and into the liver to ascertain internal body temperature.

The battered conditions of the victims were one thing; the unforgettable stench was another. As impersonal as it sounds, the victims were then only considered evidence, and all courtesies of human contact were out the window. All physical conditions mattered: the positions the victims were in, their wounds, their clothing and jewelry or lack thereof, any blood patterns on the bodies, their liver temperatures, rigor mortis, and postmortem lividity. It was all evidence.

Note: The liver temperature of a decedent is but one factor that can be used in determining an approximate time of death. Normally, the temperature will drop approximately 1.5 degrees per hour under most circumstances. However, there are several variables that are considered, including the victim's physicality, age, how he or she is attired, his or her general health, the substratum (ground), and the ambient temperature.

Once a person expires and his or her heart ceases to pump blood, the body goes through the process of stiffening of the muscles that occurs as a result of the coagulation of muscle protein. It is called rigor mortis, and it is another possible time-of-death determinant. This process usually begins some five to six hours after death, starting in the upper neck and jaw area, then moving down through the body. It takes some ten to twelve hours to complete. Rigor mortis then begins to recede from the body the same way it was introduced and is completely gone in some twenty-four to thirty-six hours.

Another time-of-death factor can be postmortem lividity. Here, when the heart stops pumping blood, the blood eventually sinks to the lowest point in the body due to the forces of gravity. Discoloration will result where the blood settles on the body and become fixed in two to three hours. Fixed lividity can also be used to determine whether or not a body was moved after death.

By the time the coroner's people began their investigation, the bodies were already coming out of rigor mortis. Their liver temperatures were consistent and revealed that death occurred sometime in the very early morning hours of July 1.

Once the coroner's team trussed up the bodies in body bags and placed them on the gurneys, they were carried down the staircase and wheeled over to the wagons, where the media went bonkers trying to assess the perfect shot angle. With the bodies loaded up and the coroner's wagons on their way, Lange and Souza assessed the scene.

The criminalists from SID, along with the latent print and photo people, had done all they could at that point. Although the detectives would no doubt return, this was the only time they would have complete control over the crime scene.

Lange and Souza knew they would have the lab people back to spray ninhydrin throughout the entire premises. Ninhydrin was a chemical that could draw latent palm prints or fingerprints out of porous interior surfaces at a crime scene. The toxic solution reacted to amino acids that form on the epidermal ridges of a human finger or palm and turns purple, making them visible.

Note: At the time, this was a lengthy process that took days to complete.

The investigation would also need a cartographer to compose schematics of the entire residence, inside and out, all to scale. To that end, well-known LAPD cartographer Howard Huckman would be employed. The detectives realized any subsequent work at the scene would be thoroughly scrutinized by the defense, not to mention the media and the public at large.

It was a wrap at Wonderland. The sun had set again, and the homicide detectives secured the location as best they could. Warning stickers designating a crime scene were affixed across the front door jamb, and crime scene tape was draped across the area. A black-and-white police unit with two uniformed officers from the Hollywood Division was assigned to stick around, at least for the night. Lange and Souza certainly didn't want any curious folks, including the media, stumbling around inside their crime scene.

Standing out front on Wonderland, the two weary detectives discussed their plan of attack. Some rest was high on the list after being without sleep for more than thirty-six hours. The news media were lying in wait with cameras rolling. Several frenzied reporters yelled questions and requests, talking over one another:

"Hey detectives…give us a statement."

"Detectives, do you have any suspects yet?"

Lange and Souza ignored the questions and the herd of media dogging them as they made their way to their vehicles. Once inside the cars with their windows up to drown out the questions, they drove away into the night.

Five

THINGS COME TOGETHER

Friday, July 3, 1981.

It was early morning on day three, and Lange and Souza were at their desks in room 321 at Parker Center. The phones were ringing nonstop and people were moving about with a defined sense of purpose. Ron Lewis had assigned a few more people to help Tom and Bob with the phones. Background checks on the victims were continuing. This was an essential element in profiling the victims. Delving into backgrounds on all the players could perhaps lead to additional motives and other facts crucial to piecing the case together.

The decision had been made that Bob Souza would keep tabs on Susan Launius at Cedars-Sinai Hospital. She was certainly not out of danger in a medical sense and continued to be under the watchful eyes of Metro Division officers night and day for her protection against the possibility that someone might want to complete the Wonderland slaughter. Visitation was restricted to immediate family and investigators on the case. Officers had been instructed to detain any visitor who showed up wanting to see Launius. Souza or Lange would be notified, and that visitor would be thoroughly vetted and interviewed.

The LAPD Records and Identification Division (R&I) revealed that Ron Launius and Bill Deverell had extensive criminal records in the state of

California. Both had several arrests and convictions for robbery, assault, drug dealing, and possession of drugs. Joy Miller currently had a drug possession case pending in the Los Angeles court system. No criminal records were found for Susie Launius or Barbara Richardson.

Homicide Special detective John Helvin was one of the detectives assigned to assist in the investigation. He was a tenacious senior detective with the division and had a reputation as an outstanding robbery and homicide cop.

Souza had been mentored years before by Helvin when assigned to a specialized unit in South Central Los Angeles. A series of murder/rapes of elderly women attributed to the Westside Rapist had involved several geographical divisions, and Helvin and Souza were part of that investigative task force. Both Lange and Souza were happy to have him on board.

In 1979, John and his partner at the time, Leroy Orozco, were assigned to the murder investigation of one Victor Weiss, a well-known Los Angeles sports promoter. His bullet-riddled body had been found in the trunk of his vehicle, which had been left in a parking structure at Universal City Studios for approximately a week. Wonderland victim Ronald Launius had surfaced as a strong possible suspect in that case and, at the time of his death, had not been eliminated as the killer.

———

Many potential "clues" were being documented by detectives answering the phones at the Robbery/Homicide Division. Every call was screened as to viability. While many callers may have felt they had pertinent information, many were dismissed for all the obvious reasons. These included basic crank calls and calls from the media, including tabloid folks looking to juice their stories. Once again, it was show time in the City of Angels.

The detectives answering the calls had been given a few facts known only to the killers and the police. These facts were often referred to as "investigative keys" and would be utilized for elimination purposes. Also, in any high-profile case, there were always those who wished to confess to the crime, even though they were not involved. While this seemed to be more of a sociology matter than a police concern, it had to be dealt with regardless. All leads on the Wonderland case were documented, and extensive background checks were completed on all persons involved, including the persons reporting the various incidents.

It was late afternoon just a couple of days out from the murders when a call came in for "one of the detectives" handling the case. The detective answering the call yelled for Lange to pick up. When he did, the male caller identified himself as "Fat Howard." Souza was listening to Lange's side of the conversation and smiled when Lange said into the phone, "Hey, look, while nicknames are fine, I'd like your real name."

The caller responded, and Tom said, "Howard Cook. Great, that's a good start." Souza was busy assembling the first murder book on the case. In the end there would be four additional volumes in large blue three-ring binders. Cook told Lange that he was with someone who had important information on the murders, and it "can't wait." He further stated that the person with him had a girlfriend at the location of the killings who was one of the victims. Cook then said he could bring his friend in, but he happened to "have a case" with the LA District Attorney's office and would like some consideration on it.

Lange told him they could discuss his case later and asked him where he was calling from. Fat Howard told him he was "at the house."

Lange: "What house?"

Cook: "You know…where it happened."

Lange asked, "On Wonderland?"

Cook replied, "Yes."

Lange told him he was on the way, so "Stay where you are!" Lange hung up, telling Souza, "Let's go!" as he slapped the desk to get Bob's attention. Ron Lewis, sitting at his desk nearby, joined the two of them. Lange spelled out the phone call, and the three men were on their way out the door.

Once again, the sun was setting behind the hills as Lange and Souza arrived at 8763 Wonderland. Lieutenant Lewis drove his own car and pulled in behind them. A lone male was seated in an older Cadillac El Dorado parked directly in front of the location. "Howard!" Lange called out. Cook acknowledged and stepped from the caddie. Souza patted him down casually for weapons. It was readily apparent how Fat Howard got his nickname.

Lange took the lead. "So, Howard, where's your friend?"

He responded, "He's in the house. I told him it wasn't a good idea, but he's headstrong." Lange, Souza, and Lewis all eyed one another.

During the brief discussion, a black-and-white LAPD unit with two officers inside happened by after handling a nearby radio call. They pulled over after recognizing Lange and Souza. They were told to notify communications and to stick around since someone was inside the house who, had to be confronted. One of the officers was also instructed to keep an eye on Cook and to run him and his license plate while they checked the pad.

Lange, Souza, Lewis, and one of the uniformed officers drew their weapons and approached the front door of the house. The coroner's crime scene warning sticker across the door jamb had been forcibly removed, and the door was ajar. Scuffling noises were heard from inside the house as someone was apparently moving about.

Moving into the kitchen area, they observed a male biker type around forty down on all fours, gathering up what appeared to be pills and tablets from the floor and filling his pockets. Lange and Souza shouted at him identifying themselves, but he was apparently oblivious, crawling around on the floor like a squirrel gathering nuts. Souza yelled louder and pointed his weapon at the intruder. The man was stocky with a shock of dishwater blond hair. He was dressed in jeans with a chain attached to the wallet nestled in his rear pocket, biker style.

As he stumbled to his feet, he was clearly upset and even distraught to the point of distraction, but not combative. Souza performed a cursory search for weapons and handcuffed him. Lange informed him he was under arrest and removed his wallet to identify him. David Clay Lind said that his "old lady" was in the house at the time of the attack, and he wanted to know how she was and where she was hospitalized.

Note: The media reported that there had been a lone survivor in the attack, a woman. Lind believed at the time that the survivor was his girlfriend Barbara Richardson.

Lange and Souza withheld the fact that Lind's girlfriend was not the survivor alluded to in the press. Lind was advised he was going to be transported to Hollywood Station for questioning. He appeared to have no objection, regardless of the fact that it wouldn't have mattered anyway. The detectives, with their prisoner in tow, moved outside. The field officer with Cook informed the detectives that Fat Howard's 1973 El Dorado Cadillac was registered to Howard Leslie Cook at a West Hollywood address. Cook was not wanted and agreed to follow them to the station. Cook looked over at Lind in handcuffs. Lange reacted. "Lind goes with us." Howard didn't argue.

Upon their arrival at the Hollywood Division station, Lind was escorted into the detective bureau and placed in a straight-backed metal chair, in the so-called free and voluntary room (a little dry cop humor of the time). It was also known as the interrogation or interview room. Souza passed Lind's California driver's license to a Hollywood detective to run record checks and general background information through local and federal sources.

Lange removed the handcuffs, and they were joined once again by Ron Lewis. The small, drab interrogation room was void of any amenities with the exception of a small metal table surrounded by four aluminum straight-backed chairs. The now-crowded room projected an image: this place is for business only.

Wanting to get right to the business at hand, Lange looked directly at Lind and asked him if he wanted to know about his girlfriend, Barbara. Lind had been nervous and asking about her the entire way in to the station. His voice was quivering, and his eyes were burning. He asked, "How bad is she hurt?"

Note: Here was a badass biker, highly charged emotionally, no doubt in and out of jail his entire life. He would not respect any detectives who played good cop/ bad cop or any other phony games with him. Lange and Souza needed him to be straight with them, and they would be straight with him in return.

Lange was at him, hard and fast. "She's dead, David. She was beaten to death."

With this, Lind jumped to his feet, knocking over his chair. As Ron Lewis leaped to his feet, Lind hollered, "They said on the news there was a woman survivor. It had to be Barbara! She never did anything to deserve this!" Sobbing, he asked, "Why?"

Souza responded, "We're hoping you can tell us why."

Lind jerked his chair upright and sat down hard, slumped in the chair. He pulled a pill from his pocket and showed it to the cops. "See this? It's a fuckin' 'lude!" He popped it into his mouth. He again dug into his pocket and threw a fistful of assorted capsules and pills onto the room's small table. He grabbed a capsule. "See this? That's a rainbow!" Again, he popped it into his mouth. Ron Lewis was uncomfortable with Lind's actions, but Lind kept going. Next, "It's a red devil," and into his mouth it went. He jumped up again. The wild-eyed biker was fighting back the only way he knew how to at the time.

Lewis was unsettled and nervous and once again jumped to his feet. Souza told Lind to sit back down and "be cool." He complied.

Lewis started to leave the room and motioned for Bob to join him. They exited and closed the door behind them. Lewis and Souza spoke in the Hollywood squad room. Lewis was not pleased with how the interview was going. "Bob, that psycho in there is throwing illegal drugs all over the room. We're in a police station…this guy is dangerous."

Souza smiled at his boss and consoled him. "Ron, we don't want to put you in the middle on this. This sure isn't quite within policy, but this guy is ready to talk, and I want to hear what he has to say. I can handle him, and I'll shoot the son of a bitch if I have to." Souza loved to shock his straitlaced lieutenant.

Lewis had that familiar look of hopelessness on his face. "OK, I trust you guys. But be careful. I'll be on the air for a while, so call if you need anything."

Note: Granted, this was an unconventional way to interview a witness, but Lange and Souza believed in doing what needed to be done and not to "bother with the deck chairs when the ship was going down."

Unless someone was totally out of his or her mind, let it ride. Lange and Souza needed Lind to trust them. They also had an in. That was to exploit the death of his girlfriend. As tasteless as that sounded; they would use it. It was clear that Lind was the key to what had really gone down and why. They needed to play this out or risk ending up with nothing.

Souza returned to the free and voluntary room carrying a hot cup of coffee for Lind. He was grateful for the coffee and now had something to focus on other than the business at hand and the death of his girlfriend.

Note: It was always good practice to find common ground with someone who had important information relative to an investigation. As it turned out, Lind used to hang out in the Sacramento area, and Bob Souza was raised there. They were actually familiar with some of the same biker types. In the past, Souza and Lange had discussed similarities in their short childhoods and rocky beginnings over beers and realized the importance of connecting.

The Sacramento banter went back and forth. Souza threw out a couple of names matter-of-factly. "Hey David, you know Snap and Springtime, a couple of lightweight Hell's Angels?"

Lind came right back. "Yeah, I know those dudes, from Sacto. Shit, they rode with Sonny Barger out of Oakland for a while."

The two of them were connecting.

Souza: "They hung out in West Sac to get away from the downtown cops."

Lind: "They weren't hiding from the Sacto cops; they were chasing young tail and looking for grass in West Sac. It was easier to find on that side of the river."

The patter was reminiscent of two guys raised in the same city but on opposite sides of the street.

There was a light tap on the door. A Hollywood detective entered with Lind's driver's license and several other sheets of paper regarding his background. The detective couldn't take his eyes off the pills scattered on the table. A quick glance at the rap sheet indicated David Lind had arrests and convictions for burglary, robbery, auto theft, drug possession, and dealing…and that was just the first page.

Souza scanned the rap sheet and placed the papers face down on the table. "Wow, you've been a bad boy, David."

Lind was getting higher by the minute and told Souza, "Yeah, well, it's the life, man. I ain't proud, but what the fuck?"

Lange went at Lind. "Tell us what's going on up at Wonderland. What happened? Who would kill Barbara?"

Note: Using his girlfriend's first name made it personal. An important connection had been made.

The sobs came intermittently, but he wanted to talk. Lind was still a potential witness in a murder investigation, and until things changed, he would be treated as a witness regardless of his past. The detectives let him drop pills and were not about to admonish him regarding his use of drugs in their presence as long as he cooperated and didn't go ballistic on them.

Lind was beginning to open up more and told the detectives about staying at Wonderland with Launius, Deverell, and the women. According to him, everyone in the house was doing drugs, and they were dealing out of the place. They had been setting up robberies of dope dealers in the Los Angeles area and taking the dealers down. They also dealt in stolen property. About this time Lind began to sob again. The drugs were doing a number on him, and Lange and Souza were lapping it up. They had the witness they needed and weren't about to shut him down. Lind told them over and over again how much he loved his girlfriend, Barbara. Their hook was set.

Knowing they were moving in the right direction, Lange asked him outright, "Who did the murders?"

He stated he knew "exactly" who was involved. He told them, "John fuckin' Holmes and his sand-dude gangster buddy" did the murders.

Souza asked, "The porn star John Holmes?"

Lind responded, "Porn star, my ass. Porn punk, maybe." Lind went on to say that porn actor John Holmes had set up a robbery at the home of Ed Nash, a local drug dealer who lived in Studio City. He further stated that Nash sold drugs out of his home and that he, Bill Deverell, and Ron Launius had ripped Nash off for dope, money, and guns "a couple of days ago."

Lind was outraged and jumped to his feet once again. He had worked himself into a frenzy. He grabbed another pill from the table. "A Christmas tree!" He popped it into his mouth. He was clearly frantic but no threat to the cops.

Souza stood again and exited the room to run down Lieutenant Lewis to tell him they had suspects and a strong motive. Lange made small talk with Lind, who was rapidly coming apart from despondence and drugs. Lange took notes while Lind ranted on and became a bit concerned when Lind kept repeating himself, saying, "I don't give a shit!"

Lange was thinking, "Could be good … could be bad."

Souza returned to the interview room and told Lange that Lewis had left for home but had yet to arrive there. There was no response when he tried Ron on the police radio. The detectives continued with Lind and were prepared to go all night, as long as Lind was coherent. Both detectives were amazed that one man could do so many different drugs in that quantity and still be conscious.

The pill-popping biker opened up completely, providing more and more details. He laid out the Nash robbery as well as all the activities at Wonderland. However, all the pills he had been popping were having an effect on his speech and thought process. Among Lind's revelations was that the Nash robbery getaway car had been driven by a guy called Tracy McCourt, one of the Wonderland regulars. Lind was also clearly hateful of John Holmes and his wormy antics.

Lind believed Holmes had rolled over on him and his partners to Nash and that Nash sent people over to Wonderland for payback and retrieval of his property. He prattled on about Holmes being terrified of Ron Launius and very upset over the fact that he and McCourt only received a small share of the booty from the Nash robbery.

Lange and Souza had Lind go over the robbery details a second time to check out his memory and test his veracity. The detectives hoped that one day, Lind would testify in court. He most certainly would have to come off as straight and forward, regardless of his checkered past.

Lind also continued to drop several names, one being "Cherokee," a friend of Ron and Susie Launius from Sacramento. It was Cherokee who had called the Wonderland house and spoken to Souza when the crime scene was being processed. According to Lind, another visitor to the Wonderland house was Chuck Negron, lead singer with the rock group Three Dog Night, and his wife, Julia. Lind chuckled when he told the detectives that Joy Miller had a crush on Negron and it irritated the hell out of Billy Deverell.

Chuckling, Lind said he had Nash and his bodyguard (Greg Diles) on their knees and begging for their lives after he accidentally shot and grazed Diles during the robbery. He knew he'd pissed off Launius. He explained how Nash was humiliated when he was forced to open his safe and turn over his drugs and a large amount of cash. He also mentioned that Launius had wanted to kill Nash, his bodyguard, and a young woman who was staying at the home during the time of the robbery, but was talked out of it by Deverell and, to some extent, Lind himself.

Lind was proud of using a stolen San Francisco police badge as a ruse to gain entry prior to committing dope rip-offs. As it turned out, the Wonderland gang had been using this mode of operation, or modus operandi, in several rip-offs of dope dealers around the Los Angeles area. It had served them well.

Note: Obviously, Lind and his group didn't realize, or maybe didn't care, that that particular ruse could tie them to other robberies, making them stronger candidates for investigation, arrest, and eventual time in prison. It was always interesting to note that most robbers never seemed to realize that the more robberies they were tied to, the greater the chance that they would be caught. This, of course, was due to larger police concentration on a larger number of crimes committed with the same MO. It appeared that a lot of these thugs never realized the value of mixing their methods of operation.

Souza grabbed another cup of coffee for Lind and had him sit tight while he and Lange excused themselves and stepped outside the room. They had a decision to make, and Lind's future was in their hands. If they booked Lind for something, anything, there was the possibility he would feel like they betrayed him. If they kicked him loose, he might get into the wind, and they would never see him again. There was also the possibility that he would end up at the coroner's office as one of their customers if he went after Nash. It was a crapshoot, but they decided to kick him loose and let Fat Howard play babysitter for a while. Cook needed a favor with the DA's office, and the detectives would hold that in abeyance. They would play it out and keep Fat Howard on a tight leash.

Lind had dozed off in the free and voluntary room. The detectives roused him and gave him the usual admonishments about not leaving town after telling him they weren't going to book him. This was after they explained to him that he could be returned to prison after forcing his way into a secured crime scene that had been officially and lawfully closed off to everyone. He was told to stay close and keep in touch with the investigative team and Fat Howard. They made it clear that they wanted to be able to reach him with one call to Cook. For what it was worth, he agreed.

Howard Cook later proved to be a valuable source when it came to getting background information on the Wonderland bunch and their associates. He had been doing business with the group for some time. It's the kind of business the cops called RSP (receiving stolen property).

The Casting Office was a bar about three miles, as the crow flies, from Hollywood Station. Lange and Souza found themselves there some twenty minutes after Fat Howard took off with David Lind. It was a good time to catch their collective breath, have a cold one, and put their heads together. They had both found that these little sessions were not just for the sake of morale but were essential in forming any upcoming game plan.

When homicide detectives are officially off the clock and wrapping things up for the day, going home isn't always the easiest thing to do. Complex cases have a tendency to hang around twenty-four seven. If detectives didn't gear down and brainstorm from time to time, they would be much the worse for wear, physically and psychologically.

Six

It was going on 9:00 a.m. the following day. Souza and Lange pulled into the driveway of a large estate just off Laurel Canyon Boulevard in the Mount Olympus area of LA. As they drove in through the tall, decorative pilasters and up the winding driveway, they discovered that the palatial entry was one thing; the grounds were yet another. Approaching the main house, it was apparent the place needed to be under the care of a decent landscaper. The outward appearance of the house was no different. It was a very large, ornate structure, no doubt built back in the 1920s. It was in serious need of some tender loving care and a little paint.

The detectives' newly acquired and highly regarded witness, David Lind, had led them there with an assist from Fat Howard. Cook had filled in a few blanks following Lind's interview. He was definitely in the know about a lot of things regarding a lot of people. Two of those folks Howard and Lind knew were Chuck and Julia Negron, who also paid the rent on this Mount Olympus monstrosity. Chuck Negron had been the lead singer of the rock group Three Dog Night before the group split.

Chuck answered the door in his bathrobe. Lange and Souza identified themselves, and he let them in. It was as if he was expecting the detectives and didn't question their presence. He appeared disheveled and a bit confused, like he might have had a rough night. Oddly and without provocation, Negron turned away from the detectives and placed his hands in the small of his back in the standard handcuffing position. Lange quickly told him to relax and that they were not there to make an arrest.

Fidgeting with his robe, Negron told Lange and Souza he would get dressed, but they told him not to bother. Lange spoke first. "We just have a few questions."

Before anything else was said, Negron stated, "Oh. This is about the thing in the canyon? I figured you guys would be by."

Chuck's wife, Julia, suddenly appeared and joined the trio in the foyer. Her overall appearance and demeanor were much the same as her husband's. She was cooperative as well.

The detectives separated them and spoke with each separately. Lange escorted Julia to the kitchen area, and Souza stayed with Chuck. Splitting them up was a basic investigative technique that avoided the situation of one witness influencing the other witness's recollections. The detectives would compare notes later and decide whether or not to make a second visit.

Chuck Negron related to Souza how he had first met Joy Miller three years earlier, just after her divorce, in the West Los Angeles area. He stated that Joy was his connection to the group up at Wonderland. "I scored some 'ludes from her at first. Light weight shit. Later, me and Julia scored blow and smack and whatever else we needed. Christ, Julia and I went through over a million bucks in smack in two years!" Chuck further stated Joy was "a sweet lady" who had the "hots" for him, and that had upset her boyfriend, Billy Deverell. Negron stated that once while at Wonderland, he heard about "a fat guy who fences stolen shit" through Joy and the others at the house. He also told the detective, "Joy was in way over her head, man." He identified Howard Cook as the fence and said Cook had introduced Joy to Billy Deverell. According to Negron, "Joy didn't know how fast that crowd was."

Negron became more relaxed, as though he was getting a huge load off his mind. He continued in his effusive manner, stating that on another occasion up at Wonderland, he saw a biker type, "Dave," come in with his girlfriend, "Barbara," who he believed was killed at the house. He had heard that Dave was doing burglaries with "Barb," who would crawl into homes through people's pet doors, then let Dave in to plunder.

Note: This was never confirmed or raised by others.

Julia Negron was talkative as well, and Lange was busy taking notes. She stated that Dave had "kidnapped" them on one occasion because they owed him money. However, things were "straightened out" shortly thereafter. Julia believed Dave wasn't a "bad guy," but there was a "wacko" named "Ronnie" who was "mean and vicious and lived there."

Chuck Negron later stated that he believed Joy was "the best thing that ever happened to Billy." Billy had "cleaned his act up" for a while but then began "chipping" and before long was back doing the "hard stuff." Then Joy had gotten involved with the same bad drugs. Chuck said that on the very night of the murders, just hours before everyone was killed at Wonderland, he had received a phone call from Joy. She wanted the Negrons to come over and partake in a "righteous score." Chuck said they had declined because they were "too sick." Later, they found out just how fortunate it was for them to have been "too sick." Lange and Souza both knew the kind of "sick" Negron referred to was drug sick.

Chuck was asked if he knew John Holmes. He did. He stated Holmes was a porn actor who was a regular at Wonderland, "He's always broke" and "scheming to scam for cocaine." Negron elaborated, explaining that Holmes was a "wannabe" and tried to act "tough." Holmes was always bringing stolen items into the house, such as radios, television sets, and even guns. Other observations by Negron included Ron Launius slapping Holmes around on various occasions. Also, Billy was trying to run their dope business like a legitimate undertaking. One time, Billy had been furious with Joy because he learned that she had given Holmes a key to the Wonderland house.

Julia Negron closed out her interview with a bit of a jolt. She admitted that during the later morning hours of July 1, she had gone by the Wonderland home and seen the front door ajar. Evie, the pit bull, was loose. She stepped into the home after knocking and observed the bloodied body of Barbara Richardson. She turned around quickly and fled. She stated that she had told a neighbor about her discovery and assumed the neighbor would call the police. It didn't happen.

Note: It is important to mention here that sometime after these murders occurred, Chuck Negron left whatever drug-induced, mucked-up life he was a part of and decided to change for the better. He apparently still tours and was last known to perform in Rancho Mirage, California, in November of 2016.

———————

The workload was piling up. Information on victims and potential suspects was pouring in fast and furious. Lange and Souza were getting some help from others in the unit, but those detectives also had their own cases that needed attention. It was decided that Souza and Lange would split up temporarily and divide the workload on the Laurel Canyon case. The all-important autopsies had been scheduled, and it was critical for a member of the assigned team to attend the postmortem exams. It was decided that Souza would stand the "posts" while Lange tended to all the other matters flooding into the office. Much of the info was time sensitive and in need of immediate attention.

———————

The address was well known to every homicide cop in the County of Los Angeles: 1104 North Mission Road in LA. It was the Los Angeles County Medical Examiner's Office, simply referred to as the coroner's office. In 1981 it was headed by world-renowned forensic pathologist Dr. Thomas Noguchi, Chief Medical Examiner, also known as the Coroner to the Stars. It's there that the homicide investigator learned all about just *who* the victim was and *how* he or she died. Also *when* and perhaps *where* the victim had died, and, with any luck, glean evidence to those ends. Detectives learned *what* the injuries were and *which* were fatal as well as *why* and *how* they produced death. The autopsy was a critical evidentiary examination, and an investigative officer had to attend in every case.

Note: Dr. Noguchi had personally conducted postmortem exams on Marilyn Monroe, Robert Kennedy, and Sharon Tate. He had also conducted exams in prior cases assigned to Detectives Souza and Lange.

Souza arrived at the coroner's office and parked in the rear of the facility. He was early, which in itself was a rare feat for him. The coroner's office is a part of the sprawling Los Angeles County Hospital complex in nearby East Los Angeles. Souza entered through the rear where the bodies were normally wheeled in. Once inside, it was not unusual to see one to two dozen bodies lined up in the corridor, sometimes two or three to a gurney. This was especially true on weekends. It was a 365/24/7 operation. Souza was met by pathologist Dr. Ronald Kornblum, a senior medical examiner. He was expected by the doctor as they had four examinations to perform that day. They got right to it.

Souza did not particularly enjoy this part of his job (no one really did), but when you had no choice, that made it easier. With most detectives it was the foul, nauseating odor of the specimen preservative mixed with the stench of decomposing human remains. This was where many cops learned to smoke cigars!

Throughout the lengthy procedure, Souza was to take extensive notes, ask many questions, and closely observe a photographer from the coroner's office, who would memorialize all facets of the examination. Most importantly, during all this Souza would have to dodge the inadvertent splattering of human blood and entrails.

Note: At the time of the Laurel Canyon autopsies, attending detectives were not required to be "gowned" or to wear rubber gloves, masks, or protective footwear. Later, the era of airborne pathogens changed all that.

Standing in the main autopsy room, Souza watched two other autopsies being conducted by two other pathologists. It was a busy day at the "canoe makers," as cops called the place. Bob recalled a young auto theft unit detective who had aspired to work homicide when Souza was assigned to the Hollywood homicide unit. The detective asked to accompany Souza to a postmortem exam on one of his cases. Souza took the young and inexperienced detective along. After the exam had commenced, the rookie detective turned yellow and green, became dizzy, and finally fainted as the pathologist began his *Y* incision. The young cop later decided to forego a stint in the homicide unit and stay with the auto theft section at Hollywood.

Each body to be examined was placed on a stainless-steel gurney. The gurney had a six-inch curbing around its entire circumference to capture any fluids or other evidence. Prior to the exam, each body had been washed down, weighed, measured, toe-tagged, and photographed. This also included close-ups of any wounds or infarctions to the body. For obvious reasons the autopsy room was well lit…and very busy.

Toxicology testing was to be completed on all victims, utilizing their blood and tissue samples. Certain substances would be checked for, such as alcohol, poisons, and narcotics. The results took some two to three weeks to process.

Needle marks or "tracks" (evidence of drug use), some new, some old, were evident on three of the four victims. None were apparent on Richardson. Ron Launius's right arm was abscessed due to the injection of drugs. Billy Deverell's needle marks were observed on the insides of his arms. They were somewhat obscured by tattoos, many of which he probably received while in custody and were intended to cover the needle tracks. Souza knew well that junkies often went to extreme measures to hide their tracks.

All four victims had been repeatedly beaten in the head with apparent blunt objects. The worst of the group was Joy Miller. Her head had been battered flat from the eyebrows back. The only victim with apparent defensive wounds was Bill Deverell. It was clear from the crime scene observations that he had been able to fight back against his attackers to some extent. Some of Deverell's fingers and ribs were also fractured. That would be indicative of him attempting to defend himself while engaging his assailants.

A scalpel was used to cut a *Y* incision into the thorax region of each victim, beginning at the top of each shoulder and slicing downward at an approximate forty-five-degree angle across the chest toward the navel where the two incisions met. After the large flap of flesh that was the chest area was separated with the scalpel and peeled back over the face and head, the bones of the rib cage were exposed. The entire rib cage was then cut out and removed utilizing what appeared to be an everyday hedge clipper with a small two or three inch crescent-shaped blade.

Utilizing the scalpel, the internal organs were then cut out of the thorax region and removed for cross sectioning. This created a "canoe" effect in the chest cavity. Samples were then sliced from each organ for toxicology examination and placed in specimen jars. The stomach was sliced open and checked for contents. If any were discovered, they would be examined thoroughly in an attempt to indicate what had been consumed as a final meal.

Note: This can assist in determining the time of death vis-à-vis the last meal as it relates to the digestive process. Sometimes, the contents themselves might later figure in as evidence.

The head of each decedent was propped up on a wooden "pillow." An incision was made with a scalpel, roughly from ear to ear, slicing the scalp around the back of the head. The scalp was then pulled forward and down over the face of each body, leaving the skull exposed. Utilizing a small handheld circular saw and raising a deafening high-pitched whine, an assistant then cut into the skull, moving the saw around the entire circumference of the cranium.

Note: This was where it became important for the detective to know where not to stand. Getting blasted with "skull dust" was not desirable.

Once this procedure was complete, the skullcap was pried off and removed, exposing the brain. Because all the skulls of the decedents had been repeatedly bashed in, this became somewhat of a challenge. For the most part, the skulls of all the victims had been cracked and shattered. Striation marks were evident in some portions of their skulls.

As would be expected, all the victims had blunt-force trauma and extensive brain damage exerted by blunt instruments. Dr. Kornblum believed these wounds were characteristic of the threaded end portion of a metal pipe. He further opined that the pipe inflicting the wounds measured 0.75 to 1.5 inches in diameter.

Once each examination was complete, all the organs were placed into plastic bags. The bags were then placed back into the chest cavities, which were sewn closed with heavy twine.

Before leaving the coroner's office to join Lange in the RHD office, Souza spoke with Dr. Kornblum. The doctor believed it would be beneficial for him to examine Susan Launius, dead or alive, for evidentiary and comparative purposes regarding her wounds. Bob agreed and advised Kornblum that he would speak to Dr. Saunders at Cedars-Sinai and pave the way for the examination.

Note: Unknown to some people is the fact that the coroner in Los Angeles County is the number one law enforcement official in the county. It is not the district attorney, the sheriff, or any police chief. The coroner makes the call in all instances of death.

Back at Parker Center, Souza parked his vehicle in one of the homicide callout spaces and walked over to the nearby car wash at the rear of the police building. He walked through the remaining soapy water left from the last car washed. Souza and Lange often used the car wash to eliminate any residue of the coroner's office left on their shoes. He then entered Parker Center and walked to the basement shoeshine stand to shine up his ostrich Tony Lama cowboy boots.

Note: Booties were still a thing of the future, at least as far as homicide cops attending autopsies knew.

All the tiered customers' seats were empty that late afternoon, and Souza greeted Horace, the Shine Master. Horace had a perpetual smile and a great gig, owning the shoeshine concession at Parker Center for several years. He liked cops and gave a good shine for a good price. Cops would never walk away from Horace without leaving a good tip.

He was an older gray-haired black man, happy to have a permanent position. He shined everybody's shoes from Chief Daryl Gates on down to the rank and file and never complained about anything. Souza climbed up on one of the raised chairs.

"How's it going, young man?"

Souza replied, "Fine, just fine. Same old shit, my man."

Horace asked, "The usual?"

"Yes, sir," Souza responded.

———

The next day, Lange was back at his desk, putting more info together on the four victims. He was also taking calls screened by others in the office that sounded productive. Souza was on his way to Cedars-Sinai Hospital to meet up with Dr. Kornblum and Dr. Saunders to discuss the condition of Susan Launius and compare her wounds with those of the four decedents.

Upon his arrival at Cedars-Sinai, Bob met Dr. Saunders in his office. For a talented neurosurgeon of his stature, Saunders was very congenial and down to earth. Souza was glad to see that the one survivor, Susan Launius, was under his continued care. It was obvious to Souza that Dr. Saunders was not eager for a pathologist to examine his patient. Saunders consented but insisted on being present with Kornblum during the examination process.

They were joined shortly by Dr. Kornblum. Souza and the two doctors were seated in Saunders's office. Souza noticed the stark contrast between a doctor who worked on live humans and one who examined dead bodies. Souza had stood clinical autopsies performed by doctors in hospitals before, and there was no comparison to the canoe makers on Mission Road.

Saunders and Kornblum discussed the specifics of the day's examination of Ms. Launius. Dr. Kornblum related that he would like to examine her and document her injuries to determine if they were consistent with those of the decedents.

Ever protective of his patient, Dr. Saunders produced x-rays of Susie's wounds. That led Kornblum to relate that he needed to examine the patient firsthand. While x-rays were helpful, a personal examination would be preferable. Foregoing any possible legal entanglements, Dr. Saunders relented.

Souza watched with fascination as Dr. Kornblum conducted his examination of the still-comatose Susan Launius. Miles Saunders was apprehensive, holding out a warning hand and stepping between Kornblum and Susie when the pathologist got too close to a particular wound. Kornblum documented his findings and observations on a clipboard with the schematic of a female body. Throughout the process, Dr. Saunders intervened from time to time, suggesting that Kornblum was coming too close to Susie's fragile skull; however, his intentions were altruistic and not in any way meant to stymie Dr. Kornblum's efforts. The finding: Susan's wounds were consistent with those of all the decedents. It was determined also that a common type of murder weapon had been used on all five victims…a metal pipe.

In delving into the past histories of the Wonderland victims, the number one badass appeared to be Ron Launius. Detectives John Helvin and Leroy Orozco, Homicide Special detectives, expanded on information regarding Launius as a suspect in the killing of Los Angeles sports promoter Vic Weiss. The team had an informant who related that Launius had showed up at a home in Long Beach to pick Weiss up and transport him to a party. Days later, Weiss was found shot dead in the trunk of his vehicle. If true, that would mean Ron Launius might have been the last person to see Vic Weiss alive. While Helvin and Orozco continued with their investigation, that scenario clearly had more questions than answers.

It was soon discovered Launius had a court date in Sacramento on July 2, 1981, on drug charges. The Yuba County Sheriff's Office in Northern California was contacted regarding Launius. One of the detectives who had known Launius for several years sarcastically stated that the death of Ron Launius was "a real loss to the greater community of criminals, an act of poetic justice."

The same detective stated Launius had received a bad conduct discharge from the US Air Force. He related Launius had also been involved in several drug heists as well as other robberies and possibly even a murder for hire.

Bill Deverell had a criminal record dating back to the 1950s for robbery, assault, burglary, drugs, and drunk driving. His estranged wife and daughter resided in the San Gabriel Valley. He also had a son in the US Navy. His criminal record aside, it appeared he was, at least for a time, a family man. He had been employed in construction for some twenty years. The local dope cops had made a couple of buys through Deverell, and he had a local drug case pending.

In a recorded blog interview on March 8, 2014, Deverell's son, Kevin, stated that his dad had a problem with alcohol while working the oil fields of Taft, California. Kevin referred to the senior Deverell as "into trouble chasing trouble." He also was well known for "playing with fire." Kevin further stated that his dad had been "good buddies" with one Paul Kelly, who was "linked up with some bad shit."

Kevin Deverell was interviewed by Lange shortly after the murders. At the time, he wasn't quite as revealing as he would be thirty-three years later in the 2014 blog interview. He stated in the latter interview that he was somewhat upset that he had not been given more information on the case, presumably by the detectives.

Note: This is understandable, and it is frustrating for the relatives of a murder victim. However, it is also imperative for the detectives working a case to keep everything close to the vest to ensure the integrity of their investigation.

Joy Audrey Miller had been married to a successful Westside attorney and was the mother of two daughters. Now and again, she worked at her parents' liquor store. She had a few drug arrests and one for driving under the influence—these after hooking up with Bill Deverell. She had also battled cancer, and it was noted at her autopsy that she had undergone a double mastectomy. Her family did not have positive vibes when it came to Bill Deverell.

Barbara Richardson was from a suburban working-class family in Sacramento, California. She had no criminal record, and her family knew little of her boyfriend, the much-older David Lind. She had tied in with Lind after a very brief marriage. Here, another victim's parents and family were decimated at the loss of a loved one and would always be haunted by questions surrounding the unspeakable crime against their daughter.

During the investigation of a murder, one of the key sources of information can be the field interview card that is completed primarily by officers in the field following some type of police action. A check of this file, yet to be automated by R&I at the time, revealed a contact with a Paul Kelly and a girlfriend, Maggie Gifford. The names had been associated with Lange and Souza's new pal, Fat Howard Cook.

The detectives ran down Maggie Gifford in the Burbank area, just northeast of Los Angeles. She told them that on at least one occasion, Kelly had threatened to kill Ron Launius. The threat had been made contemporaneous with the murders. Kelly had not only threatened Launius but others at Wonderland as well. When asked if Kelly could be involved, Gifford related that she felt it was possible but could not place him at Wonderland at any time. Later, Lange and Souza realized that if there were a trial, the defense would have this guy out front as their number one suspect in the Laurel Canyon murders.

Lange got Howard Cook on the phone with Souza listening in. Lange braced him regarding Kelly. He became a little snarky and cagey. Souza yelled at him to "quit fucking around and tell us about Paul Kelly." Howard was intimidated the first time he met Souza, and Bob's physical stature and temperament must have come to mind because Howard's phone demeanor vastly improved. Cook soon arranged a meeting for Souza and Lange with Kelly.

Paul Kelly didn't really want to talk with a couple of homicide cops investigating a quadruple murder. But he did. He came up with a fairly decent alibi that checked out. He did know the victims and Lind, no doubt through "business" dealings up at Wonderland. Lange and Souza had dealt with a bunch of bad guys over the years, and this guy was clearly one of the nastier ones.

However, the vibes were not there, nor was the evidence. The detectives didn't believe he was involved simply because there was then, and is now, nothing of a substantive nature to link him to the murders.

Note: A lack of evidence wouldn't stop the defense attorneys once the case went to trial. The reciprocal discovery rules the police had to abide by would have them turning Paul Kelly over to the defense like a turkey on a platter.

Seven

WARRANT SERVICE

On July 8, 1981, Souza and Lange were contacted by the Los Angeles County Sheriff's Office Narcotics Bureau. The LA sheriffs had an informant who had recently purchased cocaine at Ed Nash's home on Dona Lola Place in Studio City. They had also obtained a search warrant for the residence as a consequence of that buy. The sheriff's department viewed Nash as a major distributor of narcotics in the Los Angeles area. Having knowledge of the recent savage murders on Wonderland Avenue and realizing LAPD's interest in Nash, they asked if the RHD detectives would care to accompany them during the service of the warrant. The detectives jumped at the opportunity.

Later that day, Lange, Souza, and Deputy District Attorney Ronald S. Coen conducted a three-way phone conversation relative to the upcoming warrant service with the Los Angeles Sheriff's Office. Coen was a bright young deputy DA who was a fastidious dresser, articulate and with a solid competent demeanor. He had assisted the sheriff's office with the writing of the warrant. He worked out of the downtown criminal courts building in LA. Working closely with area policing agencies, the district attorney had a section that handled major violators and organized crime, such as they exist in Los Angeles. Having worked with Coen in the past and knowing him to be an exceptional deputy district attorney, Lange had been keeping him abreast of the Wonderland investigation.

Note: When working on any high-profile case, it was always a good idea to get the district attorney's office on board early. They needed to be prepared to assist with warrant preparation, the filing of a case, or legal advice at a moment's notice. In order to do this, law enforcement needed to keep them aware of the flow of their investigations and the evidence as it developed.

Bob Souza had never met Ron Coen. Lange introduced the two during the three-way phone conversation, and all three decided to meet for lunch that day to discuss the case. Lange told Coen they would pick him up outside the courthouse at noon. In a light moment closing out the conversation, Bob, flashing back to an old Hollywood spy movie, told Ron to "wear a red rose" in his hair so he'd recognize him.

Lange and Souza were right on time at high noon, driving up Broadway to the courthouse when they spotted Coen, standing on the corner of Temple and Broadway, adorned with a red rose…in his hair!

Coen and the sheriff's office had sought and been granted a so-called "no-knock" warrant from the courts. Whenever a policing agency felt there was the possibility that evidence would be destroyed or another exigency existed, such as when the occupants of the dwelling to be searched are believed to be armed, a no-knock warrant would be requested and usually signed by the judge. This warrant endorsement precluded a knock-and-notice warrant, which required the involved law enforcement agency to give any occupants present reasonable notice of their intention to search.

———

In the early-morning hours of July 10, 1981, the day the search warrant was to be executed, Souza and Lange met up with their Los Angeles Sheriff's Office counterparts at the field command post a few blocks down the hill from Nash's home. Also present was the LA County Sheriff's elite Special Enforcement Bureau. The LA Sheriff's SEB was the equivalent of the LAPD's SWAT unit.

The LA homicide team was also joined by Deputy DA Coen. It was still dark. The plan was to hit the location just as dawn was breaking. Prior to that, the sheriff's SEB deputies were to approach the home on foot in a stealthy manner, surround the location, and await the signal to enter. Some twenty in number, they were all hooked in with ear bud communication devices and would be commanded by their field supervisor.

The signal to forcibly enter was to be a flash-bang grenade that would be activated at the front door of the residence. When detonated, the grenade would be very loud. It was a smoke-producing device that was meant to distract and disorient the inhabitants. When this occurred, the front door would be forced in, as would every point of entry around the entire circumference of the home. Wearing full protective body gear, the heavily armed deputies would then enter to confront whoever, or whatever, was inside.

Just as the sun was breaking over the hills east of Dona Lola Place, a thunderous explosion disrupted the peace of the entire neighborhood, people down the hill and around the corner for several blocks, and into Laurel Canyon. Within seconds of the blast were the sound of glass breaking and the shouting of various police commands. The deputies had entered and were making their presence known. Then three rapid gunshots were followed by what sounded like two shotgun blasts. Then silence.

The field commander had contacted the command post. An entry team had taken gunfire from inside the home on the east side of the property. Lange and Souza, along with Ron Coen, were to stand by until the residence was secured. Some ten minutes later, the all-clear was given, and the detectives, with the deputy DA in tow, were instructed to come on up the hill to the location.

Preceding them up the hill were several squad cars and SEB tactical vehicles. As Lange and Souza approached the front of the residence, several law enforcement types were moving in and out of the home, along with the LA County sheriff's narcotics unit with the warrant. Detectives were then joined by two investigators from the Los Angeles City Fire Department arson unit. They, of course, were attached to the US District Attorney's Organized Crime Strike Force. And, as usual, the Los Angeles press showed up.

Souza and Lange entered through the foyer. The inside of the house was a shambles. The deputies had forcibly entered from at least six separate contact points, and they all involved glass. In addition to the busted-out windows and sliding glass doors, furniture was overturned throughout. Drawers and closets were being searched, and their contents were tossed into the center of the rooms.

———

In the middle of the living room, lying nude on his stomach on a pool table, was three-hundred-pound Nash bodyguard Gregory Diles. His hands were cuffed behind his back. A deputy picked up the eight ball out of one of the pool table's corner pockets and set it on the table in front of Diles, exclaiming, "Hey. Look who's behind the eight ball." Perhaps it wasn't professional, but it was funny.

One of the entry points on the east side of the home was the bedroom of Diles. He was apparently roused from sleep as the deputies knocked out a glass sliding door with a long metal extension pole. Diles had grabbed a nine-millimeter handgun and opened fired on the deputies. The deputies then returned fire with shotguns. No one was hit. Diles was lucky to be alive. That incident raised a question: Did Diles think that this was yet another rip-off? Was he merely trying to defend himself? It really didn't matter because he was later convicted of assault with a deadly weapon on a police officer. He was sentenced to three years in prison.

Note: Of some interest here is the irony that if the Nash robbery had been reported, Diles might have had a reasonable defense argument during his trial for assaulting the sheriffs: self-defense, believing them to be robbers who had returned and not cops serving a search warrant.

Ed Nash had been handcuffed and was seated in a chair toward the rear of the living room. Nash, a gaunt figure of a man in his early fifties with a sallow complexion, was looking around at the interior of his home. At first he was thoroughly dismayed and then really pissed off. Disheveled didn't begin to describe his appearance. "Why? Why do you guys fuck with me? I'm not the only guy with coke in my house. I'm a friend of the police." (That statement would later come to have a deeper meaning.)

Meanwhile, seated in another chair and handcuffed was a new face. He was wearing a scowl, clearly not happy. Amnon Bachsihan was the reputed godfather of the Israeli Mafia. He had apparently been taking part in the previous night's partying and didn't look any better than Nash. Amnon was also lucky to be alive.

As the front door came down and the entry team stormed in, Bachsihan had grabbed up a .32-caliber Beretta handgun. If he'd had a chance to aim and fire the weapon, it would have been embarrassing…and fatal. Amnon had left the loaded magazine for the weapon out front in his Mercedes Benz, securely locked up in the vehicle. Later, detectives asked themselves just why an Israeli would even associate, let alone party, with a Palestinian. What was Bachsihan doing there with Nash? The answer was simple enough: business. Business was business, especially when it came to narcotics. The detectives heard this refrain again a few years later.

Note: Working organized crime murders was always a little different from those cases involving the usual serial killer, robbery, gang, or rage types of killings detectives were used to handling. It was usually wise to step lightly and never overplay your hand. It was always about business here, and message killings were certainly a part of that mind-set. This was true with the Laurel Canyon murders and with another investigation Lange and Souza handled later.

In late November of 1984, a Columbian national, Juan Restrepo, and a Venezuelan national, Leando Jonama, made their way to Los Angeles from Miami. They had arrived in LA to do "business." It was the kind of business that keeps the US Drug Enforcement Agency (DEA) and law enforcement across the country constantly on the move.

Juan Restrepo was the son of a reputed Colombian drug lord who, along with his wife, was under federal indictment for various illegal drug activities at the time. They were restricted to Dade County, Florida, pending trial. They were also associated with a major drug cartel out of Colombia.

A few days after their arrival in Los Angeles, the bodies of Restrepo and Jonama were dumped in the street at two different locations near Dodger Stadium in Elysian Park. Both had been tortured over a period of time with a very sharp cutting instrument and the lit end of a cigarette. They were also extensively beaten about the head and body. At the end of their prolonged and obviously painful ordeals, they were both shot in the head with a small-caliber weapon. Their bodies were then trussed up in plastic tarps and rope. Of interest was the fact that both had been found still wearing expensive jewelry and had several hundred dollars in cash left on their persons. Message sent!

Souza and Lange flew to Miami, Florida, to interview the Restrepo family. After arriving at the Restrepo home, the detectives were ushered into the large, expensive, and highly fashionable condominium in the Coconut Grove section of Miami. The living room area was massive, with a 180-degree view of Biscayne Bay.

The family was surprisingly gracious and offered the detectives food and drink. They spoke openly and sincerely with their lawyers and armed bodyguards standing nearby. Restrepo Sr. did most of the talking. The interview was pretty standard stuff until Lange and Souza got to the part about who might have murdered their son. Restrepo looked both detectives directly in the eyes and stated, "You must understand. I loved my son very much. The family is in mourning. But business is business. We will handle this matter on our own."

In discussing the interview later, the detectives agreed that the "business" would be handled, and the "message" would be sent. There would be no arrests, no trial.

———

Bob Souza walked over to Nash with the LASO deputy serving the warrant. They assisted him to his feet and explained that they wanted him to open the safe in his bedroom closet. Souza and the deputies were already leading him in that direction. Nash complied. It was a floor safe, and as Nash kneeled, his handcuffs now off, Souza removed his weapon from its holster, holding it at the ready position. It was well known that the first thing a thug would have access to when they opened a safe would be a handgun. Nash was instructed to move slowly, and as the lid of the safe was removed, he was pulled aside, and a handgun was revealed lying atop a large stash of powder cocaine.

Nash was re-handcuffed by a deputy and continued to protest even while the gun and coke were being removed from the safe: "Why me? Why are you doing this?" Lange glanced over at Nash's unmade bed. Stuffed clumsily beneath the bed were numerous papers and documents. Everyone agreed that the papers might just make for some interesting reading after they'd done a little housekeeping under the bed.

As Lange began to remove the papers, he quickly realized they were all legal documents, police reports, law enforcement intelligence information sheets, warrants, affidavits, and the like. When the police served a search warrant, such as on that particular day, they were required to leave a copy of the warrant with the person being served, but not the affidavit that laid out probable cause for the search. The names of witnesses and confidential information needed to be protected.

The affidavit portion of a warrant describes details of the investigation that should only be known to the person authoring the warrant and those involved in the investigation of the party named. It alludes to evidence the affiant is searching for and why. The affidavit may also contain crucial information regarding witness data and informant disclosures. These are all critical areas in any investigation. Many of the documents recovered from under Nash's bed had several different persons named on them. It was particularly alarming to find confidential LAPD intelligence reports. It now seemed apparent that Nash had someone inside the LAPD and on his payroll supplying him with sensitive information.

Note: This sparked an internal investigation leading to the LAPD Records and Identification Section and other possible sources. Although suspicions remained high with some, no provable case of wrong-doing was ever uncovered.

Ed Nash posted bail and was out of jail and back at 3315 Dona Lola Place before the sun had set. The sheriff's office would be filing criminal charges with Ron Coen over at the district attorney's office relative to the service of their warrant. The narcotics guys assured the LAPD detectives that they would continue their surveillance of the Nash operation and use their informants to stay on top of him.

Eight

Down and Dirty

At this particular point in time, still early in the investigation, it was more than clear that Lange and Souza needed to talk with Ed Nash. That, of course, did not mean he would talk with them. However, this type of suspect, clearly a narcissistic sort with violent tendencies, needed to realize that the cops would not be intimidated. Souza and Lange believed they could traumatize his overly sensitive ego, and he'd say something stupid. The detectives knew they wouldn't get anywhere unless that attempt was made. Nash had been well insulated over the years and knew many people, influential people. From what the detectives knew, some were cops.

While on loan to Hollywood detectives from a specialized division years earlier, Souza had seen the influence of Ed Nash. It was commonplace in the late '60s and early '70s for Hollywood's finest to frequent Nash's clubs, the Seven Seas in particular. Detectives drinking and eating were never given a bill, and it was customary for detectives on and off duty to leave only a minimal tip for their server. While a complimentary meal wasn't a major issue, the provider of that meal may have been, at least to those who had possibly been easily impressed or manipulated.

Note: Well into the investigation, Lange and Souza were visited by a retired Los Angeles police detective from the old Organized Crime Intelligence Division.

He walked right into their office wearing his retired police identification card pinned to his lapel. Introducing himself, he told the detectives he was concerned about the reputation of Ed Nash. He said he had known Nash for many years and did not believe he could in any way be involved in the Wonderland murders. He stated, "That's just not who Ed Nash is." This was in spite of the fact that Nash had been referred to widely in the media as a major drug dealer, under federal indictment in an arson scam…and a suspect in the murders.

Lange and Souza mused over this former cop offering to be a character reference for gangster Eddie Nash. At first the detectives couldn't believe the guy was on the level. When they realized he was serious, they figured he had probably gotten his share of free drinks and dinners at one of Nash's joints back in the day and just perhaps, much more. This retired detective with the brass nuts left them his business card in case they needed "anything else" from him. The only thing preventing Souza and Lange from naming this individual was a lack of evidence tying him to anything nefarious when it came to Nash or, for that matter, any crime.

The detectives had decided if they were to ever get to Nash, they would have to interview him, as opposed to conducting an interrogation. An interview of a potential suspect was generally conducted in an attempt to glean inconsistencies in the subject's story. Things were meant to be non-confrontational. There was usually no evidence to directly confront the suspect with. Any inconsistencies that arose could then be used later at trial to impeach the suspect's story or alibi.

On the other hand, an interrogation would be considered if there were inculpating evidence to confront a suspect with. An interrogation is meant to be confrontational, even good cop/bad cop. In the case of Eddie Nash, after he had been advised of his constitutionally protected Miranda rights, detectives ran the risk of him invoking his constitutional rights against self-incrimination. If that occurred, the detectives would walk away with zip, which would not be a good scenario.

Note: During the investigation of the O. J. Simpson double murder case this became an issue with some individuals who, with little or no knowledge of police investigative tactics or interview-and-interrogation techniques, criticized the detectives' interview with Simpson. These same self-appointed "experts" never addressed the fact that there were more than a dozen substantive inconsistencies and inculpating circumstantial statements gleaned. These could have, and should have, been used at trial. But that was another story.

When Souza and Lange confronted their boss, Ron Lewis, about jamming Nash, he was skeptical. The two detectives wondered why. Lewis felt it was necessary that they first speak to their commanding officer, Captain Bill Cobb. Ron was in and out of Cobb's office so quick with an answer, the detectives didn't even have time to sit: "Don't talk to Ed Nash!"

As Los Angeles police officers and homicide investigators, Lange and Souza had always functioned with near-total autonomy in their murder investigations. Why the roadblock? The time to get at Nash was then, not later. Why then would Cobb nix the whole idea?

Captain William H. Cobb was chosen to be the commanding officer of the Robbery/Homicide Division by Chief of Police Daryl Gates. He was a tall and rather distinguished-appearing man who would never be caught with a hair out of place. He carried himself with a certain air of vanity even while at work in the office. He would never walk out even for a moment without his jacket on and buttoned. While this would appear professional to some people, it left the captain wide open to being the butt of a little tomfoolery by the troops.

On the desk of the division's watch commander, one Lieutenant Don Foster, was a large coffee container that for some months had been kept filled with sunflower seeds. Throughout the day, nearly everyone in the office would come forward, reach into the can, and remove a handful of the seeds. Some were attempting to cut back on their smoking, while others simply enjoyed a salty snack. Every morning just past 10:00 a.m., with jacket on and hair coiffed perfectly, the captain would stroll out of his office and proceed to the front of the squad bay and the sunflower can. He would dip his hand into it and remove a handful of the seeds. Then, after glancing about the room and maybe making a comment or two to someone, he would return to his office.

Detective Jerry "The Frog" LeFrois was a senior cop working the RHD robbery table. He was also an avid runner with a pretty healthy sense of humor. Every morning at 5:00 a.m., Jerry would run through the hills of the police academy in Elysian Park. On one particular morning, he came across a large gopher snake lying in the middle of the roadway, dead. Never one to pass up a good gag, he grabbed up the snake and placed it into a paper bag, then went to work with the dead snake in tow.

Just past 10:00 a.m. on that particular day, Bill Cobb walked out of his office, as he did every morning, and strode to the ever-present sunflower seed can. Glancing about the room, he nonchalantly reached into the can, grabbing a handful of dead snake. Jumping backward and quickly releasing the reptile, Cobb went one way, and the snake went the other. With a flushed face and loud profanity not expected from a man of his ilk, he returned to his office. He was not happy, but everyone else was.

———————

C ertainly there was a tremendous amount of publicity on the quadruple murder case. The detectives wondered if perhaps the brass upstairs were concerned with the department's image only. Would the investigators appear overbearing? Would detectives' efforts seem untoward for some reason? Or was it something else? It was no time to be tiptoeing through a quadruple murder investigation. Lange and Souza braced Lieutenant Lewis with their strong objection regarding an interview with Nash, but their rebuttal was not welcome. A year or so later, this same failure to act reared its ugly head in another case Bob and Tom were involved with.

———————

A young nurse by the name of Elaine Graham had been kidnapped in the city of Northridge in the San Fernando Valley. She was snatched right off the campus of a large California state university in broad daylight on a workday (Saint Patrick's Day) in 1983. Her vehicle had been found the following day, some sixty miles south in Orange County.

The older VW bug had been in poor running condition, and Lange and Souza felt that a suspect would not have transported a young kidnap victim in her own vehicle in broad daylight, perhaps kicking and screaming, for that distance. It was because of this that the detectives focused their attention on a hilly wilderness area just a couple of miles north of the university. Fearing the worst, they believed that area appeared to be the most likely and accessible dump spot a suspect with depraved intent to molest or murder might consider.

On the Sunday morning following the crime, Lange and Souza accompanied the lead detectives, Leroy Orozco and Paul Tippen, and drove north on De Soto Avenue into Browns Canyon. The detectives' hunch was that the victim had been dumped in the area shortly after her abduction. The terrain was rugged yet accessible. A search on horseback would be ideal. Detectives would set up a command post and coordinate the search not far from the access road.

As luck would have it, the LAPD horse detail was set for a training day. After contacting the officer in charge of the unit, Lieutenant Larry Welch, Lange and Souza decided to combine the unit's training day with a search for Elaine Graham's body, with the presumption she was deceased. An airship (helicopter) would also be deployed. It was a two-for-one. An administrative coup! Lieutenant Ron Lewis would join the search with his horse and become a part of the cadre. Lewis was also a member of the LAPD mounted search and rescue detail.

With everything in place, Lewis approached Captain Cobb with the plan. His response was swift and to the point: "No! It's too remote!" Lange and Souza were livid. Although not a sure thing, it would be a proactive undertaking. There were no other leads of any substance in the case. No doubt the brass upstairs were concerned with what the media would say about squandering the taxpayers' money and the department's time and resources if nothing was found. Apparently, it was not what the police did but how they looked doing it that mattered. It was imagery.

Spring turned to summer, summer to autumn, and then it was winter. The rains came. Mud, dead vegetation, and all types of debris flowed down through the hills above the San Fernando Valley. It was two young hikers who first saw the bones—human bones—scattered over the hillside by animals and the winter rains. Elaine Graham's remains! The bones were discovered within sight of the detectives' proposed command post from months before, just days after the abduction.

Somewhat akin to the Laurel Canyon murders time wise, it took more than twenty-two years before a suspect, Edmond Jay Marr, was convicted. However, the detectives certainly would have found the victim's remains early on, as well as having the benefit of a fresh crime scene to work with. Important evidence that had otherwise been lost due to the passage of time and the elements would have been recovered.

After receiving the hands-off warning on Ed Nash, detectives continued their investigation. Acting on information received from bad dude yet straight-shooting Dave Lind, Souza and Lange were led to Tracy Ray McCourt. He was incarcerated in the Los Angeles County jail system for grand theft. Tracy was the kind of guy you wouldn't trust with last week's newspaper. He was a mousy, skinny hype who couldn't keep his hands off other people's property.

When Lange and Souza first met up with McCourt at the main jail in downtown Los Angeles, he appeared happy to see them. He hadn't gotten a lot of visitors, so he was happy to see anyone. That was about to change.

Since the detectives already knew where McCourt fit into all this, they would first probe Tracy with a little "acid test" to see if they could pry anything of relevance out of him. Under this scenario the detectives did not want to alienate McCourt or anyone else. Souza and Lange knew they would need them down the road. Although Lange and Souza normally did not abide bullshit from those they interviewed, they still treated those folks with a modicum of respect in most instances. They braced Tracy right out of the gate to let him know they were there for serious discussion of a serious matter.

They wanted to know everything he knew about the goings-on up at Wonderland. He lied at first, saying he knew "nothing about Wonderland"

and didn't even know where it was. They knew it would take a different tactic to get Tracy's head straight. Good cop/bad cop was a simple strategy and worked well in many cases. A seasoned detective could sell it with some convincing playacting. Lange was always the good cop. At six feet four inches, probably six feet six inches with his boots on, and 240 pounds with a natural stone face when needed, Souza was more intimidating. Souza was the bad cop, and he was wearing his boots that day.

Souza got right up in his face and glared at him. "Hey, Tracy. Do we look stupid to you?" The big detective hovered over the frightened addict and appeared to be pissed off.

Lange took over in a moderate tone. "Tracy, we know better. Help us out here. It'll go better for you later."

Tears began to well up in his eyes as he blubbered on about people getting killed. He said he wasn't there when it happened. He admitted scoring drugs "at the pad before" and that Ronnie was a pretty good guy when he wasn't a hard-ass. This kind of general information was not enough for the increasingly impatient detectives.

Lange continued to pump him while Souza stood nearby, smoking and blowing the smoke in Tracy's direction. "What about the Nash rip-off? You involved in that?" The detectives knew the right answer, but it had to come from him. He denied knowing anything about a rip-off.

Souza moved in again and in his face. "Hey! Shit bird! If you're gonna lie to us, lie to us about the shit we don't know!" The tears and a little blubbering came again. He was weak and a lousy liar.

With a few disgusted glances his way and a bit more intimidation, McCourt began to recount the robbery at Nash's place. He admitted he was the wheelman. He recounted that the car was a '75 Ford and that he didn't know until later that it had been stolen by Ron Launius. He said he was stressed out waiting for his partners in crime to exit Nash's. He said they took all kinds of guns rolled up in a shower curtain, and Billy had to stop a couple of times "to pick up shit that they dropped." He went on to say Deverell had stuffed his pockets with cash, and it was falling out as he ran toward the car.

As Tracy went on, he appeared to pick up the pace as he described how Launius had been "pissed" at Lind because Lind had shot a black guy, Nash's bodyguard, in the back. Running cover for Lind, Souza asked McCourt to describe Lind and what he knew about him.

Lange inquired if Tracy knew of anyone handling the gang's stolen property. He said he knew of a fence up in Laurel Canyon by the name of Rico. When pressed regarding the murders themselves, McCourt denied any involvement but said he had spoken to people who had visited the crime scene early on, initially to buy dope. When asked who those people were, Tracy began to drag his feet again, causing the "bad cop" to get back up in his grill: "Gotta do better than that, asshole."

Tracy was appearing more and more frightened of Souza, but he had been eye-balling his cigarettes ever since the cops had arrived. McCourt began to whine for a smoke. Souza picked up on his need and placed his pack of Kool filter kings on the table. Souza lit up and blew some more smoke in McCourt's direction. He then placed his hand over the pack and pushed it toward Tracy. "Honesty gets you a smoke," said Souza. McCourt reached for the pack, and Souza lifted his hand.

Souza stepped back from Tracy and took a seat. Tracy was now smoking and talking about a guy named Whitey and another guy named Jimmy Vegas visiting the crime scene. They were there initially to take Launius "up north" for a court appearance. Meanwhile, McCourt chain-smoked, using the butt of one smoke to light the next one. He went on to say that John Holmes had been furious at Launius because of the meager split he got from the Nash robbery. McCourt said he, too, only received a small portion but did not complain. "Ronnie fuckin' kills people, man! He's way outta my league."

Wanting to squeeze McCourt for anything else, Lange pushed him to explain about "the other jobs" he and the Wonderland crew had been involved in. This was a minor crapshoot because, while everyone knew there had to be other robberies, the detectives had no details and no proof. Tracy had his hand on the full pack of Kools in front of him as he blurted out, "You mean like Arnie Newman?"

McCourt then proceeded to describe his involvement in a residential robbery that had occurred in the San Fernando Valley at the home of a guy who owned a pet store, Arnie Newman. Tracy had worked briefly for Newman at the location. He had also been to Newman's home where he had observed numerous antique rifles and handguns throughout the house. Newman also kept live full-grown alligators in his back yard, confined in a small fenced-in lagoon. McCourt had mentioned this to Launius, who immediately set up plans to rob Newman.

Sometime later, while Newman was at work, Launius and a guy named "Cherokee" forced their way into the house and roughed up the housekeeper, then tied her up and helped themselves to the antique rifles and handguns, jewelry, and other items. Tracy told Lange and Souza he "didn't want shit to do with it." With a wink and a nod, the detectives let the little fib pass.

Later on, Tracy added he had heard from Cherokee that Launius wanted to kill the housekeeper but Cherokee had persuaded him not to. Tracy went on to say Launius had then handed the stolen items over to John Holmes to sell, which Holmes did, to Ed Nash. Happy to have his own pack of smokes, Tracy told Lange and Souza that Newman's property, the antique rifles included, was part of the loot the Wonderland bunch took back from Nash during the robbery.

When pressed again, McCourt spoke more about Rico. He said he lived in the Hollywood Hills somewhere above Wonderland and had fenced a large amount of stolen property for the Wonderland gang and other people. There was no need to tell Tracy the cops already knew who Rico was, thanks to Lind.

Note: David Lind, although a hardcore ex-con, cooperated with Lange and Souza throughout much of the investigation. He had his reasons. Uppermost in his mind was the brutal slaying of his girlfriend, Barbara Richardson. He would do anything to avenge her death, even work with the cops.

Lange and Souza were content with what McCourt had told them and knew he wouldn't be hard to find if they wanted to re-interview him. Souza told him to keep the pack of smokes and that they would probably be back to talk to him again. Hearing this, Tracy appeared to be disappointed.

Later, Souza and Lange met Arnie Newman at his home to interview him regarding Tracy McCourt and the robbery at the residence. Newman was an interesting guy and gave the detectives the fifty-cent tour. He was a world traveler with photos and artifacts of his trips from around the globe. African ritual masks and crudely made spears adorned the walls. There were photos of him posing with headhunters and cannibals in Borneo and Africa. His home was a virtual museum. He was a collector of all things bizarre.

He insisted the cops go out back and meet his pet alligators. The two beasts were huge. He described their diets as he threw them some unknown type of meat over a less-than-sturdy-looking fence. Lange and Souza wondered what the animal rights folks would think of that setup...not to mention the neighbors.

Arnie was also able to communicate with the gators by making various clucking sounds with his hand over his mouth. The gators actually responded! After the tour and the interview, the first moniker of the case was christened: Alligator Arnie.

Nine

HOLMES AND COMPANY

On July 12, 1981, while back in the office, Lange took a call. It was his boss, Ron Lewis. Lewis told Lange that John Holmes had been picked up at a motel in the San Fernando Valley and was being held at an unknown location. Two other detectives from the Homicide Special Section were talking with him. Lewis felt that Holmes was about to give up the killers, and he was on his way back to the office. Lange was incredulous and slammed the phone down. He briefed Souza on the strange call from their boss, and they awaited the arrival of Lewis in disbelief.

When Lewis returned shortly after the phone call, Souza and Lange walked over to his desk. They demanded that Lewis tell them just who was going to handle the case as it related to John Holmes. Lewis assured the detectives that it was their case, but it had to be a "team effort." While Holmes was a central figure in the investigation, the assigned team needed to get into him. After all, Lange and Souza had all the facts and a true grasp of the evidence. Appearing a bit defensive, Lewis believed since the other team was interviewing Holmes, they might get a confession or at least more information on the killers.

Note: Under most circumstances Detectives Lange and Souza would take any and all help they could get, but John Holmes was a major player, and they needed to take the lead. Having other detectives stepping in at that point was a serious departure from protocol, not to mention a slap in the face to the primary investigators on the case.

After a bit of prodding and some salty remarks, Lewis told Lange and Souza that Holmes was downtown at the Los Angeles Bonaventure Hotel with his girlfriend, Dawn. He was being guarded by the LAPD's Metro Division. He had also been joined by his wife, Sharon. Souza couldn't believe Lewis would tolerate such a transgression on the investigation. "What the fuck, Ron? Are you taking us off this case?" Lewis refuted Souza's statement, then worked on smoothing the matter over for the detectives. Both had a hard time reconciling his poor judgment and believed Lewis favored Helvin due to his seniority over the assigned detectives.

Lange and Souza proceeded to the Bonaventure Hotel, where Lewis would not allow them to enter the room where the other team was hosting Holmes and his women. This angered the detectives further, and Souza was considering dropping out of the case. The group's stay at the Bonaventure was brief. The metro division tactical officers didn't approve of the layout. It was something about ingress, egress, and too many people involved. Incredibly, Holmes had also complained about the size of their suite. It was too small.

Lange and Souza knew they were expected to cooperate with whatever their bosses came up with. To that end they knew of a retired LAPD supervisor who was now employed as a security consultant at the iconic Biltmore Hotel just a few blocks away. After they solidified their contact, they were actually able to score the vice-presidential suite. It was the ideal answer to all the security concerns, and the metro detail approved, as did Holmes.

Once the move was complete, Holmes made himself at home with all the opulent surroundings. Sharon and Dawn had apparently formed some type of an alliance. While Lange and Souza were still reeling from the interference with their case, Holmes was ordering room service several times a day. Lange and Souza scoffed when they heard Holmes favored expensive single-malt scotch, provided compliments of the LAPD. The idea was to make Holmes feel comfortable and at ease so he would loosen up, but the expensive scotch was pushing the envelope. They cut off the scotch.

Note: The Biltmore Hotel and the scotch brought back memories of an investigation on the twelfth floor of that very hotel a few years earlier. The room involved was just below the suite Holmes and the women now occupied. Lange was working the central division homicide unit at the time. A young man checked into the hotel in the early afternoon and requested a room on the highest floor available that would supposedly afford him a scenic view of the city. Once in the room, he ordered a bottle of Johnnie Walker Red scotch from room service. When the bottle arrived, he opened it and proceeded to make every effort to drain it.

The young man then drew a warm bath. Still working on the scotch, he disrobed and climbed into the tub. He then produced a straight razor and slashed both his wrists. He lowered his hands into the warm water to allow the blood to flow more freely. Apparently, things were moving much too slowly, so he rose from the tub, walked to the open window overlooking a very busy West Fifth Street, and dove head first through it to the busy street below. A mangled mass of human flesh and bone in the middle of the street is nothing to be viewed by the faint of heart, as many drivers found out on their way home after a busy day at the office on that late afternoon.

———

Lange and Souza respected Detective John Helvin and his seniority in homicide. Ron Lewis truly believed Helvin's cool and level-headed demeanor would gain Holmes's confidence and prompt him to open up. Regardless of Lewis's confidence in Helvin, the situation did not sit well with Souza and Lange.

While Helvin was an outstanding homicide cop with a great deal of experience, the investigation was the responsibility of Lange and Souza, who felt as though they were losing control. That old time-worn refrain of "too many cooks in the kitchen" came to mind.

After a considerable amount of time was spent schmoozing Holmes, he seemed to settle in and eventually told Helvin that he would discuss details about the killers and the motive for the murders. Holmes related he would only cooperate, though, if the detectives could ensure that he and the two women would be put into a witness protection program. Helvin agreed, even though he would have no control over that decision. Covering himself, Helvin promised that he would do anything and everything in his power to make that happen.

Holmes began his so-called admission by alluding to complicity in the robbery of Nash. He stated he had drawn a diagram of the Nash residence for the Wonderland bunch and left a rear sliding-glass door unlocked for them to enter. Holmes also admitted to receiving more than $2,000 in cash and some cocaine as his take in the robbery. He discussed his relationship with Ed Nash further, stating that he also scored cocaine at the home and fenced stolen property there from time to time.

Regarding the murders themselves, Holmes claimed he had been coerced into leaving the front door of the Wonderland house unlocked on the morning of the murders.

Note: Of import here is the fact that "duress" is not deemed to be a defense for murder. Additionally, Holmes had to know what the intentions of the persons entering the Wonderland home were prior to the murders.

When Helvin pressed Holmes for more information on the killers, Holmes backed down and refused to provide any further details. He refused to name names, and then he refused to talk at all, even after Helvin told him that being prosecuted for the murders could be in his future.

Throughout his stay Holmes had demanded special treatment and played up his role to the hilt. It had been five full days of talk and, basically, five days of nonsense with John Holmes and his women. Now there seemed to be some friction between the two ladies. This wasn't difficult to understand, and things were getting a bit claustrophobic for everyone. Sharon Holmes had had enough. She gathered her few belongings and headed out the door to return to Glendale.

Lange and Souza continued to complain to Ron Lewis about the interference in their case. They didn't believe the VIP kid-gloves strategy was getting them to first base with Holmes. Souza and Lange had a different approach in mind. They felt an interview situation, somewhat akin to that of David Lind, would be more successful. They believed that removing Holmes from the luxury of the Biltmore Hotel and getting him back out on the street would have been a good start. Treating him as any other potential witness or suspect, without the celebrity status, would be effective.

Holmes was soon released to deal with his grand theft charges. He had been out of custody on his own recognizance (no bail established). He bailed Sharon's car out of an impound lot, and he was in the wind once again, but it would not be for long.

During these types of investigations, detectives usually monitored and documented all the players and their observed activities at staggered times when it was plausible. A very large player in the Wonderland case was Ed Nash. Driving or walking by his residence at any hour of the day or night, Lange and Souza checked for any activity. They also jotted down the license plate numbers of any vehicles at the home to be checked later for owner information. Documenting these types of things told detectives who had been there on a particular date at a particular time. Sometimes these little bits of intelligence helped to fill in the blanks later on. Any truly good cop is also a nosy cop.

On that particular evening, just hours after Holmes was kicked loose from the Biltmore, he was back at Nash's place on Dona Lola. After he told Helvin all the details of his participation in the robbery and the murders, Souza and Lange wondered if Holmes had also shared any of those supposedly factual details with Nash. They presumed he had not. The detectives believed there was just about the same chance of that happening as there was of Holmes testifying in court.

Note: Driving by Nash's place very late one night to check on activity, the detectives noted a new vehicle parked in front. Registration later revealed the car belonged to a well-known local television newsman who had been reporting on the Wonderland murders.

—•—

It was early morning. Lange had just picked up his regular partner, Frank Tomlinson, and they were driving to work downtown. Frank had been on a scheduled vacation, and Lange brought him up to speed on everything that had occurred since he'd been away. Lange's update included the questionable gathering at the Biltmore Hotel and what little it had produced.

Frank, a tall, quiet, soft-spoken man with a well-controlled demeanor, was not happy. He could not understand why Ron Lewis would agree to treating

Holmes with such deference and excluding the assigned detectives. After Lange provided Tomlinson with a few more details, he sighed and told Lange he believed it was time for him to retire. Cops say those kinds of things all the time, but when Frank said something, he usually meant it. Very little was said during the rest of the trip in to work.

———

On July 16, 1981, Souza and Lange were once again contacted, this time in letter form, by a member of the Los Angeles County Sheriff's Department. The deputy wrote that while working as a patrol officer in West Hollywood in 1973, he had responded to a number of criminal complaints at the Starwood nightclub, located at 8151 Santa Monica Boulevard. The letter further described how certain people who wished to make brutality complaints against that club's bouncer, Gregory Dewitt Diles, had been talked out of following through with their formal complaints to the sheriff's office. The club was owned by Ed Nash.

The complaining patrons from the club stated they had been assaulted by Diles with a "billy club or some type of a stick." The deputy was never able to recover a weapon at that time. Subsequent to this, the deputy related that he had made a traffic stop on Diles in his vehicle pursuant to these complaints. He wrote that he had found a length of steel pipe, with one end encased in a rubber bicycle handlebar grip, on the floorboard of the car. Diles was arrested, booked, and eventually convicted in Beverly Hills Municipal Court for possession of a deadly weapon.

Note: This incident clearly demonstrated a circumstantial evidence tie to Diles and the purported type of murder weapon used in the Wonderland killings.

———

On July 24, 1981, Jamie McGuan, the same young woman who had been present at Nash's home during the ill-fated robbery, was interviewed by an LAPD officer regarding a beating she had suffered and was being treated for. During this interview, while stating that Ed Nash had threatened her physically, she declined to say that he had actually beaten her.

McGuan related to the officer that Nash had stated to her, "One got away from the robbery, and he is running, and you know too much." She also stated to the reporting officer that Nash had been robbed of drugs and money and had not reported it to the police. McGuan described John Holmes as a friend of Nash who scored drugs at the Nash home. She also stated that after the June robbery at Nash's, he had had Holmes beaten by his bodyguard, but she didn't know why.

Note: The chances of having the young woman testify to these statements in a subsequent murder trial were probably nil and nil.

Interestingly, sometime later, Jamie McGuan wound up at Cedars-Sinai Hospital after a serious traffic collision she had while driving one of Ed Nash's vehicles. She was treated in the emergency room by Dr. Miles Saunders. He, of course, was the same physician who was treating victim Susan Launius. While McGuan was being treated, Nash entered the ER and demanded to see the doctor treating McGuan. Apparently, however, Nash had been concerned about McGuan's injuries, and he wanted her treated immediately. Nash probably never knew that Dr. Saunders had also been treating Susan Launius. Eventually realizing a potential problem, Dr. Saunders had another doctor take over and handle McGuan's treatment in the emergency room.

———

On August 4, 1981, Souza and Lange actually had a little time to speculate on a few things and do some digging. That didn't happen often enough in high-profile cases. With meetings and briefings and the case in chief, time for snooping and pooping, as they called it, was usually at a minimum. Follow-ups on theories or so-called clues that had come their way were often left on the back burner.

On that day the detectives decided to go up to Nash's neighborhood. After checking to make sure they weren't followed by the media, they drove to the area and parked down the street, out of sight of Nash's house. Many of those in the press were a sneaky lot and certainly not above tailing cops while they attempted to follow up on an investigation.

On Dona Lola Place once again, the detectives walked around to speak with a few neighbors. They laughed at the thought of running into Ed Nash watering his roses out front. Lange and Souza were firm believers that the harder you dug, the luckier you got, and they'd take luck any day.

Most of the neighbors who spoke with them claimed they did not know of a "Mr. Nash" who lived up the street at the top of the hill. A few did but were a little reluctant to gab on about their neighbor. The cops certainly didn't blame them.

They worked their way up the hill and came to Nash's neighbor directly to the east. The home's entrance was recessed and could not be seen from the Nash property. A fifteen-year-old boy answered the front door. He was a nice, bright kid who wasn't intimidated by cops showing up at his home. He said he knew the neighbors. He told the detectives they had noisy parties and such, but they never seemed to bother anyone.

The boy did recall an incident sometime in late June or July when he was out front and his neighbor, a large black man, had approached him and asked if he could use the family's phone. The man had stated to the boy that he had been robbed and showed him what he described as a gunshot wound to his side. The man (no doubt Diles) also told him that the robbers had posed as police officers and had handcuffed him and Mr. Nash. The man told the teen that the robbers had cut their phone lines and robbed them of cash and other items.

Note: Later, the boy's story was somewhat corroborated by a building contractor detectives found working in the area down the street. He had apparently glanced up the hill a month or so prior and had seen the boy and a large black man conversing.

Diles was allowed in the boy's house and used the phone for several minutes. The boy said he did not over-hear Diles's phone conversation. The teen's parents were not at home, and detectives left a business card with the youth.

On August 7, 1981, the detectives received a phone call in the office from the boy's mother. She stated that their neighbor, Greg Diles, had approached her son once again on the day of her call. According to the mother, Diles told him to forget any conversation he'd had regarding the robbery. He also told the teen that everything had been taken care of and there was nothing to be concerned about. While the mother expressed some concern, she was told that all this information would be kept strictly confidential.

Note: This information was never used nor did it become an issue; however, the neighbor's phone records were requested. A check of the records revealed nothing of any consequence to the investigation.

———

On the morning of September 18, 1981, Lange was in the office trying to make sense of an ever-growing case file. Picking up a ringing phone, someone yelled, "Lange on one." It turned out to be another call coming in to the office from someone with more alleged information on the case. While many of these calls were bogus, detectives never knew for sure. The assigned detectives didn't have the luxury of a screener, so it was up to them to document everything. This could eventually play havoc with the discovery process, wherein they would be required to turn everything over to defense attorneys prior to a trial.

The guy on the other end of the phone said he was calling from the federal detention center in San Diego. He was on the wrong side of the bars. His name was Jerry Van. Jerry said he had something good on the murders "up in the canyon." A jailhouse snitch was not really the type of witness cops were looking for in any criminal investigation, especially murder. These jailbirds would hawk their own dead grandmother's jewelry right off her body for a get-out-of-jail-free card. Now and then, one could have legitimate, useful information, but the informant certainly had to be carefully vetted.

Van told Lange his straight-up name was Jerry Anthony Van Hoorelbeke. He claimed to have inside information on Ed Nash and to know others who had worked for him. He also happened to be in the federal cage for arson, courtesy of the US Attorney's Organized Crime Strike Force. He was one of Nash's indicted arson-for-hire stooges.

The three-hour drive down to meet with Van Hoorelbeke at Club Fed in San Diego was a shot in the dark but couldn't be counted out. Jerry Van was what was known in prison circles as a "keep-away." He was isolated from all other prisoners due to his status as an informant. Releasing him into the general population would be a death sentence.

Van Hoorelbeke seemed almost jovial for someone who had been incarcerated for several months and was awaiting trial. The federal facility and its accommodations were the Ritz Carleton compared to the likes of Corcoran, Soledad, San Quentin, and Folsom where Lange and Souza had interviewed more dangerous prisoners. Club Fed, as they called it, wasn't bad for a con like Jerry Van. He told the cops that he hailed from Flint, Michigan, and had been the starting quarterback on the Michigan State University Spartans football team several years earlier. That actually turned out to be true.

Van Hoorelbeke was the overly talkative type and spoke as though he had a limited amount of time and didn't want to miss any points he had planned to make. He said Nash knew many influential people, and they all "protected" him. He told the detectives most everything they already knew about Nash. Nash was a bad guy, couldn't be trusted, and was one of the most prolific dope dealers in the Los Angeles area. He gave the detectives everything without telling them anything. All that he had could have been picked up listening to the 11:00 o'clock news on any television station that was reporting on the case. Federal prisoners were all given television viewing time. While the detectives were patient, they certainly had not learned anything new. They told him, "Thanks. We'll get back to you."

On the return trip to Los Angeles, Lange and Souza discussed what had just transpired with the newest "witness" on their case. To begin with, Jerry Van Hoorelbeke was supposed to be a protected federal informant. As homicide detectives investigating a crime, Lange and Souza had not been screened to any great degree while getting into the lockup in San Diego. No questions were asked of them by any authorities, but more importantly, the detectives were not aware of any approvals being made by the Feds for their visit. If Lange and Souza had an informant, they would have wanted to clear any interview with him involving another law enforcement agency well in advance. Was his handler ever notified? Being an informant, this guy was also a con man. Did he really believe he could get away with giving up all the nonsense he did and still have the detectives buy in to it? Lange and Souza suspected that something else was in the mix, and it was beginning to smell. Later, as things played out, this all began to make more sense.

———•———

On Sunday, November 8, 1981, Lange and Souza were at home on days off. Calls came in to both detectives just after noon. The North Hollywood division of the LAPD had received a DB (dead body) call at 3315 Dona Lola Place in Studio City, Ed Nash's residence. By now Dona Lola was a familiar address, not just to the cops, but to anyone who read a newspaper. Because of the ongoing Wonderland investigation, the North Hollywood homicide cops wanted RHD to respond and handle the investigation.

Arriving about an hour later, Lange was met by the North Hollywood detectives. They were joined shortly by Souza. North Hollywood had not started an investigation while awaiting the RHD team. Lange and Souza knew the North Hollywood cops didn't want to touch anything in view of the Wonderland murder investigation. It was a good call on their part.

As the detectives entered Nash's home, things seemed different. Nash had never been known to be a neat freak or a tidy housekeeper, but his place looked immaculate. Nothing was lying around on the floor, and things appeared to be in their proper places. The dishwasher was even running. Everything appeared to be in order, except for the dead body in the guest bedroom.

Nash appeared agitated now that his weekend had been disrupted and Lange and Souza had returned to investigate a death in his home. He stated that the dead guy, Dominic Fragomeli, twenty-six, had been in the guest room with Jamie McGuan. Detectives learned the deceased was employed by Nash as a sound technician at the Starwood Club.

Their investigation revealed that Fragomeli had a heroin habit and had reportedly fixed some fourteen hours prior to the arrival of the police. Nash told the detectives McGuan had slept through the whole affair. The zombie-like response from McGuan more or less confirmed it.

Fragomeli was lying supine in bed. He had been bleeding profusely from the nose. He was in full rigor mortis, indicating he had been dead for probably well over twelve hours. There was a hypodermic needle on the night stand adjacent to the bed.

The room looked as though someone had gone through it thoroughly and cleaned things up. It looked a little too pristine for a couple of heroin addicts who had spent the night there. Detectives were not buying the fact that the dead guy was shooting up in bed while the other just slept through the whole ordeal. The scene looked as though it had been staged. Lange and Souza huddled up and, judging from the evidence at hand, agreed there was a possibility it was a hot shot (a deliberate overdose) administered by persons unknown with the intent to kill. They agreed that if Fragomeli had raised the ire of Ed Nash, this would probably be the style used to take him out. On the other hand, there was also the possibility that the cleanup had been arranged to keep Nash out of another narcotics beef.

For a period of time, the possibility of locking down Nash's pad and seeking a search warrant was considered. The warrant affidavit could also be broadened to include Fragomeli's workplace, just to squeeze Nash a bit more. But seeing how Nash and his bunch had obviously gone through the entire premises before the cops arrived, it would probably be just a waste of time. Absent this extenuating circumstance, the death investigation would have probably been drawn out more.

The detectives also didn't want it to appear as though they were harassing Nash just for the sake of it. While they wanted him nailed they also wanted the evidence in the case to do the talking and not some harassment accusation. They decided to complete the investigation and write it up as an undetermined cause of death, pending the autopsy finding. At that point it would be up to the coroner's office to make the call.

The coroner's office later ruled the Fragomeli overdose an accidental death. It was always very difficult to prove a so-called hot shot case. There certainly needed to be something to corroborate the suspicions reached by the cops after their investigation. This would have included direct witness testimony and/or physical evidence and perhaps coroner's findings to some extent.

Regardless, rumors swirled for months that Dominic Fragomeli was the recipient of a hot shot for upsetting the wrong guy, and the wrong guy lived at 3315 Dona Lola Place, but the hard evidence was never there.

Ten

"Making Friends"

On November 18, 1981, Henry Hoskins walked over from the federal building across the street and up to the Robbery/Homicide office at Parker Center. He was the supervising agent for a contingent from the Bureau of Alcohol, Tobacco, and Firearms. His unit was on a loan status to the US Department of Justice and the US Attorney's Organized Crime Strike Force based in Los Angeles.

Hoskins came on as a slick operator with a good-old-boy southern drawl. He was tall at six feet six inches and gaunt with hawkish features. It was obvious he used his size and demeanor to intimidate and get his way. He was expecting complete cooperation from "the locals," as federal agents liked to refer to city police officers. Souza and Lange were wary from the start, knowing full well the Feds wanted all the information they could get and would never share anything they had in return.

After the introductions and some small talk, Hoskins got right to the reason for his visit. His group and the US Strike Force had Adel Nasrallah and twenty-one others under federal indictment.

The charges included arson for hire as well as other racketeering counts laid out in a Racketeer Influenced and Corrupt Organizations (RICO) federal indictment. Nash had been charged with orchestrating the torching of various businesses in Southern California and Las Vegas for the insurance money. From what Lange and Souza understood, a local firefighter might have died while fighting one of the blazes. If this was true and arson was involved in the death of a firefighter, it would be a first-degree murder charge.

Hoskins came across as almost too stern and didn't really seem to comport himself the way most law enforcement types did when in the company of one another.

It was soon apparent he was not in the RHD office to invite Lange and Souza out for drinks. He wanted any and all information the primary detectives had on Ed Nash at that point in their investigation. Souza was no slouch at intimidation, and he maintained a steady glare at Hoskins as Lange explained to him that they did not release or divulge any information on an unsolved murder investigation. Hoskins appeared miffed. "Hey, look, fellas. I'm just an old country boy who believes in total cooperation between our agencies." Lange and Souza were not impressed with his routine.

Hoskins explained that their federal investigation was still ongoing and that there were other suspects and charges they were pursuing. Souza held his stare as Hoskins insisted the detectives' cooperation would not only be welcome but could be crucial in convicting Nash and the others. He persisted with wanting the LAPD detectives to be "on board." His empathy ploy fell short.

As an experienced federal agent, Hoskins should have known better than to take on seasoned homicide cops. No law enforcement agency in its right mind was going to give up any information on an unsolved murder investigation to anyone unless ordered to do so by the courts. Even then, it would be a stretch. Hoskins was steadily losing ground and appeared to be containing his anger.

Lange and Souza realized that the three of them would not be grabbing a beer together after work any time soon. Hoskins abruptly turned and stormed out of the office without as much as a handshake.

The LA cops had no intention of cooperating with Hoskins in the future as they had bad vibes about him after their initial contact. They decided to feed him innocuous information if pressured. Souza told Lange, "My grandmother told me that when a man says he's just an old country boy, grab your wallet and hang onto your girlfriend; the bastard can't be trusted." Lange smiled in agreement.

———

The US District Attorney's Organized Crime Strike Force was comprised of several law enforcement agencies, including not only federal prosecutors but also the Federal Bureau of Investigation, the Bureau of Alcohol, Tobacco, and Firearms, the IRS, and the Los Angeles City Fire Department Arson Unit. This was because some of the arsons charged had been committed in the city of Los Angeles and had been investigated by the LAFD arson unit.

The Los Angeles City Fire Department was headed by the Los Angeles City Fire Commission. The commission called the shots regarding department resources, policy, and general oversight. In short, it ran the whole show. One of the commissioners, appointed by then Los Angeles Mayor Tom Bradley, was a Burbank attorney by the name of Dominick Rubalcava. Mr. Rubalcava had a client by the name of Ed Nash.

While Nash was under a federal indictment on arson-for-hire charges, he was also being represented by a criminal defense attorney who happened to be the president of the Los Angeles City Fire Commission. The commissioner's own arson unit was investigating *his* client! While Mr. Rubalcava certainly appeared to be a reputable attorney, there was still the appearance of impropriety here because of an obvious conflict of interest.

The relationship of Rubalcava to Ed Nash was leaked to the media, and Mayor Bradley was braced with the obvious question: Did he see a conflict? "Certainly not!" responded the mayor.

Bill Cass was a senior arson investigator for the Los Angeles City Fire Department. He had been assigned to work with the USDA's Organized Crime Strike Force, which was looking into the aforementioned arson-for-hire cases alleged to have been set up by Nash. Lange and Souza met with him and his partner at his office.

Cass believed Nash had a considerable number of people in the public sector running interference for him, including political and law enforcement types. Regarding the appointment of the president of the fire commission (and Nash attorney) Rubalcava, Cass told the detectives that he and others had a big problem with the apparent conflict of interest. They had been pursuing Ed Nash on allegations of arson for hire for a considerable amount of time, and he was being represented by their boss, the president of the fire commission.

Cass went on to relate that he and his unit had been told by their superiors not to pursue Nash independently. They had been instructed not to focus their investigation on him. They were told to go after Nash only if he was caught up in the larger context of organized crime activity. Did this include a conspiracy? No one really knew. What the detectives *did* know was that Cass and his arson unit, were outraged. They were professionals who took a great deal of pride in what they did. They did not appreciate this appearance of conflict and impropriety or the interference in their investigation. Souza and Lange certainly understood at that point the element of interference.

———•———

The drug business at 3315 Dona Lola Place had not slowed. Patrons were coming and going at all hours of the day and night. About the only thing that could have sped things up for Nash any more would have been a twenty-four-hour drive-through alongside his home. His biggest concern should have been that half the dope cops in Los Angeles County were watching.

By late November of 1981, the LAPD had ramped up its surveillance on Nash's home and several of his nightspots as well. Narcotics detectives were busy putting together a damning affidavit defining their observations, witness statements, and informant information. Once again, they had obtained a no-knock search warrant. This time, it would be an all-LAPD show.

It was Wednesday, November 25, 1981, the day before Thanksgiving. Cops involved with the raiding party had adjourned their roll call and were at the same spot as before at the bottom of the hill below Nash's home. Berry Drive was a secluded residential street just off Laurel Canyon Boulevard concealed beneath several large trees and made for an ideal command post. Souza and Lange pulled in just before dawn. The SWAT unit was already there. They were double-checking their weapons and gear. Adam Dawson, the news reporter, was also there and double-checking his note pad and pen.

Lieutenant Jeff Rogers, the field commander for the SWAT unit, had been an LAPD academy classmate of Souza's. Rogers and Souza had been in contention for top shooter in their class. Rogers had beaten Souza out by a few points. But a little class rivalry was one thing; taking down armed thugs was another. Jeff was concerned about a reporter being at the scene, but Souza assured him it would not be a problem. The reporter was not interested in police procedure. It was Nash he wished to exploit. Rogers was unhappy. SWAT priorities were totally different from those of homicide cops trying to put a case together, and with good reason.

Lieutenant Rogers had been in touch with his counterpart in the LA Sheriff's Special Enforcement Bureau. The operation would be similar to the one conducted just days after the murders. At first light SWAT would proceed up the hill and approach from the front. They were to bail out and rapidly deploy around the circumference of the residence. When the flash-bang grenade was initiated at the front door, they would force entry at their pre-designated targets: windows and glass-sliding doors.

Just as the sun began to reveal the new day, everyone was in place. The flash-bang was ignited, and once again, the front door went down, and every window and glass slider in the house was smashed in, followed immediately by the entrance of the heavily armed cops.

Unlike the last time, Greg Diles didn't even get out of bed. There was no resistance. This time, there were no guns in Diles's room, just a broken pool cue. Nash was dragged from his room, and just like before, he was mad as hell.

"Why? Why me again?" blustered one of the biggest cocaine dealers in Southern California.

Souza took the time to answer, further agitating the gangster. "It's against the law to deal coke in California, Eddie."

Nash was escorted to the now well-known floor safe in his bedroom. Nash opened it. It was filled with loose cash and more than two pounds of powder cocaine. Apparently, the coke had been delivered the day before, just in time for Thanksgiving. It was simply sheer luck to find the safe stuffed with dope. Souza and Lange enjoyed the thought that Nash would think he had a snitch in his midst due to the recent delivery. Drug dealers didn't really buy in to happenstance.

As Nash and Diles were led away from the front door of the home in handcuffs, they were again met by the media, cameras clicking away. That was the part SWAT Lieutenant Jeff Rogers didn't care for or understand. Eddie Nash on the front page of the *Los Angeles Times* in handcuffs did more for the murder investigation than keeping the press at bay. Deputy District Attorney Coen was also present. He would be staying close to any law enforcement activity that involved Ed Nash. He intended to file any and all criminal charges he could justify in his attempt to rid society of one well-entrenched dope-dealing hoodlum.

———

Clearly, at this point, there were two central figures rapidly emerging as persons of interest. Souza and Lange were stepping up their efforts regarding the backgrounds of Ed Nash and John Holmes. They wanted to know everything that there was to know about these two unsavory sorts. Well aware of the expression "Knowledge is power," they knew that in a murder investigation, someone's knowledge could also be evidence or lead to it.

While Nash's whereabouts were pretty much common knowledge, Holmes's had proven tougher to nail down. The word *flighty* best described the roving actor.

The Los Angeles Police Department had two specialized entities who reported directly to Daryl F. Gates, the chief of police at that time. A cop's cop, Gates was known to take no guff from anyone. He was respected by the rank and file but pretty much despised by the media, Mayor Tom Bradley, and several other groups who fancied themselves as voices of the people or, as some would opine, rank apologists.

Note: Of interest was the fact Tom Bradley was a retired LAPD lieutenant who was later elected Los Angeles city councilman prior to his terms as mayor.

Daryl Gates was a chief who demanded to be briefed by the assigned detectives in any particular case he had an interest in, usually those of a high-profile nature. Most of the rest of the brass would take what they thought they needed through their chain of command, from their lieutenants and commanding officers. Lange and Souza had briefed the chief personally on other cases and were always well received. Following one meeting, Souza had been chastised by a superior for wearing his moustache too long and overly bushy. During that particular meeting, it had been evident that Chief Gates could not have cared less about Souza's moustache. It was all about the progress of the case at hand. For that particular complaining superior, it was all about appearances.

Note: Although retired for some two years, Chief Gates would call Lange from time to time during the O. J. Simpson case. He would share his thoughts and make recommendations based on the particular climate of the day regarding the case. He was always there for his people, even in retirement.

The two specialized entities alluded to earlier were the Administrative Vice Division and the Organized Crime Intelligence Division (OCID). Their titles told it all. Ad-vice handled specialized investigations involving illegal activities such as prostitution, gambling, and pornography. OCID was interested in organized crime activities and building intelligence dossiers on organized crime figures.

These were a couple of groups Lange and Souza wanted to get close to because of Holmes (pornography) and Nash (organized crime). Both of these sections also operated largely on intelligence. Intelligence meant informants. There are informants, and there are confidential informants. The homicide team was interested in the latter group.

Souza had an in with both divisions since his brother was assigned to Ad Vice at the time and had worked OCID for several years. Nine years his senior, Souza's brother Glenn had come on the department in the late 1950s and had investigated many organized crime figures in Los Angeles, Eddie Nash being one of them.

John Holmes was also a familiar name to Glenn because of Ad Vice's interest in the pornography scene throughout Los Angeles. Lange and Souza learned that Holmes was a high-end confidential informant. According to Glenn Souza, he had always been "handled" by Detective Tom Blake in Ad Vice.

Back at their desks on the Homicide special table, Bob Souza called the Ad Vice office while Lange wrote up a statement from one of their possible witnesses. While the detective at Ad Vice told Souza they had an extensive package on John Holmes, he was reluctant to give any specifics. He informed Souza that it was against Ad Vice policy to release any info regarding a confidential informant.

Note: Confidential informant was another way of saying paid informant.

Sensing a run-around, Souza got steamed. He explained to the vice guy that the detectives were involved in a quadruple murder investigation. This did not seem to resonate with the vice cop. While sounding somewhat empathetic, he said they did not give up their sources. However, he told Souza that Holmes was not his area of expertise. Somewhat impatient, Souza stated, "Let me talk to Tom Blake." There was a brief hesitation on the phone. The vice cop then told Souza that Blake was in the field. Souza didn't believe him. He said they needed to talk to the detective who was handling Holmes and also told the Ad Vice guy to get hold of Blake. Then he told him they were on their way down to Ad Vice.

Lange and Souza made their way over to Fort Davis on East Fifth Street (Skid Row), the home of Ad Vice. It's also the home of the Central Division of the LAPD. The building had been named for the former chief of police, Ed Davis. Central Division was where Lange had made his bones, spending several years working the streets there and investigating his first murder case in 1975.

Lange and Souza needed to find John Holmes. Tom Blake, who handled Holmes, was out of the office. Souza left a personal message on his desk for him to call them at RHD. As Souza and Lange headed back to their office, they decided to put Holmes on the front burner with Blake and Ad Vice. Nash and the OCID inquiry would have to wait, at least for a short time.

With the cops now trying to find Holmes, the media had somehow gotten wind that porn star John Holmes might be a suspect in the killings. The detectives' acquaintances in the news business were lapping it up.

They wondered how the news folks could have gotten onto something like Holmes being a suspect so soon. The answer was as old as cop work itself. It's called a leak.

Note: Looking back on their careers, Lange and Souza could not recall a single high-profile case in which there was not some type of a leak. For whatever reason, it was usually at the most inopportune time. The media always liked to call the leak "a source close to the investigation." That always got a chuckle. Too many fingers in the pudding meant that someone was going to walk away with sticky fingers.

The Robbery/Homicide squad bay was a large, open room with approximately fifty detectives, located on the third floor of Parker Center. Each detective had his or her own desk area and phone. The room was segmented. It included the Homicide Special Section, Robbery Special Section, Bank Robbery Section, Highjack Section, Major Crimes Section and the Sex Crimes Section. All sections had city-wide oversight of their respective specialties. There was also a small administrative unit. The doors to the office were never kept locked, nor were the desks and cabinets. The only security in the entire building was on the lobby level and at the front and rear entrances to the building itself. People came and went at will.

Here, RHD detectives investigated some of the most sensitive and high profile cases of the day, and it appeared as though everyone was on the honor system. Lange had complained about the lack of security since he was assigned to the division. He was not alone. Several assigned detectives continuously requested a secure "war room," but the requests had all fallen on deaf ears. It simply wasn't a high priority in the annual budget, which was certainly indicative of a pure bureaucracy: we'll worry about it when it happens.

Holmes's "handler" from Ad Vice had returned the detective's visit with a phone call, and Lange and Souza readied to meet with him at his office. Detective Tom Blake was a senior investigator in the Administrative Vice

Division with a solid reputation. Although a bit brusque on occasion, he was a straight shooter.

The detectives returned to Fort Davis and within the hour had parked and entered the facility. Walking in, the detectives briefly discussed how far superior the security situation there was to that at Parker Center.

Blake walked out to meet them in the lobby and introductions were exchanged. He then escorted them back to his personal office. His appearance screamed lax grooming and dress standards. Blake was a respected veteran who had been around for a while. There was an unlit cigar butt sitting on his desk, and the air reeked of cigar stench. His office would never be awarded the *Good Housekeeping* seal of approval. It was cluttered with case files, photographs, and a whole lot more. He had also forgotten to empty his ash tray … that year. Both detectives were grateful he didn't fire up the fat stogie he held in his mouth.

Blake was an affable kind of guy. His attire was not inspired by *GQ* but rather knock-off Tommy Bahama. He addressed Souza first. "So you're Glenn's brother. Good man. Best whore man we've got. What can I do for you fellas?"

Once they were all seated, Lange got right to the point and inquired about Holmes in a general sort of manner. Neither one of the homicide team wanted to throw his weight around or be pushy with Blake. By his demeanor they could tell he was a savvy street cop and certainly no push-over. If they wanted anything, it would be smart to show some respect for him and his position.

Referring to Holmes by his first name, Blake told the detectives he knew him "pretty well."

Lange explained they wanted "everything": associates, vehicles, where he scored, association with Ed Nash and any other crime figures he was aware of, and, of course, "Where is he now?"

Blake asked them to consider the position he was in. Holmes had been a good informant, turning all manner of solid intelligence for the unit. Blake's lieutenant and his captain both liked the info he had come up with while utilizing Holmes. That information made everybody happy, right up to the Chief of Police.

They once again explained they were investigating a vicious quadruple murder that could soon have a fifth dead victim. The media was all over it. They related they were more than certain the news folks would love to hear Holmes was a snitch for the LAPD and that he was now being protected because he helped the "vice squad" make porno cases. Lange asked Blake if he believed Chief Gates would go along with covering for Holmes under these circumstances.

A light came on, and it appeared that Tom Blake, the tough-guy vice cop, had an epiphany. He removed his feet from the top of his desk and sat up. He told Lange and Souza he'd run Holmes down but that he was sometimes hard to find. Lange re-emphasized that no one wanted to see anyone get embarrassed, including the Chief, just because of a "porn snitch."

Note: The detectives knew any good cop would try to protect his or her informant at almost any cost. Wonderland was a different situation, and Blake had been around long enough to realize when it was time to blink.

———

In any high-profile case there are numerous "clues" coming in at all times. Since Lange and Souza obviously could not track every one of them down to a successful conclusion, decisions had to be made as to viability. Such was the situation when they received info from law enforcement in Florida. An informant had knowledge as to Holmes's where-a-bouts in the southern part of the state.

Two days later, Lange and Souza were on their way to Miami. Once they had arrived and met up with their federal law enforcement contact, the so-called "hot" Holmes clue fizzled out, as so often happens in high-profile cases. Two days of travel time coming and going wasted. Somewhere in south Florida, a federal informant was going to have some explaining to do. However, the detectives were able to build a little rapport with the locals. That was always good. One never knew when they might need some out-of-town assistance on a particular case.

On the morning following their return to Los Angeles, Lange was in the office and received a phone call. When he picked up, he heard, "Hey, Tom. How was Miami?"

Lange didn't recognize the caller's voice and realized that no one was supposed to have known their whereabouts over the last few days. "Who's this?" Lange asked.

"Adam Dawson. You dig up anything on Holmes?"

Adam Dawson was a reporter for a local San Fernando Valley newspaper and had introduced himself early on. While concerned where he had gotten his info, Lange just played along. He told the nosy reporter they had nothing to report and no comment. Lange and Souza would hear from Adam Dawson again, many times.

Note: Adam Dawson had the reputation among cops as a "real" reporter. He was considered a throwback to an older generation who could be trusted to sit on a story if needed. He was also very good at what he did.

———

William "Rico" Vlick lived less than two blocks from the Wonderland crime scene. Lange called him at home. He was a bit guarded talking with homicide cops but agreed to meet with them for lunch anyway. His terms were Musso and Frank's, the following day, at noon. Apparently, he was more comfortable out in public.

Musso and Frank's was the oldest restaurant/bar in Hollywood. It was considered the in spot for celebrities of a bygone era. It wasn't hard for the detectives to spot Bill Vlick, nor for him to spot them.

Vlick was in his early fifties, average build and height. He dressed like a gangster at a race track. He wore lots of gold jewelry, not the expensive stuff, but swag. He couldn't understand why Lange and Souza wanted to meet with him. That was interesting in that he *was* meeting with them. Vlick also had an annoying way about him and was less than blessed, with an abrasive personality.

Shortly after the three were seated and a drink order was placed, Souza got down to the subject at hand. He told Vlick the detectives "understood" he did business with the folks at Wonderland.

Vlick was indignant. "Who the fuck, told you that?"

Souza ignored the question. "You know anyone who would want them dead?"

Vlick mellowed out a bit and told Lange and Souza he didn't know them "that well." He did know Launius liked to play the "big shot" and was a bad guy. He also believed Launius was a gun for hire - a free lance hit man.

It became obvious Vlick was just marking time, and he no doubt agreed to the meeting in an attempt to find out what the cops had in mind, for his own benefit. Lange and Souza were certain he knew more about the victims, but about the actual murders, probably not so much.

He threw around as many clichés as a Raymond Chandler novel, and with the nineteen-fortyish backdrop of Musso and Frank's, the detectives were beginning to feel as though they were in a Humphrey Bogart movie.

Realizing Vlick was a receiver of stolen property and probably nothing more, the detectives soon wrote him off as a peripheral player only. Vlick talked a lot but said little. As things began to wind down, he insisted on picking up the tab. "It's my party," he said. "You guys don't make any money." Lange and Souza would later regret ever going there.

Eleven

Closing In

Back in the RHD squad room, Lange and Souza were boning up on what they had so far and where they needed to go regarding the investigation. The subject of Holmes's whereabouts still lingered, and they had heard nothing from Tom Blake over at Ad Vice. They decided to put out an NCIC (nationwide want) on Holmes for charges of grand theft and receiving stolen property. These were charges he had pending. They also notified Administrative Vice, LAPD Detective Headquarters Fugitive Detail, OCID's airport detail, the Los Angeles and Los Angeles Sheriff's Narcotics Bureaus, and all LAPD divisions of the nationwide want.

The search for John Holmes continued as the detectives circulated the informational wanted flyer:

WANTED: John Curtis Holmes, Male, White, age 37, 6-0, 145, brown hair and blue eyes. Driving a 1970 Chev Malibu, 2-door, faded blue. Felony Warrant # A028750 charging (1) count each Grand Theft and Receiving Stolen Property - L.A. Superior Court, Santa Monica, Ca. – L.A.S.O. - Fugitive handling. Subject last observed on 8-13-81 at the San Fernando Valley Inn, a motel located at 10911 Ventura Blvd., Studio City - Frequents motels along Ventura Boulevard - Possibly armed with unknown type handgun. Holmes is a burglar with an addiction to cocaine free basing, is hurting for money and knows he's hot. Possibly in the company of one Dawn Suzanne Schiller - Female, White, age 21, 5-2, brown hair and blue eyes. If located stake and notify R.H.D. detectives Lange, Souza or Tomlinson, extension 2531 (LAPD - ph. 213-485 2531).

One morning the detectives took a drive over to Glendale to visit John Holmes's wife, Sharon. Although they believed John Holmes was running with his girlfriend, Dawn Schiller, they saw the possibility that he might try to contact Sharon. She was polite and appeared cooperative.

She told Lange and Souza that Holmes was driving her vehicle and gave them the license number and description. Sharon said John had friends all over Southern California and family still living in Ohio.

When asked about his "friends", Sharon related that a porn director by the name of Bill Amerson had a very close relationship with John. She also informed them that Amerson lived out in the San Fernando Valley. She had always thought Amerson was boorish and did not care for him personally.

Referring back to the time of the murders and before the debacle at the Biltmore, Lange asked her when she had seen Holmes last. She told the detectives it was on July 2. Prodding her, Lange asked for more. Sharon said he came by the house "bloody and bruised" and had asked her to draw a bath for him. She went on to state that John told her he had been to the Wonderland house "where the people were murdered." She said John was "scared," and she had never seen him so upset. According to his wife, Holmes did not provide her with any more specific information, and she didn't ask.

Note: Detectives believed it was possible that Sharon had gotten the dates confused and Holmes had actually come by her home on the first of July (the day of the murders), and not early the morning of the second. She seemed forthright, and detectives believed she was simply mistaken. As things turned out, her possible confusion of the dates was irrelevant. Sharon Holmes was not about to testify to anything regarding John Holmes in a court of law nor could the law compel her to do so.

In reviewing statements from the likes of David Lind, Tracy McCourt, Cherokee, and others, as well as taking a close look at the physical evidence (antique rifles, palm print, etc.), there appeared to be the makings of a fairly solid case against John Holmes for murder.

Note: As to the aforementioned antique rifles recovered from the closet in Ron Launius's bedroom at Wonderland, the detectives were now able to link the weapons up from the robbery at Alligator Arnie's by Launius and Cherokee to John Holmes, who had sold them to Ed Nash. They were then forcibly taken back by the Wonderland bunch during the robbery of Nash's home and ended up in Launius's closet. While this was not evidence of murder, it was circumstantial evidence tying Nash to the victims through Holmes, with the common thread being the antique rifles.

"A finding of murder in the first degree can be sustained although all the evidence presented was circumstantial, and where no body is produced, no direct evidence of death is produced, or the criminal means used, and where there was no confession (People v. Scott, 176 Cal. App. 2nd 458)."

In a scheduled evidentiary meeting with Deputy DA Ron Coen, the detectives decided that when the time was right, they would seek a warrant on four counts of murder and one count of attempted murder against John Holmes. They would articulate their case and the evidence in an affidavit. If they were able to eventually convict Holmes, they might be able to get him to roll over on Nash and the other killers. It would all come down to his cooperation with the prosecution. With his conviction, through his attorneys, and with the court's compliance, his sentencing could become contingent on his testimony. The dice were about to be tossed.

———

Once again, the cops were all out searching for John Holmes. The media loved that kind of stuff. On a hunch, Lange, Souza, John Helvin, and Leroy Orozco wound up at the Palladium Theater in Hollywood at the Porn Actors Screen Awards Show. The popular comedian Paul Lynde was the emcee. Through a source in that industry, detectives heard that although he was not nominated for any kind of an award, Holmes might show up, his ego being what it was.

Looking closely at all the attendees on the plush red carpet, it was clear that the get-together was more about who could out-porn whom. Every deviant form of dress (or undress) was on blatant display. The detectives agreed that Billy Graham probably wouldn't make the gig.

As the detectives "badged" their way in through the very large and noisy crowd, it was evident they weren't fooling anyone as to their presence. Holmes didn't show. Having a big ego didn't necessarily include wanting to go to jail for murder.

In a follow-up interview with Sharon Holmes, she revealed that John had previously phoned her collect from the Pendleton, Oregon area. At the time, John was in trouble and needed money. Also, Dawn Schiller had family in the Pacific Northwest. His cash-flow issue was apparently the impetuous for the visit there with Dawn. This being the only viable lead at the time, it was decided that Souza would travel to Pendleton with Frank Tomlinson and check things out. Lange stayed behind to handle incoming information as well as the incessant meetings that came with handling a major case.

Frank and Bob left out of LAX on a commercial passenger jet bound for Portland, Oregon. They then caught a connecting flight on an eighteen-passenger twin-engine prop job for the final leg of their journey. While flying over the Cascade Mountain Range, the puddle jumper experienced very rough turbulence as it flew through blizzard-like conditions. The small aircraft shook violently and bobbed abruptly up and down. With no door on the cockpit and Souza and Tomlinson near the front of the plane, it was apparent to Souza that even the pilot and co-pilot were nervous about the situation. Some passengers, like Bob Souza, were terrified.

Frank Tomlinson was a man of deep religious faith. He made no secret of this. He traveled with the Holy Bible and on occasion prayed on his knees with victims and suspects alike. As most of the aircraft's passengers were in panic mode, the plane continued to lose altitude and twist and jerk in the fierce winds. Frank calmly read his Bible. He noticed that his temporary partner, Souza, was shaken. He told him, "Don't worry, Bob. God's in charge. We'll be fine."

Souza was beside himself and responded with, "That's fine for you, pal, but I haven't talked to God in a long time. If we make it through this, I'm driving back!"

Arriving in Pendleton safely, Bob took a while to shake off the rocky ride. Speaking to a flight attendant, Souza learned that the employee had been flying for twelve years in the area, and that flight had been the worst he had ever experienced. However, for Frank, the flight was ancient history, and he was ready to go to work.

It was the frigid season in Oregon, and the detectives had to run around for most of the day to determine that Sharon Holmes's information about John was stale. Dawn Schiller's family members were welcoming and cooperative. They all seemed to be forthright with the detectives and eager for John to be in custody where he, but more importantly their daughter, would be safe.

Souza and Tomlinson also spoke to Dawn's younger brother, Wayne. He related he was very upset with Holmes because John had beaten his sister on several occasions. He also offered that Holmes had painted Dawn's car a different color in what Wayne believed was an attempt to evade capture. The detectives also learned Holmes had been in Oregon only briefly and then took off for what the family believed was Los Angeles with Dawn.

Although Holmes was once again in the wind, this trip would not turn out to be a complete waste of time. Tomlinson and Souza had made a very positive connection with Dawn Schiller's family that would pay off later.

———

Since the media was much involved, Lange and Souza were still receiving all manner of leads on Holmes that had to be checked out. After handling dozens, and sometimes hundreds, of these so-called clues in high-profile cases, experienced detectives gradually developed a system to deal with the never-ending flow of information. Of course, this information was all grist for a defense team at trial. It was "discoverable" meaning it all had to be turned over to the defense team per the rules of reciprocal discovery prior to any trial. These little, sometimes innocuous-appearing bits of information, had been known to create "red herrings" and cause much chaos for the prosecution at the trial level, usually when it was least welcomed.

In breaking down these so-called clues, priority numbers one through three were assigned to each one. A one meant the clue needed immediate attention. This would include a named individual, a suspect, a witness, or a license number and description constituting a solid lead. A two would be important enough to follow through on but with less information than a one. A three would be an Elvis sighting, and the King was having lunch with John Holmes.

Frank Tomlinson had kept in touch with Dawn Schiller's family in Oregon. He had always had a calming and credible rapport with witnesses. Frank phoned Dawn's younger brother, Wayne, and told him he could be a tremendous asset in helping get his sister away from Holmes. Wayne was more than enthused to do just that. Yes, he had heard from his sister. She was in south Florida with John, somewhere in the area of North Miami Beach.

Frank explained to Wayne that he believed Dawn's life was in danger. He told him that traveling with Holmes was a tremendous risk she should not be taking. He explained that Ed Nash was not going to allow Holmes, or anyone with Holmes, to talk to law enforcement for fear they might testify against him. Frank related that John and Dawn were only marking time before something bad happened to them. Wayne decided to offer up more information. Dawn's family in Oregon had recently received two collect phone calls from her that originated in the northern Dade County, Florida area.

Note: The collect-call phone numbers had been retained on a phone bill.

Meanwhile, at Cedars-Sinai Hospital, Susan Launius was showing signs of recovery. Dr. Saunders believed she could be interviewed, at least on a limited basis. Lange and Souza discussed how they should best approach the obviously delicate situation with her. They were not certain of her allegiances. It was decided that Bob Souza would handle the interview alone. He would become her confidant and use his Sacramento roots to gain her trust. He would also be her protector and the one person she could rely on. Having one permanent contact among the investigators seemed to be a better fit for Susan, and the investigation as a whole.

Twelve

Miami or Bust!

Wayne Schiller agreed to fly to Miami and meet Lange and Tomlinson in an attempt to locate his sister, Dawn. The detectives hoped this would lead to the apprehension of Holmes. On November 30, 1981, Tomlinson and Lange were on a flight to Miami International Airport. Later that night, they were to meet up with Wayne Schiller there.

Note: Wayne had lived in the Miami area for several years and attended local schools, solidifying relationships with many acquaintances along the way.

In the midmorning hours of December 1, Lange pulled their rental car to the curb in front of the Carol City Stop and Go Market. Wayne Schiller jumped out and walked the mile or so to the residence of a Mr. and Mrs. William Smith. The Smiths had befriended the Schillers years before, and their children had attended school together in Carol City, a suburban area northwest of Miami.

Note: Carol City and Liberty City in Miami had been the sites of violent riots the year before when four local cops were acquitted in the purported beating death of a local black man. Several citizens had died, and local residences and businesses had been burned and looted. Tensions remained high, with sporadic disturbances occurring from time to time.

Lange and Tomlinson were scheduled to meet with local Drug Enforcement Administration agents who had offered to assist the Los Angeles detectives in locating Holmes. The contact had been set up by the Los Angeles area Drug Enforcement Agency office. In their initial meeting with the agents it became clear any assistance from the local DEA office would be limited at best. Unfortunately for Lange and Tomlinson, the local agents were hip deep in a multiple murder investigation involving six local Colombian cocaine dealers who had been murdered a week or so prior to their arrival. At that particular time, the Miami area was considered one of the hottest cocaine distribution points in North America.

One of the two phone calls from Dawn Schiller to Oregon mentioned earlier had come back to a phone registered to a real estate office in Surfside, Florida. Surfside was a tiny community of rundown motels and hotels along Collins Avenue with the Atlantic Ocean as a backdrop. The town was bordered on the south by northern Miami Beach and on the north by the Dade County line. This was not where the elite meet to eat. Instead, the area was frequented by many folks attempting to support their drug habits by committing burglary and all manner of theft. The few out-of-town tourists who frequented the motels were usually on fixed budgets and did not stick around town long after they became victims. This, of course, made prosecuting the crooks difficult. While Surfside was a haven for thieves, it was also a headache for law enforcement.

The Surfside Police Department had seventeen sworn members. One was Detective Sharon Richards, one of three detectives on the force. She had eleven years with the department and during that time had not developed what one might consider an appreciation for her profession. This was not difficult to understand when the folks running the show were perhaps more concerned with the traffic congestion problem (and the revenue it generated through the writing of traffic tickets) than with the proliferation of dope and burglars. Detective Richards offered to assist Lange and Tomlinson in any way she could. Any cooperation or assistance the detectives could get when out of state was always greatly appreciated.

Richards accompanied Lange and Tomlinson to the Surfside Realty Office, where one of Dawn Schiller's phone calls had originated. Detectives interviewed the few employees there separately. None were able to identify Holmes or Schiller and did not profess any knowledge regarding the phone call made from their business. Although a telephone is readily available for public use on a countertop, detectives were told people just walking in off the street were not allowed to use it. Since the phone in question was not under constant observation, there was a clear flaw in that policy.

Note: The second phone number came back to a public phone in the same vicinity.

Tom and Frank found themselves back at the Surfside Police Department in the detective bureau to regroup. The room reminded them of a converted broom closet without the broom. It did have an air conditioner, which would always come in handy in Florida. They discussed the possibility of showing the Holmes and Schiller mug shots around the various motels, but that plan got shelved as impractical and probably a waste of time. Richards told the LA cops that her ex-husband, Bob Richards, was a detective with the Metro-Dade Police and was deployed just north of Surfside. She believed he would assist Lange and Tomlinson. She phoned him immediately and set up a meeting for that very night.

The detectives also had a meeting scheduled that evening with the Miami-Dade police regarding the aforementioned multi-six dope murder that had occurred the previous week. The in with that department was the Wonderland murders. Although remote, detectives wanted to look into the possibility that the cases could be connected. With Holmes hanging somewhere in the Miami area, they wanted to cover that possibility and be able to discern if there was any connection. Also, it was a viable reason to hook up with the local homicide cops to build a rapport for the present investigation and any future endeavors.

Metro-Dade homicide detective Jose Diaz was as busy as any young murder cop could be. He had six cocaine-dealing victims tied and gagged, then summarily shot in the back of the head. The grisly message murders had occurred in Perrine, a suburb southwest of Miami. Diaz was trying to get organized. The incoming phone calls were incessant. The brass wanted answers. The media wanted interviews. His partner wanted more assistance. Diaz just wanted some sleep. Unable to find any tie-ins with their investigation and with a great deal of empathy, Tomlinson and Lange took their leave.

In trying to cover all bases, their next stop was the Miami Beach Police Department's narcotics unit. After being contacted by Sergeant Jon Anderson, they were informed that one of Anderson's men had an informant, a one-time porno actress who had "performed" with John Holmes in the past. The two had an off screen non-romantic relationship, and she could be of some help. The problem, however, was that the former actress, called Lucy, had an association with a major bad ass narcotics dealer who was also suspected of some dope-related murders that were unsolved in the Miami area.

A subsequent stakeout involving the snitch and Mr. Badass had finally ended, and the informant wound up with the Miami Beach dope cop at a local pizza joint over a couple of beers. Lange and Tomlinson joined the two. The introductions were less than dignified as Lucy went into a profanity-laced rant about her erstwhile relationship with John Curtis Holmes. She was high, nasty, and not in any mood to cooperate. Besides, she hated Holmes. She had heard he was involved in "murder or something" on the West Coast.

From the dope cop: "C'mon, Lucy. Don't be a fuckin' slut. We know you've seen him."

She stated, "I swear to you I haven't seen him and don't want to. I hope the motherfucker dies!" Wrapping up her comments, she glanced out the large picture window onto Alton Road. Genuine fear registered on her face. The detectives all turned toward the window, and there was Mr. Badass, glaring down at her through the glass, much as a cobra would a mouse.

Next thing the detectives heard from the dope cop was, "OK, Lucy. See you later. Stay loose." Lange, Tomlinson, and the dope cop were up and out the door.

Earlier, Frank and Tom had put Wayne Schiller up at the Palms Beach Motel, located just a few blocks from the Northeast Station of the Metro-Dade police at 162nd Street and Biscayne Boulevard. Wayne had spent the day with his family's lifelong friends, the Smiths. He told them that he had run away from Oregon and would remain in the Miami area at least until he was able to see his sister. Had they seen her?

Yes, they had. They saw Dawn some two weeks earlier when she had dropped by their home with another young woman. Her friend worked as a dancer at the Aquarius Lounge on the Tamiami Trail, near Coral Gables.

Note: There was concern in using family (Wayne) under these circumstances. The detectives did not want to put anyone in jeopardy. If they approached Dawn too early, she could implode. However, she was very close to her brother. She might listen to him and hear his true concerns. She could then be convinced to give Holmes up for the safety of herself and her family.

Dawn had further explained to the Smiths that she was living with the other woman temporarily and caring for her children. After the visit the Smiths observed Dawn and her friend drive off. They also noted the two women (her friend was driving) were in an unusual-looking blue Ford pickup truck with a camper in the bed of the truck. The camper shell was actually a miniature log cabin.

Note: It appeared the detectives had their first solid Florida lead in locating Dawn Schiller. Her roommate danced at the Aquarius Lounge on the Tamiami Trail and drove a blue Ford pickup with a log cabin for a camper in the bed of the truck.

It was 10:30 p.m., and it had been another long day, but the LA cops were not through. They entered the lobby of the Northeast Station at Metro-Dade. Bob Richards came out and introduced himself. He was in his mid-thirties with boyish looks and a somewhat withdrawn demeanor for a cop. Richards looked like anything but a cop. He would do well in any undercover-type assignment. He got right to work and determined the Aquarius Lounge had dancers working every night, and the club closed at 3:00 a.m. Lange and Tomlinson planned to go there that night and attempt to locate Dawn's friend and her miniature log cabin truck. If the truck was located, they would stake out on it and follow the driver home. Wayne Schiller had also given a fairly good description of Dawn's friend that had been relayed to him by the Smiths. That would help. Bob Richards told Lange and Tomlinson the club had a less-than-stellar reputation for fights, shootings, stabbings, and the like.

He mentioned they would probably not want the patrons to know who they were.

If the truck was located in the parking lot, the plan was to enter the club individually and attempt to identify Dawn's friend while she was dancing. Richards would remain outside in the lot with eyes on the pickup. Lange and Tomlinson would no doubt be moving in and out of the club several times to stay in touch with him, since a police radio in the club would not have been a good idea.

Note: While Lange didn't know the bar, he knew the location. It sat on the southwest corner of the Tamiami Trail (Southwest Eighth Street) and Lejeune Road. Before moving to Los Angeles in 1961, Lange had lived just blocks from that very intersection while attending high school in Coral Gables.

It was going on midnight as Lange and Tomlinson drove slowly through the Aquarius parking lot. Then they saw it. The blue Ford pickup with the miniature log cabin in the bed was parked in the lot. All of a sudden, they were no longer tired. After a day of strikeouts, it looked like they had just gotten hold of one, and it was headed for the fence. Richards ran the license plate for the owner information as well as wants and warrants. It turned out the truck had earlier been reported stolen out of Akron, Ohio. There was no local owner information available. The detectives would have to stay on the truck and follow the driver to wherever she took them. Some things never seemed to come easy.

Frank and Tom entered the bar separately. Richards remained outside, keeping an eye on the pickup. Sitting at the crowded bar next to Tomlinson, Lange ordered a Budweiser. The non-drinking Tomlinson had ordered a draft beer and was touching the glass to his lips, but not swallowing any beer. When the bartender wasn't looking Lange poured Frank's beer into his glass so as not to give the wrong kind of impression.

The interior of the Aquarius was adorned with three circular stages accommodating three nude dancers. The stage platforms could all be viewed from anywhere in the club. The three young women performing were hard at work. The cops didn't have to worry about feigning a conversation because the place was packed, and no one could hear anything anyway above all the loud music and commotion. The whoops and catcalls from the well-oiled young male patrons added to the overall confusion.

The main attraction seemed to be the female dancing totally nude on the center stage. The shapely young woman balanced herself on her hands as she did splits in the air. She then moved across the platform on her hands to the edge of the stage and ever so slowly lowered her legs down and around the necks of two joyous (and drunk) patrons. If you were a practicing Catholic, what happened next would have had you in the confessional at your local church early the following week, just for watching. It was after one in the morning, and the detectives were thrashed. They decided to get some fresh air and watch the pickup truck from their car. Richards was alone in his vehicle. Lange and Tomlinson had police radio communication with him. The next couple of hours dragged on for the cops but probably not for the customers inside the Aquarius.

It was 3:00 a.m. when the target exited the club, this time in clothes. She walked directly to the pickup. She was accompanied by a young male. They got into the truck, pulled out of the lot with the woman driving, and headed south on Lejeune Road toward Coral Gables. Using their handheld radios, Tom, Frank, and Richards continued communication. Richards, driving alone, took the lead.

They soon discovered that the easiest part of police work did not include following a vehicle at 3:15 a.m. on a dark, deserted residential street without being detected. The pickup finally pulled up in front of a darkened home in sleepy Coral Gables and stopped. The headlights remained on. A few minutes passed before the male exited the truck and went into the residence. Frank had stopped down the street with his lights off. The pickup then made a sudden U-turn and accelerated back toward the detectives' car at a high rate of speed. The truck flew by, and within seconds it was out of sight. Since Richards was paralleling the detectives' car one street over and was unable to follow the truck, they blew the tail. She was gone. Another night staked out at the Aquarius did not sound appealing.

Frank pulled out on to Lejeune Road and sped north, trying to pick her up. At that point they didn't know whether or not she had spotted them. As they flew by Majorca Avenue, Lange was struck with a bit of nostalgia.

Note: As an eight-year old boy in 1953, he had stood on the street at that very location and shaken the hand of the new president of the United States, Dwight D. Eisenhower. The motorcade was slowly passing by, and the president was seated in the left rear of an open convertible. On a whim Lange had run out into the street and stuck his hand into the car, and the president grabbed it and shook it. Back then, things were a bit different.

With their luck apparently running high, they spotted the pickup truck directly ahead. They pulled in behind it and continued to follow it north past the Aquarius. Being on a major roadway, there was more traffic, making their task a bit easier. At this point Lange and Tomlinson lost all communication with Richards. Weak signal? No signal? They didn't know, so they just stayed with the target. The Los Angeles team had no legal authority in Florida, so they were eager to contact Richards.

They followed the pickup for several minutes until the driver pulled into a Denny's restaurant across the street from Miami International Airport and parked. The dancer exited and joined four males in the parking lot. All five then walked into Denny's for an early-morning breakfast. While their communications were down, the pay phones out in front of the restaurant were up. Lange was able to connect with Miami-Dade communications, and within a few minutes, Bob Richards joined them.

At 4:15 a.m. when the group exited Denny's, the female climbed into her pickup and proceeded northbound on the Miami Turnpike alone. The detectives were close behind as she exited at NW 182nd Street. The truck then proceeded into a still-dark, quiet residential area, causing the detectives to back off in order to avoid detection. At one point Richards cut his headlights as he followed closely.

The pickup finally pulled into a single-family residence encircled with colorful twinkling Christmas lights. Richards pulled in closer to get an address as the lights were doused. It appeared the target was in for the night, at least what remained of it. Was Dawn Schiller inside? Lange and Tomlinson would follow up after some rest.

Thirteen

Holmes in Cuffs

At 5:30 a.m. Lange and Tomlinson pulled into the River Town House Hotel across from Miami International with the intent of grabbing a couple of hours of sleep before they picked up Wayne Schiller at 10:00 a.m. As they entered the hotel, it was still dark when they were braced by a surly security guard whom they had inadvertently aroused from a nap. Their rest was put on hold as they were forced to explain their very early, or very late, entry onto the hotel premises. After things were cleared up, they entered the hotel, only to be turned away at their room. The door would not open. They discovered they were locked out due to a five-dollar deficit in the hotel room deposit. The little glitch was cleared up in minutes, and they were finally left to crash for three hours.

By 9:50 a.m. the detectives were en route to pick up Wayne Schiller and deposit him, hopefully, at his sister's current residence. At around 10:30 a.m., they met up with Bob Richards with Wayne Schiller in tow. Lange and Tomlinson laid out their plan over a bite to eat, and by early afternoon, they were ready to go. Wayne proceeded to Dawn's girlfriend's home in a rental car. The three cops were waiting outside and ready to follow. Approximately forty-five minutes later, Wayne exited the home, alone.

They followed Wayne as he drove away and shortly thereafter pulled into a church parking lot and stopped. Per the plan, Wayne was to drive the rental car with Dawn as a passenger. He was to gradually talk her into pulling over with him and talking to the LA cops, who would be following them. Dawn Schiller would then give up John Holmes, and Lange and Tomlinson would return to Los Angeles with their fugitive. It sounded reasonably simple, but simple didn't always work.

The detectives hooked up with Wayne. He told them Dawn was at the home but couldn't leave until 4:30 p.m. because she was watching her girl-friend's kids. Wayne had told her he would return at that time and they would go for a drive. All was not lost. Dawn told Wayne she had been staying at the location for several weeks. She said Holmes was in the Miami area, but she hadn't seen him in about two weeks. Wayne related that they hadn't discussed the purpose of his trip or how he found her, but he would bring that up later during their drive.

By 4:45 p.m. the rented tan sedan was eastbound on 168th Street with Wayne at the wheel and Dawn in the front passenger seat. Tomlinson and Lange were right behind in their rental, followed by Bob Richards. Wayne pulled over near a small market, and Dawn ran in and grabbed a six-pack of beer. She was back shortly. They were cruising once again.

The plan was for Wayne to be ready to pull into a small park near Dawn's current place at around 6:00 p.m. At 6:05 p.m. Lange and Tomlinson observed some furtive head movements on the part of Dawn in the car. A jerk here and a rapid head movement there, a quick glance in the passenger's side-view mirror and they knew Wayne had dropped it on her. He pulled into the park and stopped. He then hesitatingly exited the car and walked slowly back toward the detectives who had pulled in behind them. Frank and Tom got out and walked slowly forward. Wayne had that questionable look on his face that said, "I don't know. She's not happy with me."

Lange approached the passenger window and reintroduced himself. He got a gruff reproach with, "I know who you are!" It was not a friendly reply. But they talked. She listened. Lange and Tomlinson explained the problems

Holmes had gotten himself into and said she should not have to shoulder them. They explained that she had her entire life ahead of her. The threats were real. She shouldn't get drawn in.

For a spell Dawn was defensive. She told the detectives Ed Nash had cops in his hip pocket. Dawn said, "Maybe you are working for Nash. How do I know I can trust you?" This was certainly a reasonable question under the circumstances. The cops would have to be convincing.

Tomlinson keyed in on Dawn's anger with Holmes and his self-centered ego, his lies, and his taking advantage of her. A few moments passed, and she finally stepped out of the car and leaned against it. She listened some more and asked to speak with Wayne. A few minutes later, after some reflection, she walked over to Lange and said, "OK. He's at the Fountainhead Motel on Collins Avenue, room 41. He's there under the name of John Wade. He's dyed his hair black. His car is parked and locked up at the Standard Station two blocks away. It's been painted black. We did it when we were in Montana before we came here."

As it turned out, the Fountainhead Motel was in the heart of Surfside. Dawn went on to tell Lange and Tomlinson that Holmes was doing some handyman work at the motel to pay for his keep. Wayne Schiller had come through in a big way and had greatly aided the detectives in turning his sister.

The Miami-Dade police did some background work on the Fountainhead Motel. It was an older nondescript two-story building located on the ocean side of Collins Avenue. It was also currently closed for renovation. Room 41 was on the second level, just off an outside lobby. It was clearly visible from the west side of Collins Avenue.

By 8:15 that evening, eight detectives from the Metro-Dade Northeast station had assembled in their squad bay. They were joined by Frank, Bob Richards, and Lange. After speaking with Dawn and going over past experiences with Holmes, the detectives felt he just didn't seem like the type to go down with guns blazing. They decided to stake out the location from the excellent vantage point on the west side of Collins Avenue and wait for Holmes to show.

Meanwhile, the cops would secure the area around the entire motel, choking off the north and south areas along the east side of Collins Avenue. There would also be a couple of undercover types, along with Tomlinson, roaming up and down the street in front of the motel, keeping an eye out for Holmes. Holmes had never seen Tomlinson before.

At 8:50 p.m. Bob Richards and Lange pulled into the only available parking spot on the west side of Collins Avenue. The location afforded an excellent view and line of sight to room 41 across the street.

After checking out their communications, the group settled in for what could be a long night. However, as it turned out, things went down quickly. Not five minutes after the cops set up, John Holmes appeared in the doorway of room 41. He had altered his appearance some. He had a scruffy beard and had dyed his hair, as well as his beard, black.

Holmes walked next door and entered the neighboring room, where the door had been left wide open. A small party was in progress. Greetings were exchanged. He then walked back into his room, leaving his door wide open in an apparent attempt to catch the cooler evening air. Things were looking up.

Lange notified the others, who had taken up positions in and around the motel. Ten minutes later, Lange took up the familiar barricade position against Holmes's door jamb and leveled his two-inch Smith & Wesson .38 at Holmes as he lay on his bed. There was a brief look of surprise on Holmes's face until he recognized Lange, who had him roll over with his arms behind his back. He was handcuffed immediately. There was no resistance.

"I was wondering when you would show up. What took you so long?" Holmes, of course, needed to say something to feed his self-centered movie persona, Johnny Wadd. A check of his room revealed empty food containers everywhere, clothes strewn about in heaps, rotting uneaten food on paper plates, and assorted trash tossed throughout. It was a good thing the detectives were there simply to arrest him and didn't have to spend any more time in his room, which reeked of rotting garbage.

Holmes's demeanor changed from carefree to sullen rapidly once he discovered that the Los Angeles detectives were a bit more business-like this time around. Holmes was booked into the Dade County detention facility on the

Los Angeles warrants. The arrest and the booking had gone down with no problems, and the best news was there were no paparazzi in sight. A media presence would not have been advantageous at that time.

On the following Saturday morning, the judge at the Dade County Municipal Courthouse decided to take up an extradition hearing on the weekend, saving everyone a lot of time and unwanted press.

Lange and Tomlinson watched intently as a deputy public defender was appointed as Holmes's attorney. The detectives figured he would fight extradition, and they prepared to stay in Florida a bit longer. To their surprise, Holmes waived extradition. They were on their way home. Driving out to Miami International Airport the following day, Holmes was loose and talkative, even a bit flippant. Although he had been advised of his constitutional rights, Holmes waived them and told the LA cops he had nothing to do with the killings. Nash was behind all of it. The back seat of a rental car was not the best place to conduct any kind of an interview, nor was a plane. However, his remarks were documented regardless. The detectives were anxious to get back to Los Angeles to take their shot at Holmes, but kept their ears open anyway.

While on the plane, Holmes appeared to doze off as Frank read his Bible. Meanwhile, the Miami press was all over the arrest and maybe a bit miffed that they had missed out on all the action. Lange was glad he had given Souza the heads-up on their arrival at LAX. He had a pretty good idea his other partner would handle things when they landed. The Los Angeles paparazzi would be impatiently waiting and salivating for their arrival.

Once they landed in Los Angeles, Lange and Tomlinson were approached by a flight attendant who asked them to stay seated while the other passengers deplaned. They were informed that LAPD people were out on the tarmac with security and a transport vehicle. Lange smiled, knowing Souza and Lewis had come through for them. The media would be left to their own devices this time around.

On the way back to Robbery/Homicide Division Holmes mentioned to Frank that he had seen him with his Bible. He asked if Frank would pray with him. Seeing an opening with Holmes, Tomlinson agreed. While Frank truly wanted to obtain any information on the murders that he could from

Holmes, he was also very serious about praying with him, not as a murderer, but as a believer. This, of course, could have important ramifications in trial. When a detective prayed with a murder suspect in order to obtain a confession (which would be the impression here), the detective was risking having that confession thrown out. Holmes's defense team would eat it up, and so would the press.

Lieutenant Ron Lewis would have to make the call. Regardless of sentiment, the detectives all agreed that Tomlinson had a certain rapport with Holmes, even if the actor was playing a game. If Frank was careful about how he conducted the interview, he might be able to glean important facts regarding the murders and still obtain some type of admission, if not a confession. Tomlinson was confident.

Upon their arrival at the office and for reasons of privacy, Tomlinson took Holmes into the vacant captain's office and closed the door. It was Frank and the murder suspect and the Holy Bible. They prayed. They discussed Holmes's involvement in the murders. There was an important admission. Holmes alluded to letting the killers into the Wonderland house. Clearly, he had known why they were there to begin with. If properly obtained, this admission would go far in a murder trial. However, was it obtained as a consequence of prayer?

Note: Souza and Lange did not agree with this tactic. It went against protocol in that it was not being recorded, there were no notes taken, there was only one interviewer, and if the basis for an admission or any other evidence obtained was dependent on praying over the Holy Bible, they had major problems.

Holmes came across with some corroborating information, and then there was the important admission. However, when Holmes was asked about Nash's involvement and the identity of the killers, he balked. He refused to go there. He said he feared for his and his family's safety. The prosecution and the cops would need Holmes convicted if they were ever to have the possibility of him rolling over on Nash and the killers. This was far from a sure thing.

Following the interview, Holmes was officially arrested for the murders and booked into the central jail at Parker Center. Souza guided Holmes in handcuffs to a secluded back stairway on the third floor that led down to the felony section of the Parker Center jail. It didn't take long for prisoners in that section to learn of the celebrity porn star about to be booked. Souza and Holmes were greeted by the jail staff. They had been given a heads-up regarding the arrival.

Some prisoners in the lockup without a clear view of the felony processing area were on the shoulders of other prisoners to get a peek at Holmes. Felony jailers offered no privacy or special consideration during the skin-searching portion of processing. Holmes was ordered to strip down and then went through the same process as any other arrestee. There were a great many catcalls and comments shouted when Holmes was totally naked. He seemed embarrassed. When he was ordered to bend over and spread his cheeks, the jail erupted in cheers and shouts. Souza thought it strange that a man who spent hours naked in front of a video camera and crew would be embarrassed in a room full of men. He was quiet and compliant as the jailer ordered him through the entire cavity-search process.

Souza returned to the RHD squad room and was greeted with shouts from his fellow detectives:

"Hey, Souz, was it really over a foot long?"

"Who says all men are created equal, huh, Souza?"

"Kinda humbles us mortals, eh?"

Souza smiled, taking in the comments. He sat at his desk and had a single response to the room. "Holmes was pretty nervous. It was shrunk down to a lazy nine."

That afternoon, a popular disc jockey on one of the Los Angeles radio stations broadcast a news item between spinning records: "I just found out that famous porno film star John Holmes was booked for murder this morning, and it took the booking detective three hours to skin search him."

As had been arranged, Deputy DA Ron Coen filed four counts of murder and one count of attempted murder for the attack on Susan Launius. Things had gone well relative to the arrest and filing. This was mostly because the district attorney's office had been onboard throughout the investigation. That was not always the case.

Note: The district attorney representing a county in the state of California is an elected position. No politician can be expected to run for that office and be reelected without being able to bring with him or her, a hefty conviction rate. Because of this, there are times when filing deputies at the DA's office played a little fast and loose.

On September 3, 1976, Franklin D. Crockett, age forty-three, was stabbed some forty-seven times, resulting in his death. The assault took place in his small hotel room at 311 East Winston Place in downtown Los Angeles, just off Skid Row.

While investigating the scene, Detective Tom Lange was approached by a neighbor of the victim who, with a furtive gesture and whispering softly, led Lange to a hotel room just above Crockett's room on the next level. As Lange approached the front door, he noticed it was wide open. He tapped on the door, announced his presence, and glanced inside. He observed what appeared to be a bloody towel hanging on a rack by the open window. It didn't take long to figure out that this open window was directly above the open window of the victim's room and was also adjacent to the same fire escape. Both rooms were easily accessed from the outside fire escape ladder.

The occupant of the room stepped toward the door and told Lange he lived there. After a short interview and denials of even knowing who the victim was, Lange confiscated the towel and continued his investigation downstairs. At that time a latent fingerprint on the window sill by the fire escape in the victim's apartment was revealed when the sill was being dusted.

Walter L. Valentine and Ernest L. Williams were subsequently arrested by Lange for the murder. The print from the windowsill in Crockett's room was soon matched to one of the men. The bloody towel found in the suspect's room was ABO typed to the victim. (Again, there was no DNA technology at that time.) Additional circumstantial evidence was obtained from witnesses at the hotel.

Lange submitted the case to a filing deputy at the district attorney's office and was rejected. The deputy DA wanted more clarification on the evidence. Clearly stating that his investigation would continue even after a filing, Lange did not impress the deputy DA, and the suspects were released.

Work on the case continued, and Lange was able to get an updated serology report confirming the victim's blood on the towel through sub-typing and some additional circumstantial evidence. He eventually returned to the DA's office and once again was rejected by a different filing deputy. Lange got into a heated discussion with the attorney and left in a huff. The attorney for the DA's office followed Lange out of his office yelling at the detective. He made a formal complaint to Lange's commanding officer about the detective's "brusque" behavior. That particular filing deputy went on to become the Los Angeles County District Attorney some years later. While Lange regretted getting involved to that extent, he still believed he would probably do it again.

Lange understood that the district attorney's office had filing protocols in place and would not want to file a case they knew they might not win. However, they also had a duty to the citizens of the community to protect them and charge persons with crimes when there was reasonable evidence to show culpability. That was what preliminary hearings were meant to determine.

On November 27, 1976, George Trammell, age forty-six, was stabbed numerous times, resulting in his death. The brutal attack took place in the third-floor hallway of his apartment at 1330 South Olive Street in downtown Los Angeles. This was a few miles southwest of the Crockett murder scene. Valentine and Williams were once again arrested for murder. A woman by the name of Barbara Blanks was also taken into custody.

Lange assembled files on both cases and took both murders back to the original filing deputy. He declined to review both cases, writing in his declination that "Submission to another filing deputy would give a fresh view of the matter." Lange wound up in the office of Deputy District Attorney Stanley Weisberg. Weisberg was eventually appointed to the bench and became a superior court judge in Los Angeles County. He went on to become involved with several high-profile cases, including the McMartin Preschool molestation case, the Menendez murder case in Beverly Hills, and the Rodney King case (People v. Powell). Judge Weisberg retired in 2008 after a distinguished career.

Weisberg filed both counts of murder on both suspects and one count of murder on the woman after discussing the matter at length with Lange. Everything was going along well until his phone rang. He picked up and was greeted by a reporter from the Los Angeles Times. *As he listened Lange watched his facial expression change from mildly interested to concerning, and then to really pissed. He hung up abruptly after a short exchange with the reporter—something about "no comment"—and then glared at Lange, asking, "Are you trying to start a war?"*

The call had been an inquiry about why the district attorney's office had not filed the original case since another victim had now been murdered after their initial refusal to file. The old "leak" had reared its ugly head once again. Were the cops trying to start a war? No, just trying to take killers off the street.

In January of 1982, in spite of all else, John Holmes was arraigned on murder charges in a downtown Los Angeles courtroom. As expected, he pleaded not guilty. He was represented by Los Angeles attorneys Earl Hanson and Mitchell Egers.

Both defense counselors were highly respected and very competent. Having these two men appointed at county expense was probably about the best thing that had happened to John Holmes since the horrendous events of July 1, 1981. Deputy DA Ron Coen had mixed feelings about how the Holmes situation should be handled by his prosecution. While he saw a fairly solid case against Holmes, he was concerned by the manner in which the interview of this now-defendant had been conducted. If Holmes could be held to answer at a preliminary hearing, there was a good possibility that some type of a plea could be negotiated with his testimony against Nash and others.

Note: Of import here is that Frank Tomlinson did not believe that Holmes was an actual participant in the murders. He did believe Holmes was complicit to a certain degree, but he viewed Holmes as more of a witness to be turned. Certainly that scenario could play out if Holmes was eventually held to answer, or even convicted.

Holding to his earlier assertion to Lange, Frank Tomlinson retired from the Los Angeles Police Department. He would eventually testify at Holmes's trial, but he would be a civilian when he did.

Frank remained firm in his belief that Holmes did not actually kill anyone. While this may have been true in layman's terms, he could still be found guilty of aiding and abetting in the crime. Tomlinson's stance on Holmes drove Deputy District Attorney Ron Coen to distraction. What would a jury think if Tomlinson testified that he didn't believe the suspect he arrested for murder actually committed murder?

Fourteen

In the Field

While in the office and not having heard from David Lind recently, Bob Souza called Fat Howard for a chat. Howard told him Lind was staying "over on Yucca" in Hollywood with a new girlfriend. Howard said the new girl's phone was out of order but gave Souza an address. This would be round two with Lind, and no doubt there would be more to come. Lange was on his way to the district attorney's office on another case, so Bob grabbed Detective Leroy Orozco to back him up. Souza and Orozco headed for the basement parking lot and Souza's car.

The address on Yucca Street in central Hollywood was an older, dilapidated apartment building. Bob rapped on the door of the apartment number provided by Fat Howard. He announced himself and called out for Lind by his first name. They heard someone approach the door inside.

It was Lind. "How do I know you dudes are really cops?"

Souza responded, "Hey David. It's me, Souza."

There was silence on the other side of the door when Leroy identified himself and slipped his police identification card under it. In a flash the ID card was whisked up, and there were the sounds of crashing furniture and someone running toward the rear of the location. Then a rear door slammed.

Souza looked at Leroy. "That asshole is running!"

The detectives were on the move when Leroy shouted, "It's my ID card. Shit!"

They ran to the rear of the apartment building, and as Souza rounded the corner, he nearly ran into Lind coming the opposite way. Souza knocked Lind to the ground, and Leroy kneeled on him and hooked him up with his handcuffs.

Souza helped Lind to his feet. "What the fuck are you doing David?" he growled.

Lind's speech was slurred; it was apparent he was stoned. "Hey, man, I thought somebody was after me."

Orozco reached into Lind's breast pocket and retrieved his ID card. He punched Lind in the chest. "We should book your ass, fucker!"

Souza steered Lind toward the front of the building, and they took him back to their car. Souza guided Lind to the back seat. "Hey, David, you really pissed off my partner."

Lind was on the nod and coming down from his last fix. He muttered, "Yeah man, I'm sorry."

Bob said to Leroy, "Bet you won't do that again."

Leroy gave him a dirty look. They returned to the office with Lind.

Once again back in the free and voluntary room, Lind was drowsy. Souza asked him about Holmes. "Did John go over to the Wonderland house often?"

"Yeah! Sometimes every day."

"Did you ever see him in Launius's room?"

"Are you shitting me? Ronnie's room? No way! He'd kill that punk bastard."

"Was Holmes allowed free reign around the house?"

"No way!"

Orozco, still annoyed with Lind, pushed back. "Why not?"

Lind explained that Holmes was a thief who was constantly "bringin' shit over to us to trade for dope. He stole from everyone, including his friends. He was a strung-out dude. Deverell and Launius were in the dope business and couldn't afford to have Holmes around, or even trust him."

Lighting up a smoke, Lind was groggy but coherent. He told Souza and Orozco a couple of guys had come by the house looking for Launius and found the bodies. He said they then helped themselves to whatever was left in the house. Asked if he knew their names, Lind replied, "Whitey and Jimmy Vegas."

Souza wanted to know if Lind knew a guy by the name of Paul Kelly. He did. He said Fat Howard also knew him. Souza asked if Lind thought Kelly could have been involved in the slayings.

"No way!" He went on to say that Kelly acted like "he was in the mob." He tried to impress people with "big-time" connections that didn't even exist. He also traded in stolen property. Lind went on, "Kelly's more bullshit and *bark* than *bite*." Souza and Orozco finished up with Lind and called Fat Howard to come pick him up.

Later, after checking a number of sources including moniker files and field interview cards, detectives identified "Whitey" as Melvin Hull and "Jimmy Vegas" as one James Adras. More background checking led them to the LAPD Valley Bunco-Forgery detectives in Van Nuys. The Valley unit had both men in custody on forgery charges. Souza and Lange headed for the Van Nuys jail to interview the two men.

Melvin Hull told the detectives he went to the Wonderland home to pick up Ron Launius and drive him to court in Sacramento. Finding the front door ajar, they entered and discovered the bodies. Hull was cooperative and told Lange and Souza that while he was checking out the back room he had stepped over the body of Susan Launius and heard her moan. When asked why he didn't do something, Hull stated he thought because of her obvious critical condition, she was going to die anyway. "Why attract attention?" he offered. Then, in a pathetic attempt to justify his actions or lack thereof, Hull stated that he told the neighbors about the bodies on his way out the front door. Adras declined the detectives' invitation for an interview.

Once again, the LA County Sheriff's Narcotics Bureau was on the move. They had identified another Nash regular through an informant and surveillance.

Dorothy "Dottie" Glickman had been seen moving to and from the Nash residence on a regular basis. Her husband, bondsman Harold "Hal"

Glickman, was a longtime Nash business acquaintance who also owned a bail bond business. He had recently been released from federal prison in Lompoc, California, after being convicted of attempting to bribe a federal magistrate on behalf of Ed Nash.

Of some interest to Mr. Glickman would have been the fact that his wife, Dottie, had had an ongoing and close relationship with Ed Nash while he was locked up. Dottie and Nash's relationship wasn't about business. She was also addicted to cocaine. Hal had accused her of looting his bail bond business while he was incarcerated and had been pursuing legal action against her through the district attorney's office; he had discovered a substantial amount of cash missing when he was released from prison. Apparently, there had been no arrests or prosecutions in the case.

By the time Hal was released, Dottie had broken off her relationship with Nash and hooked up with a biker out of Bakersfield. Hal became an ex. Since Frank Tomlinson had offered to assist in the Wonderland investigation before he retired, he and Lange decided to go to Bakersfield and talk to Dottie Glickman.

Lange phoned Dottie, and she agreed to meet with the detectives at the Bakersfield Police Department the following day. Lange and Tomlinson believed she wanted to meet at the police department because she did not trust the police in general or the LAPD in particular. This lack of trust may have risen as a consequence of her being under the influence of Nash and his dealings.

The following day, Dottie shared her addiction problems with Lange and Tomlinson. She was a nervous and somewhat mousy blonde who said her addiction was in check and she was determined to stay clean. She believed Ed Nash was the most evil person who ever lived. She clearly hated Nash but denied she had any information regarding him as a suspect in the murders. The detectives' interest was heightened when Dottie related she'd had a "late" breakfast with John Holmes on the morning of July 1. She said they had met at Tiny Naylor's restaurant on the corner of Ventura and Laurel Canyon Boulevards in Studio City.

That location was just a mile or two down Laurel Canyon from Nash's place. She told detectives Holmes was very nervous and "shook up," but he hadn't shared anything else with her.

Note: If true, at this particular time, the murders had already occurred, but the bodies were yet to be discovered. A "late" breakfast would have been several hours later.

Lange then braced Dottie with a rumor that had been floating about. Did she drive the killers to the Wonderland house in her car on the morning of the murders? She vehemently denied the rumor. Detectives lacked any evidence of her involvement or participation in the murders. While Dottie appeared forthright in her interview with Lange and Tomlinson, the cops believed she knew more than she was letting on. Their rapport with her was good, and they knew that further down the road, they would be able to re-interview her if needed.

While Tomlinson and Lange were in Bakersfield interviewing Dottie Glickman, Souza was on his way to Cedars-Sinai Hospital. Dr. Saunders had called Bob and told him Susie was awake and able to communicate on a limited basis. In keeping with the original plan, Souza would continue to be Susan Launius's lone contact with the police.

During an earlier visit to the hospital, Souza, with Dr. Saunders present, had attempted to speak with Launius, but gleaned very little. They were able to accommodate her simple questions: "What happened to me?" "Where is Ronnie?" "Can I go home?" During that time Bob had deferred to Dr. Saunders as to the amount of time he should spend with Susie. The doctor did not want her over-stimulated. The pain meds would help keep her calm, but her lack of stamina hindered any intense questioning. It was apparent to Souza that bringing Susie around would be a long, drawn-out process if the cops were to get anything of relevance from her. Here, patience would not only be a virtue, it would be a necessity.

At the hospital, as in the past, Souza first met with the on-duty LAPD Metro Division security detail officer in the hallway outside Susie's room.

The officer stated all was well and that Susie currently had a visitor. This being a bit of a jolt to Souza, he asked who the person was. When he found out the officer hadn't identified the visitor, Souza rushed into the room, only to find a buckskin-clad man lying in the hospital bed with Susie! The two were actually laughing and appeared to be getting along well.

The visitor was taken aback when he was grabbed forcibly by Souza, yanked from the bed, and thrown to the floor. The big detective was standing over him as he gathered himself and came to his feet. He had a thick head of black hair, dark skin, and coarse features. He said, "Hey man, everything's cool. Susie and I are friends." Susie was calmly lying on the hospital bed, unmoved by the action.

Souza was overly protective. "Who in the hell are you?"

The intruder brushed his thick black hair back with both hands, keeping a distance between himself and Souza. "My name's Cherokee."

Souza demanded identification, and Cherokee pulled out his wallet and handed his driver's license over to the detective. Souza learned the man's full name was Larry Martin Hershman. He had a Sacramento address. Cherokee's features were clearly that of a Native American. He was also garbed in a matching head-to-toe fawn-colored buckskin suit.

Note: Cherokee was the same individual who had phoned the Wonderland home on July 1 and spoken to Bob Souza during the crime scene investigation.

Souza told Hershman to take a seat in the hall while he stayed briefly with Susie. Souza asked "You all right?" Susie was smiling, and it was the first time Souza had seen any emotion from the lone surviving victim. The detective wondered if she was perhaps playing possum with him. Is she really as bad off as she seems? Bob excused himself, telling her he would return shortly. Susie sat silent, holding a smug grin.

In the hallway, Souza upbraided the cop, who said nobody had given him any instructions about screening visitors. He said he did frisk Hershman before allowing him in the room. Bob escorted Cherokee down the hall and into a vacant visitors' waiting room.

Hershman told Souza he had scored drugs at the Wonderland home for about eighteen months. He knew Ron and Susan Launius from the Sacramento area. He had also phoned from the jail in Arizona in order to talk with Ron Launius to tell him he was on his way to Los Angeles. Hershman was cooperative and even somewhat overzealous in his discussion of the Wonderland pad. His demeanor reminded the detective of a professional snitch. Souza decided to drive him downtown for a formal interview. Cherokee didn't object and then told Souza he was hungry but didn't have any cash. On the way to Parker Center, Souza drove through a fast-food joint and bought him a hamburger meal. In a general conversation, Souza asked about Cherokee's suit. Cherokee commented on the buckskins, raving about it being his favorite of many he owned.

At the Robbery/Homicide Division, a background check of Hershman revealed an extensive record of robbery. He had also done hard time in the California state prison system. He was no doubt one more member of the Wonderland gang. The only difference was that Cherokee was still alive.

Souza made it clear he was not interested in Cherokee's problems with dope, not in the least. He was, however, interested in the murders and anything Hershman had to offer. It was apparent Cherokee possessed all the attributes of an informant. Under those circumstances, Souza wanted him to hang around.

Bob discovered Hershman had outstanding misdemeanor warrants, and the detective realized this was a good start. Cherokee was booked into the Parker Center jail and given two packs of cigarettes so he'd remember Souza. During the booking process Bob confiscated his prized buckskin suit, holding it on the ruse that it was possible evidence. Cherokee was obviously distraught about the suit being confiscated, so Souza figured it would be enough to keep him close.

Later, Souza returned to Cedars-Sinai to spend more time with Susie. He was still bothered about her behavior with Cherokee. Susie told the detective they had been friends for years and she thought he was "really cute." Souza believed the more visits he made, the more trust and confidence she would have in him. While Launius appeared to be cooperating in a reasonable fashion, Souza believed she was holding out when it came to her husband, Ron, and perhaps key elements of the butchery at Wonderland.

Her reluctance to fully cooperate would be understandable, but the detectives still had many more questions. Did she know any more details about the motive for the attack? What else did she recall about Holmes and his activities around the time of the murders? Could she identify any of the suspects or provide better descriptions? What *specifically* had her husband shared with her about the goings-on up at the Wonderland house prior to his death? Who else might the investigators talk to? Answers to any of these questions could lead to more questions. Souza would have to be patient and play it out.

Susie's condition had improved to the extent she was released from Cedars-Sinai with Dr. Miles Saunders's approval. She was transferred to the Rancho Los Amigos Rehabilitation Hospital in the city of Downey, east of Los Angeles. She would be housed in the major head trauma clinic where she would initially be restricted to a wheelchair and a hospital bed. The section where she was receiving treatment was more of a large dorm with several patients, all recovering from traumatic head injuries. Some patients were ambulatory, some were bedridden, and a few more were nearly in vegetative states. The living accommodations at Rancho Los Amigos were far more conducive to normal living than those at Cedars-Sinai. Souza would continue with his visits.

The security for Susan Launius continued for a short time but was soon canceled. This was largely because most of the people out on the street who had run with the Wonderland bunch had come to believe that Susie was still comatose and would remain that way. Obviously, Souza and Lange were more than happy to perpetuate the rumor. Dr. Saunders was reasonably confident that over time, Susie could very possibly recall important facts heretofore lost in the fog of the assault.

Over the weeks that followed, Launius appeared somewhat guarded and even defensive when it came to discussing her late husband and his activities. It had seemed strange that Susie didn't seem to mourn Ron's death or any of the others' staying at Wonderland. She always bragged about what a "badass" Ron had been but never showed remorse for his death. There were, however, times when she did open up.

She recounted one day how she and Ron had attended a party near Sacramento before his trek down to LA. At the party Ron was smoking his pipe, and a Mexican Mafia gang member was "eye-fucking" him. Ron "shined him on" for a spell, but eventually the guy braced Launius and stuck a gun in his face. Susie said that Ron took his pipe, tapped the spent ashes out of the bowl onto the barrel of the weapon, and said to the guy, "Where do we go from here, Vato?" According to Susie, the guy backed down and left the party.

Susie also related another incident that supposedly occurred in Mexico. She had accompanied Ron on a trip that involved a fairly large drug deal. Once in Tijuana, the people Launius was dealing with felt he was cheating them, and they demanded more cash. Susie called it an "okey-doke." "Ronnie was pissed off." Susie said she was held by these guys as some kind of collateral and during the ordeal had been sexually abused. According to her, Ron had returned and rescued her. While she said she never saw anything to verify it, she did believe Ron had killed them all.

Note: Whether or not any of this was true is unknown. What was known is that Ron Launius was feared by most people who knew him.

On one occasion, answering a question from Bob, Susie ended her response with "Anyway, that's what I was telling your buddy."

Souza asked, "What buddy? Who are you talking about?"

Susie responded, "The other cop. The one here on security."

Realizing that no one else was authorized to speak with Launius, Bob followed up. His inquiries led him to Officer Jim Pearson, who was a member of the security detail.

In short order Souza ran down Pearson and asked him why he was questioning Susan Launius regarding anything. Without hesitation, Pearson responded he was writing a book on the case and believed Susie had a compelling story to tell. He stated he would also like to talk with Souza about the case.

Incredulous, Bob explained the facts of life when working murder cases and closed with "You're off the detail, and stay the hell away from my witness!" Even after the confrontation with Souza, things didn't sink into Pearson's skull. He was disappointed and, unbelievably, attempted to interview her again.

It was apparent to Souza that Pearson still intended to write the book and that he wasn't going away, and he didn't.

Note: Officer Jim Pearson went on to work a Los Angeles Police Department security detail at the 1984 Olympics in Los Angeles. Other than the Russians dropping out of the competition, Pearson became the focal point of perhaps the biggest scandal of that entire Olympics. He had discovered an explosive device on one of the Olympic team buses. He was heralded as a hero for saving the day. The only problem was that he was the one who had planted the bomb to make himself look like a hero. While the bomb wasn't real, his dismissal from the LAPD was.

Everyone wondered if he put that in his book.

Fifteen

More Jailbirds

Larry "Cherokee" Hershman had been on the phone with Souza more than a couple of times since he was booked on his warrants. Now that he'd be getting out of jail, he wanted his buckskin suit back. Bob told him he'd work on it, but he needed to clear up a few matters first. After a couple of minutes with Cherokee, he was able to document answers to a few questions that had lingered regarding the victims and their "business ventures."

Cherokee had remained a good source as long as the cops vaulted his buckskins. He was now out and back in circulation on the streets. He would become a de facto "source close to the investigation" in their efforts.

Soon after Larry Hershman was released in Los Angeles, Souza received a phone call from a bail bondsman in Kingman, Arizona. Cherokee had previously made bail there on the grand theft auto charge and fled to LA, where he'd been promptly arrested again by Souza for local warrants. Because of his Los Angeles incarceration, Cherokee hadn't made his court date in Arizona. The bondsman was livid. He stood to lose a good deal of money. He told Bob if he could get Hershman back to Arizona for him, he'd make it worth his while. Souza scoffed, knowing that if he cooperated with the bondsman, he would be the one to end up in the crapper.

Things usually had a way of working out. Arizona decided to decline extradition due to cost. This absolved the bondsman financially, and the cops were able to keep Cherokee on a hook. Cherokee actually believed that Lange and Souza had pulled his fat out of the fire in Arizona. Now he owed the detectives, and that was the way they wanted it.

———

The Mount Olympus section of Los Angeles was an older but high-dollar area in the Hollywood Hills. It was where Hal Glickman called home. Hal's rap sheet was lengthy. It mirrored that of someone who could be considered a member of an underworld criminal empire. It included early convictions for statutory rape and grand theft and later charges of criminal breach of fiduciary duty, not to mention his stint in the can for attempting to bribe a federal judge.

Glickman's application for a bail bond license and association with Ed Nash traced back to 1968. At that time he managed several nightclubs owned by Nash. Apparently, though, he did a bit more than merely manage the clubs.

Glickman's bail bond license had been revoked following his conviction for attempting to bribe the federal judge. He had tried to obtain a more lenient prison sentence for a drug dealer associate of Nash. Apparently, Glickman was still able to conduct his bail bond business through a fictitious business name filed in Los Angeles County. The bail bond business was being run by associates of his.

The day had come for Bob Souza and Tom Lange to visit Hal Glickman. It was planned as a cold call, so they went early. That way, Glickman wouldn't be prepared and probably didn't even realize the detectives wanted to talk with him. The cops really didn't know what to expect, but sometimes surprises could be interesting and fruitful.

The ringing of his doorbell brought the barking of more than one dog on the other side of the door. Then the somewhat muffled response from Glickman: "Who is it?"

Standing off to the side of the entrance just in case, Souza responded, "LAPD homicide."

The voice told them to wait while Glickman put up the dogs. That was appreciated.

Moments later, a disheveled Hal Glickman, clad in wrinkled, ill-fitting sweats, opened the door and invited them in. As they entered the cops were met by a stench reminiscent of the Los Angeles Zoo before the cages had been cleaned…in August! A quick scan of the living room confirmed the smell. There were numerous piles of dog excrement, some old, some newer, spread throughout the room. The contrast of the feces with the expensive-looking light-beige-colored carpeting was striking.

Lange told Glickman the detectives were investigating the deaths of four people who were killed on July 1. The bondsman responded with a half-assed sardonic reply: "You think I did it?"

Lange, explaining that everyone was a suspect until the police knew better, stated that yes, he, too, could be a suspect. Lange mentioned they had information concerning his wife's possible involvement in the case. Glickman cut him off in midsentence to clarify that she was an ex-wife.

Glickman was obviously upset with Dottie, telling Souza and Lange that Dottie had taken up with Ed Nash while he was in prison. He also complained that she had looted his bail bond business of some $200,000. He then began to complain about the cops not doing their job when it came to Dottie looting the business. Glickman then abruptly became antagonistic and slipped into a profanity-laden rant about his ex-wife and the cops' presence in general.

Both Lange and Souza attempted to bring Glickman back around to their investigation, but he became even more agitated. He told the detectives, in no uncertain terms, that he couldn't care less about their murder investigation. Trying to switch gears, Lange slipped in a question regarding his association with Nash. Hal went on a rant and told them to find the door.

As they exited, almost on cue, the dogs went bonkers once again. On the way out, Souza called back over his shoulder, "Hey Hal, why don't you clean up this dog shit?"

As expected, Glickman had talked out of both sides of his mouth. In spite of his anger over Dottie's supposed infidelities and the looting of his bail bond service, Hal would not let that interfere with any "business relationship" he might have had with Ed Nash. Once again, that old organized crime refrain came to mind: "Business is business."

Just prior to and during the time when things were heating up at 3315 Dona Lola Place, another person of interest had been spotted by Los Angeles sheriffs' surveillance. His name was Scott Thorson. A fairly frequent visitor to Ed Nash's home, Scott had his own problems with addiction. He had recently broken away from his lover, world-renowned entertainer Liberace, and the reason for the breakup was cocaine. Liberace did not tolerate drugs or anyone associated with them. As a consequence Scott was given the boot.

The usually loquacious Thorson had undergone plastic surgery earlier, urged on by Liberace to change his appearance, and looked strikingly similar to the entertainer. Scott would often be seen chauffeuring Liberace out onto the stage for a performance, driving an open limousine. But those days ended once Scott chose drugs and jail over show business. Souza and Lange both agreed that Thorson, being a regular at Nash's, would no doubt pop up again in their investigation.

Note: It was around this time Souza and Lange were put back on homicide callout for cases citywide. As frustrating as it was, they were forced to put the Wonderland murders on the back burner.

In the early spring of 1982, Nash was under federal indictment charging arson and racketeering awaiting trial, some bad guys had robbed and humili-ated him, he was getting slammed with no-knock search warrants, he faced narcotics sales and possession charges in a state trial, he was constantly either being followed or under surveillance by law enforcement, and he was being investigated as a suspect in a quadruple murder. A situation one might call a full plate.

Arson is always serious business. When a person dies as a result of an arson fire, it results in a first-degree murder charge and can potentially bring a life sentence or even the death penalty. Some fires are the work of thrill-seeking pyromaniacs, some are lit to cover up other crimes, and then there was the Nash type. They were known as friction fires: when the deed of trust rubs up against the insurance policy and sparks fly.

Bob Souza and Tom Lange had handled a couple of arson/murders, but none like what occurred on September 4, 1982, while they were still up to their necks in the Wonderland murder investigation.

———————

The Dorothy Mae Apartments were located at 821 West Sunset Boulevard in downtown Los Angeles. The four-story building was home to dozens of families who had fled their native Mexico for a better way of life in the United States.

A nineteen-year old local gang member, Humberto de la Torre, lived in the building with several family members. He had been at odds with his uncle, who also happened to be the apartment manager. De la Torre had been gracing the walls around the building with gang graffiti. This continued to be an annoyance to the uncle and other residents of the building. The uncle eventually confronted de la Torre, and it got physical.

Days later, the nephew retaliated. He purchased a small amount of gasoline from a nearby service station at Sunset Boulevard and Figueroa Street. He then walked back to the Dorothy Mae to the first apartment on the second level, the home of his uncle. He poured the gasoline on the mat in front of the door. He ignited the gas and ran out the front entrance of the building. Ironically, just as the fire was spreading, the uncle walked into the building from the rear. As the back door opened, the fire was fed by a surge of wind from the rear, causing a back draft. The ensuing eruption escalated into an inferno.

The flames rapidly shot up an elevator shaft and into the east stairwell to the third level. The now very intense flames raced down the corridor to the west stairwell and up that stairwell to the fourth level and back down that corridor. Panic stricken, the occupants ran into the three hallways. They were all incinerated midstride. Twenty-five persons, including a viable fetus, lost their lives. Dozens more were injured jumping out of upper-floor windows. Twelve of these people were related to de la Torre.

Although this was an older, dilapidated building, most if not all of these people would have survived had they only remained in their apartments. Unbeknown to the victims, the building had been refitted with Ponet fire proof doors as a consequence of a LA city ordinance. They were designed to hold back flames for twenty to thirty minutes.

Note: The Ponet door designation was taken from the Ponet Square hotel fire on September 13, 1970 at 1249 S. Grand Avenue in downtown Los Angeles. Nineteen people perished in the arson fire and many more were injured. The hotel had been built in 1907 and condemned in 1941 due to structural deficiencies.

De la Torre had fled to Mexico. After several months of visits and much wrangling with Mexican law enforcement, LAPD detectives arrested him, and he was returned to the United States. He offered up a confession to Lange and Souza. He also gave them a videotaped walk-through of the crime scene, articulating his actions. De la Torre was convicted on twenty-five counts of murder. He was sentenced to 25 years on each count, to be served consecutively—625 years!

Sixteen

Dominos

The plan all along had been to pressure Holmes into testifying against Nash and the actual killers once he was indicted, held to answer at a preliminary hearing, or convicted. Detectives and the DA's office wanted Holmes to be in a corner, finding himself with no way out. Now that Holmes was behind bars and facing an unknown fate, it was time to see if the domino theory had any legs. It was also time to shake things up a bit and let certain people know that Lange and Souza were still around.

The next "domino" to match up would be Gregory Diles. Diles had to believe that a weasel like John Holmes, now filed on for murder and facing trial, would do anything to save his own rear end. It was a good time—maybe the only time—for detectives to test their theory and put some kind of pressure on Diles. The time was right for a probable-cause arrest of Gregory Diles. Lange and Souza would be throwing the dice, with Ron Coen backing their play.

In the best-case scenario, the detectives could end up with "dueling suspects," each attempting to broker their own deal. They would both be fighting to keep themselves out of prison for the rest of their lives, or worse. The detectives realized that if Gregory Diles was directly involved in the Wonderland murders as they believed he was any dealing for consideration on a sentence would be tenuous at best. They also knew it was possible Diles would testify against Nash to save himself from the death penalty if it were still applicable at the time of sentencing. They decided that sitting in jail for a few days would give him time to think about it.

Note: It was never believed, and there was never any evidence, that Ed Nash was ever at the Wonderland crime scene or took part in the killings. Nash was a gangster who hired others to do his dirty work, and of course, it was they who would be subject to the consequences.

The LAPD Special Investigation Section, or SIS, consisted of undercover operators whose job it was to follow suspected felons they believed to be committing felonies and those they thought probably would. This highly effective unit was also utilized to keep tabs on various individuals who were under surveillance for other reasons, such as ducking out of the country when police preferred they didn't. Such was the case with Ed Nash.

With Holmes in the LA County lockup for murder and the media all over the Wonderland killings, Nash might decide it was time for him to take his leave. With both Holmes and Diles in jail, clearly, he would realize the possibility that either one or both might decide to talk to the cops and the district attorney. Lange and Souza were concerned he would head straight for LA International Airport once Diles was snapped up.

The detectives had decided SIS would not allow Nash to board a plane and leave the country and, if necessary, would affect a probable cause arrest for murder. An attempt by Nash at an abrupt departure right after Holmes and Diles were arrested for the murders would tend to make Nash look involved with the killings. That contention was something that surely would be brought up in a subsequent trial and clearly wouldn't look good for Nash. This was another crapshoot, but the detectives were running out of options.

The plan was to nail Diles on the street. SIS would already be set up on Nash at his home. Diles would be arrested late on a Thursday so detectives would have access to him over the long weekend before the jail was forced to release him on Monday if he hadn't been charged. It was apparent there would be no criminal filing because there was no substantive evidence against Diles at that time. If for no other reason, the detectives would be shaking things up and causing key people to be looking over their shoulders. Lange and Souza also looked forward to having Diles in custody to lean on him regarding the murders. He just might have something to say.

Diles was arrested on his way up to the Dona Lola house. Shortly thereafter, Ed Nash was on the move. SIS followed him to an apartment in the San Fernando Valley. It was a new location…and another Nash associate emerged. While at the location, Nash attempted to conceal his vehicle. It was apparent he was concerned with the recent activities and was keeping a low profile.

Meanwhile, Souza and Lange attempted to interview, and perhaps intimidate, Greg Diles. He had given his mother's address in South Los Angeles as his residence. He gave the Seven Seas restaurant as his place of employment. When he was approached, he became surly and demanded to see his attorney. He refused to speak with the detectives. Lange and Souza determined two things about Diles. He had obviously been schooled on what to say (nothing), and he hated cops, Souza and Lange in particular. The two detectives closed out the interview with a tacit admonishment that they would be back to nail him for the Wonderland murders. He didn't seem impressed.

Diles was released following the weekend. There was nothing lost and nothing gained. In spite of the Diles question-and-release weekend, Lange and Souza weren't going anywhere.

A short time later, the Los Angeles District Attorney's office filed felony narcotics and assault charges against Nash, Diles, and Amnon Bachsihan in regards to the search warrant service of July 10. Souza and Lange made sure they attended the disposition hearing for Bachsihan, which was preparatory to any trial. He was represented by local counsel and in no mood to have the detectives sitting and staring at him from the back of the courtroom during the proceedings. He kept peering back over his shoulder, glaring at the detectives throughout. There was some concern in his stare and yet a great deal of discontent. It got worse when Souza mouthed an expletive in his direction as he sat alongside his lawyers. He had to be restrained by one of them. Having only a minor record locally, he was sentenced to become a part of a diversion program for the drug possession.

Detectives heard nothing more of Amnon Bachsihan until he returned home to Haifa, Israel, years later. He was shopping at an outdoor street market when someone riding a Vespa motor scooter and wearing a face-concealing helmet pulled up to him, stopped, and pumped eight bullets into his skull.

———

In March of 1982, Greg Diles was sentenced to three years in state prison for his assault on the Los Angeles sheriff's SEB unit during the July 10, 1981, warrant service at Nash's residence. Nash was still out on bond, awaiting trial on the narcotics charges from the same warrant. Other charges would be added later, and he would be tried for three incidents that had resulted in three warrant services. The narcotics cases would be consolidated into one trial.

———

The day had finally come when Susan Launius was to be released from Rancho Los Amigos Hospital. Her rehabilitation therapists had consulted with Dr. Saunders, and they felt that going back home to northern California would be the best course of action for her. She had pleaded with Souza to back her for release and to talk to the doctors so that she could return home. Souza and Lange were satisfied they had gotten all the information they could from Susie for the time being.

Susie would be staying with her parents in the northern part of the state. It had been a long and arduous journey, filled with uncertainty, pain, and anguish for the young woman. She would be traveling with her constant and now-trusted companion, Detective Bob Souza.

It was a bit of a relief for Souza to escort Launius from Los Angeles. His brother and mother had cautioned him against getting too close to her. His old-fashioned mother worried that the amount of time he spent at Rancho Los Amigos Hospital was not good for his marriage. Souza scoffed at the notion of any involvement with Launius and chided his older brother for arresting attractive call girls while assigned to the Administrative Vice Division. As for his overly concerned mom, he assured her it was all business.

Arrangements were made for them to fly out of Los Angeles International Airport anonymously and lightly disguised. The media were not informed for all the obvious reasons. Detectives and the DA's office did not want anyone to know her whereabouts, not just out of safety concerns, but also because they planned on bringing her back at the time of trial.

Dr. Saunders insisted that Susie wear a protective helmet for the trip. Her brain was only protected by a thin layer of barely healed scalp, and the metal plate she would eventually be fitted for was still down the road. Susie balked at the appearance of the device, so Souza found her a scarf to cover the unattractive headgear. She had regained most of her good looks, and her vanity was now kicking in again. After she was fitted for the helmet, she found it to be uncomfortable as well as ugly.

The airline had been briefed on the sensitivity of the matter and accommodated the two passengers by boarding them first into the first-class section. Once airborne, Susie complained again about the helmet. Souza reminded her that he had promised Dr. Saunders she would wear it at all times. Susie was manipulative and went to work on Souza. She smiled and poured on the charm. "How about I buy you a beer, and we just don't tell Dr. Saunders?"

Souza replied, "You don't have any money."

She giggled, and Souza weakened. He made her a deal. He would allow her to remove the helmet while she was seated, but if she left her seat, the helmet went back on. He helped her loosen the headgear, removed it, and placed it in the overhead.

When he sat back down, he noticed Susie had also removed her scarf, exposing short brown hair beginning to thicken since being shaved bald. She had a glass of champagne, and Souza had a beer. Because of her medication and weakened condition, the champagne seemed to take effect. She became giddy and began touching the top of her head where the thin flap of skin covered her brain. She pressed lightly in certain areas, "Oooh, that tastes like chocolate. Oh, that's a good one, kinda tickles."

A flight attendant stopped by and watched Susie briefly. She continued fingering the top of her head. "Oh, that's the sexy one there. I'll leave that alone." The flight attendant disappeared quickly.

Souza told her to stop and put her scarf back on. Susie's demonstration, whether real or something else, reminded Souza of Michael Crichton's novel *The Terminal Man*, whose title character could be stimulated by sending electrical impulses to parts of his brain. For the remainder of the trip, Launius dozed on and off, and Souza looked over his to-do list in his notebook. He laughed to himself, imagining the flight attendant sharing what she had just seen with her friends later that evening. When they exited the plane, the flight attendant was nowhere to be seen. Souza had a car waiting and drove Susie home to her happy and much-relieved parents.

While Bob was traveling, Lange was in the office going over witness statements. He got a call from reporter Adam Dawson. Dawson was back at it and greeted Tom with "Hey, Tom. What's the deal with the old man and the search warrant?"

Lange had no idea what he was talking about. He was curious about the reporter who had been calling him more and more lately. Not only did he have the RHD phone number, but he seemed to know when Lange was at his desk, and lately, it was not that often. "Adam, I have no idea what you're talking about, really."

Dawson did not believe him, but Lange persisted, stating he didn't know.

As it turned out, Dawson had been snooping around at the county court registrar's office as usual, looking at the criminal warrants filed recently by law enforcement, including the LA district attorney's office. Most were public record if they hadn't been sealed by the court for reasons articulated in the accompanying affidavits. He had come across a filing by one of Ron Coen's investigators regarding a bartender employed by Ed Nash at his Seven Seas restaurant. The employee was in his seventies and had been selling cocaine from behind the bar during business hours.

Lange thanked Dawson and got on the phone to Ron Coen. Coen told him his investigators had worked up a dope case against Nash through the bartender and sought a warrant. He told Lange it had nothing to do with the Laurel Canyon murders. Lange reminded him that the RHD detectives wanted anything and everything on Nash. Coen agreed. Lange figured there was no intent on Coen's part to hold anything back, and he wrote it off as just a slight lapse in communication.

Note: A personal axiom of Lange's: the bane of any criminal investigation is usually a lack of communication.

As for Adam Dawson, Lange pondered his intentions and was impressed with his resourcefulness and, frankly, his honesty. He made a mental note to hook up with Dawson and see what else he might know. It was all part of being what a good detective should be: nosy!

Seventeen

Tepid Trials

More than a few years' worth of work by the US Attorney's Organized Crime Strike Force culminated in the arson and fraud trial of Ed Nash in Los Angeles Federal Court on May 18, 1982, Judge William Byrne Jr. presiding. Other defendants included Paul Stechel, a San Gabriel, California, insurance broker; Michael Hensley, a Tustin, California–based insurance adjuster; and Khalil "Charlie" Khalaf, the owner of a Los Angeles restaurant.

The US Department of Justice's precept of the case was that the four defendants were members of an organized arson ring. The allegations against the group were that they would purchase a business, insure the business, burn the business, and attempt to claim losses, all with fraudulent intent. The crimes occurred in Los Angeles and Las Vegas. There were several other defendants listed in the original federal indictment.

Nash was being represented by Los Angeles criminal defense attorneys Donald Re and Dominick Rubalcava. The latter deferred to the former when asked what part he would have in the defense of Nash. Whether this had anything to do with the fact that Rubalcava had recently been identified as president of the Los Angeles City Fire Commission, an apparent conflict, was unknown.

Throughout the trial Nash was observed nodding off from time to time and generally showing a lack of interest in the proceedings. His defense team had its hands full just trying to keep him awake. Perhaps he found it difficult to sleep at night…or maybe it was something else. As usual, Adam Dawson was once again present and reminding his readers that Ed Nash was not only on the hook for the federal arson charges but being looked at critically for the Wonderland murders as well.

The US District Attorney's Strike Force prosecutor, Paul R. Corradini, was all business as Jerry Van Hoorelbeke was called to the stand. Souza and Lange had interviewed Jerry Van earlier in the federal lockup in San Diego. It would be interesting to see just how Nash's lawyers handled him in light of the fact that he was a federal informant who would presumably be testifying against the man who had hired him to commit the arsons. Van Hoorelbeke had torched a brothel in Nevada and a restaurant in El Monte, California. He was also charged with assaulting the ATF officers who had arrested him.

During cross-examination Donald Re hammered Van Hoorelbeke for being a federally protected informant who had been receiving favorable treatment. His lengthy criminal record was also brought front and center. A second arson suspect, Gregory Colbert, testified similarly to Van Hoorelbeke to feather his own bed with the Feds.

Colbert had been in federal custody in Dade County, Florida, under circumstances similar to those of Van Hoorelbeke. Lange and Souza had traveled to Florida earlier and interviewed him. As with Van Hoorelbeke, it had been a colossal waste of time. During the testimony of these two men, there was never any documentary evidence introduced that tied Nash to any of the businesses that had been torched.

On June 3, 1982, the trial of John C. Holmes for murder got underway in Los Angeles with Superior Court Judge Betty Jo Sheldon presiding. The judge had a decent reputation and was not known to be anything but fair to all parties. The even-tempered magistrate would serve both sides in this matter equally well.

In his opening remarks, Deputy DA Ron Coen stated to the eight-man four-woman jury that he would prove that Holmes participated in the murders of four persons at the Wonderland home on July 1, 1981. He described Holmes as a perpetual liar with absolutely no credibility. He also stated that Holmes had admitted to letting the killers into the home on Wonderland Avenue very early that morning to commit the murders, knowing full well what their intentions were.

Some weeks prior, in Coen's office, the detectives had discussed his opening statement because there was, of course, great concern that the prosecution had no Catholic nuns, Salvation Army volunteers, or war heroes as witnesses, only thieves, drug addicts, and hardened convicts. Coen would have to be out front with this or get hammered by the defense for putting on such degenerate witnesses. They needed some kind of a phrase that would not only explain this predicament but also stick in the minds of the jurors. After slapping this around for a while, Lange came up with "When a crime occurs in hell, you don't have angels as witnesses." Everyone liked it then and it stuck.

There certainly could not have been a more dramatic way to open a mass-murder trial than by putting on the videotape of the crime scene, raw and unedited. Lange was called to testify to all that he had observed at the crime scene while conducting the walk-through and the narrative that was part of the video. It was the first time a videotape of the crime scene had been admitted as evidence in a murder trial in the state of California. It put the case in true perspective for everyone right out of the chute. Also, it was considered a positive sign for the prosecution when there were a few gasps from the jury and other persons in the courtroom as the tape rolled.

After he was called to the stand, Lange testified that on July 17, 1981, after Holmes was released following his interview, he was back up at Nash's residence on Dona Lola Place within an hour. This was just after he told detectives that he could not name the other killers because of this incredible fear he had of Nash. Detectives had also documented several subsequent visits by Holmes to Nash's place over many months, no doubt to score drugs.

Lange also testified Holmes was released from the so-called protective custody at the Biltmore Hotel simply because he had lied about anything substantive to the investigation. In a favorable ruling for the prosecution, Judge Sheldon found that Holmes could not claim coercion as a defense for murder.

———

Every high-profile criminal trial seems to have its own court jester. In the Holmes trial, it was Al Goldstein, the editor of *Screw* magazine. *Screw* was not the type of publication readers took home to the wife and kids for their evening entertainment. Goldstein had been commissioned by *Playboy* magazine to cover the trial.

Al was loud, flamboyant, and outspoken, but he still managed to get a seat in the courtroom. He was always bedecked in colors that never seemed to match, but the gold wasn't swag; it was the real thing. Being the gregarious type, he was easy to like, but he wasn't to be taken too seriously. One day, he caught Souza and Lange out on the street and made a scene, giving the detectives T-shirts with his *Screw* magazine logo across the front in bright colors. He dared them to wear the shirts, at least on their way over to court. He would win the dare. It didn't happen.

David Lind was called to the stand. He was sober and impressively sharp for an old ex-con. When Coen asked his occupation, Lind simply replied, "I'm a robber." He went on to describe the robbery at Nash's house, articulating his words like an English scholar. He left nothing out. Lind's side of the story was crucial testimony that laid out the motive for the murders.

Note: While motive is not necessary to prove in any crime, including murder, it is always something that a jury wants to hear, if known.

Next up was Tracy McCourt. McCourt related about the same things Lind did, but he stumbled and fumbled his way through his testimony, which could make a juror question his veracity. He did, however, corroborate all the important points of Lind's testimony. He was nervous by nature. The drugs didn't help. Defense attorney Earl Hanson, being a straight and credible lawyer, cross-examined McCourt in reasonable fashion. A less-than-honorable attorney would have hammered Tracy for hours just to dirty him up as a witness in front of the jury.

Frank Tomlinson came to the stand and was sworn in. Ron Coen was confident he could elicit enough from the retired detective to bring the Holmes admissions out. Tomlinson related Holmes's statements regarding setting up the Nash robbery and Nash forcing him to admit to it. He stated that Holmes told him about Nash threatening him by copying the names and addresses of Holmes's family members to hold over him if he was ever compromised by the porn actor. Tomlinson testified that Holmes admitted to being at the Wonderland house when the murders occurred and to letting the killers in. He stated that Holmes also said he knew what was going to happen. Tomlinson then stated that Holmes had refused to identify the other killers, despite promising to do so.

Note: Interestingly, many of the details of Tomlinson's interview and how it was conducted with Holmes never became a major issue in the trial.

Frank was cross-examined by attorney Mitch Egers. Egers was interested in the parts of Tomlinson's testimony that involved Holmes's fear of Nash, especially the portion dealing with Nash copying Holmes's relatives' information from his address book.

Dr. Ronald Kornblum from the coroner's office, who had testified in hundreds of homicide cases as an expert, described in detail all the horrific wounds to the four victims that were instrumental in causing their deaths. He was followed by several experts from the Scientific Investigation Division regarding forensic evidence recovered at the scene. One of those, a latent print expert, testified to lifting a partial left-hand palm print from the ornate bed railing above the battered body of Ron Launius. The latent print belonged to John Holmes.

Additional testimony revealed that the partial palm print was in a very curious location, in that it was lifted from a position consistent with someone bracing himself with his left hand on the bed railing as he beat down on the head of Ron Launius. The animosity between Holmes and Launius was also highlighted in testimony.

Susan Launius was under constant protection and escorted to and from the courthouse by Detective Souza after being flown to LA. She appeared extremely nervous and had become aloof toward him and others. It was obvious she wanted to remove herself from the entire Los Angeles scene and the events of July 1, 1981. She appeared petite and innocent, almost childlike, as she limped her way to the witness stand. A hairpiece was in place to conceal her severely injured skull.

Susie's testimony included her recollections of what had occurred at the Wonderland house subsequent to the Nash robbery, including essentially all the narcotics-driven partying. When asked what she recalled about the attack on her, there was a palpable hush in the courtroom. Susie stated that all she could remember were dark shadowy shapes with metallic objects and then tremendous pain, much the same that she had related to Souza at Rancho Los Amigos.

In a very delicate cross-examination of Susan Launius, Earl Hanson was able to get her to state that at no time had she observed John Holmes in the company of the killers. Hanson's cross of Launius was short, to the point, and very effective. This was in spite of the fact that Holmes had already admitted to being at Wonderland during the murder spree.

Somewhere in the middle of the trial, during a lull in testimony, a lone male entered the courtroom and took a seat in the very back row. This type of thing occurs regularly in the downtown Los Angeles court in high-profile cases. But these visitors are usually not also murder suspects in the same case being tried. That lone male was Ed Nash. It took only seconds for everyone in the courtroom to realize who the most recent visitor was.

Proceedings continued without a hitch, as though Nash was just another courtroom gadfly. After several minutes he stood up and walked out. Maybe the best defense there *was* an offense.

Holmes's attorneys did not call any witnesses and most certainly not Holmes himself. Perhaps they didn't wish to gamble on the lack of angels in hell.

Ron Coen's closing statement included all the testimony from the various witnesses, the Holmes admissions, and the palm print, along with the defendant's testy relationship with Ron Launius. He wound things up with a question: "If John Holmes didn't participate in the murders, why did the killers allow him to live?" This was clearly a very basic question that will never be answered.

In his closing remarks to the jury, Earl Hanson stated that the wrong man was on trial for the Laurel Canyon murders. This had become a theme of the defense throughout the trial. He further related that Holmes had been forced at gunpoint to allow the real killers to enter the premises at Wonderland, and he genuinely feared for his life. Hanson went on to state that Ed Nash was incredibly evil. Lange mused that Nash should have been in the courtroom to listen to Hanson.

Hanson then went after the prosecution and Ron Coen. He blasted them, stating that the only reason Holmes was on trial for the murders was because of his failure to give up Nash as the real suspect. Hanson made it clear he would never allow his client to make any remarks about the case.

Deliberations in the jury room went for just over a day. Holmes was acquitted. The short time it took for the verdict to be reached meant there could not have been much argument. The jury truly believed Nash was the one who should have been on trial, not Holmes.

Once the verdict was in, Hanson, an emotional man, was brought to tears. Ron Coen, probably a bit less emotional, couldn't believe the jury would roll over for Holmes's defense. He skipped the press briefing and retired to his office. Souza and Lange joined him there.

On the evening of the acquittal, Al Goldstein threw a big party, inviting all persuasion of folks, including Souza and Lange. The detectives politely declined. Al just laughed.

Shortly after the trial, John Holmes was served with a subpoena from the Los Angeles County Grand Jury to testify to what he knew about the Laurel Canyon murder suspects. When he refused to comply, he was jailed. There was no immunity to offer due to his acquittal. According to Judge Julius Leetham, Holmes would sit in a jail cell until he testified. Lange was waiting for Hanson to shed a few more tears.

While in custody, Holmes received lots of mail. That was to be expected. The letters ran both pro and con. Among his supposed admirers was one Adel Nasrallah. Nash wrote to Holmes, describing him as his "good friend" and beseeched him to tell "the truth" about Nash. Nash already knew Holmes's mail was censored, and if anything in his letter got out, it could only have a positive effect for Nash and anything in his future regarding the Wonderland case. When a reporter asked Holmes if he had any fear of Nash, Holmes replied, "He is the evilest man I have ever known." Holmes continued to speak out of both sides of his mouth, something he was very adept at.

Just to add to all the nonsense surrounding Holmes's incarceration, he was also a target for celebrity seekers. A well-known female superior court judge had sought his in-custody autograph.

Note: She will remain anonymous to save any embarrassment to an otherwise very good judge.

In order to stay relevant in the news, Holmes announced he was going on a hunger strike. After losing a few pounds, and a remark or two from some people—Ron Coen called Holmes "the hunger striker who fasts between meals"—Holmes gave up. He was back to eating.

Not surprisingly, John Holmes was getting plenty of support from the porn industry. *Hustler* magazine publisher Larry Flynt supported Holmes in his refusal to identify the killers. Flynt was a big supporter of the First Amendment. As to identifying thugs who beat people to death with metal pipes, not so much.

On June 11, 1982, a jury in Los Angeles federal court convicted Nash's three codefendants on all charges in the arson-for-hire case. Ed Nash was acquitted. To some, the testimony of Van Hoorelbeke and Greg Colbert appeared to lack directness when it came to implicating Nash. One didn't have to look too far to see that Ed Nash led a charmed life when fingers were pointed in his direction. Or were there other forces at work?

In June of 1983, *Hustler* published an extensive article on Holmes, written by one Barbara Wilkins. She believed Holmes's jailing was due to his involvement with the pornography industry and nothing more. The detectives believed she must have missed the trial. After being questioned about his well-known problems with drugs, Holmes told Wilkins his habit had cost him dearly, both financially and personally. But now he was in control of his habit and his life. Apparently, this resonated with the writer, who continued to fawn over him.

In the article, instead of admitting to setting up the robbery at Nash's home, Holmes laid everything off on the Wonderland victims, knowing that dead men told no tales. He said he did score drugs at Wonderland, and he also attempted to sell off the antique rifles, but the Wonderland crew would not allow it. However, that was not what David Lind, Tracy McCourt, and Cherokee had to say.

Holmes went on to state that he had made the Wonderland bunch promise not to kill anyone during the Nash robbery. Holmes then told Wilkins that while in custody, he got a letter from the real killers telling him to "go ahead and testify." The entire interview was packed with laughable fantasies Holmes created to make himself look good. It really didn't jive with reality.

When Holmes had been in jail for two months, writer Wilkins composed a letter signed by her and two of the jurors from Holmes's trial, comparing his confinement to that of a political prisoner in the Soviet Union. She aligned Holmes's predicament with that of *Los Angeles Times* reporter Bill Farr, who had been jailed for forty-two days for contempt of court after he refused give up his reporter's notebook in the Charles Manson murder investigation. The detectives knew the biggest difference between Holmes and Bill Farr was that Bill Farr was an honest, reputable, and talented reporter. It was often quoted that if Holmes hadn't had a large personal appendage to flaunt, he wouldn't have qualified to be a forklift operator. The detectives felt that was an insult to forklift drivers. The letter went out to Judge Leetham, LA District Attorney John Van De Kamp, and, of course, the *Los Angeles Times*.

The Holmes on-and-off switch was on once again. He agreed to testify before the Los Angeles County Grand Jury. Ron Coen was tied up with another case, so Deputy District Attorney Bob Jorgenson examined Holmes. There was contradiction after contradiction regarding Holmes's relationship with Ed Nash. Although he once again admitted to setting up the Nash robbery, he then stated that he had never actually observed the killers who went over to Wonderland on July 1. He denied ever hearing Nash or Diles or anyone else order the killings. John Holmes was released from custody, and he moved in with his scribe, Barbara Wilkins.

Shortly thereafter, Holmes gave another interview to the soon-to-be-defunct *Los Angeles Herald Examiner*. He spewed most of the same rot from the *Hustler* interview, only in this one, he went after David Lind. He told the reporter that Lind threatened him not to testify. He also stated that when Lind was on the stand testifying, he drew his finger across his throat while staring at Holmes. The implication had been clear to Holmes. Whether or not this actually occurred was never substantiated, but it would have made no difference or had any impact on the outcome of the trial.

8763 Wonderland Avenue – Note staircase on right.

Warrant service – Ed Nash (far lt., back to camera) and Greg Diles (lt. center) are led from Nash home. Lt. Ron Lewis (center porch in tan suit), Bob Souza (rt. center) and Tom Lange (far rt.). November, 1981.

Billy Deverell

Joy Miller

Ron Launius

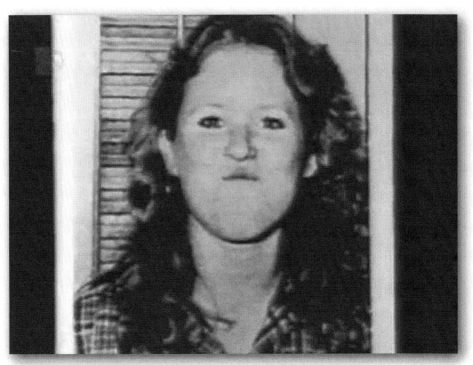

Barbara Richardson

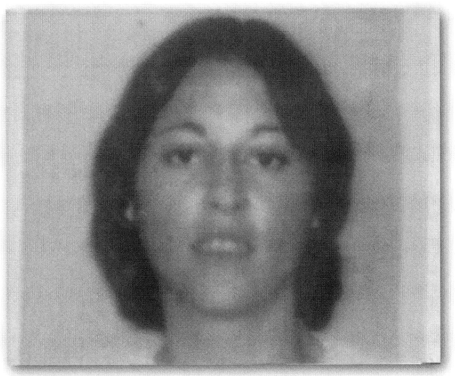

Susan Launius

Robbery/Homicide Division office – circa late 1994.

John Holmes in custody pending trial.

David Lind enters court to testify.

Tracy McCourt testifying during trial.

Ed Nash in court.

Gregory Diles enters court.

Henry Hoskins

Lt. to rt. - Tom Lange, Chief Daryl Gates, Bob Souza, Jim Grayson
and Bob Grogan (seated lower rt.) - promotion party.

Lt. to rt. - Bob Souza, Chief Daryl Gates and Glenn Souza – circa 1981.

Lt. to rt. - Tom Lange, actor Ron Masak (Murder, She
Wrote!) and Mac McClain – April, 1997.

Detective Russ Kuster – in memorial – EOW (October 1990) – Medal of Valor.

Eighteen

More Murder Madness

The 1980s were a busy period for homicide cops in Los Angeles. Unfortunately, five people getting their heads crushed didn't mean that everything else came to a halt. Several serial killer investigations were still underway from the 1970s, and many more would rear up in the 1980s and right on into the 1990s, not to mention a myriad of murders with every other type of motive.

Note: In 1992 the LAPD experienced a record 1,092 murders in the city and the remaining portions of Los Angeles County also experienced record numbers.

Many of these cases took years of investigation and many months in court to resolve. Some of the task force–type investigations were in conjunction with other law enforcement agencies. Many times, this included the Los Angeles County Sheriff's Office and its homicide unit, housed in the old Los Angeles County courthouse at Temple and Spring Streets downtown.

Note: Up until the early 1970s, the old courthouse was also home to the LA County Coroner's Office, which was located in the basement. The detectives could still recall being in court on an upper level and the elevator doors opening at the most inopportune time, providing a foul-smelling whiff of the goings-on in the coroner's office, also known as the "back office," down below.

A serial killing case is defined as having two or more separate murders at different locations committed by the same suspect(s) with no apparent motive. Motives tended to evolve and become apparent in these cases which often involved sexual gratification and domination by the perpetrators. All these cases had their own peculiar sides as defined by the unorthodoxy of the particular suspect. This is referred to as a signature. A signature can be used to link various cases and should remain confidential.

Note: Of interest is the fact that at the time the FBI's Behavior Sciences Unit in Quantico was in its infancy and just beginning to accumulate data on serial killers. Heretofore any serial killing profiling was accomplished by local law enforcement.

One serial killer of great interest was the Skid Row Slasher. It was considered one of the first cases in the greater Los Angeles area to be recognized as a serial killing, although the serial-killer phenomenon dates back centuries. In 1964 two Skid Row transients had been found dead with their throats slashed in downtown Los Angeles. There were scant leads, and this, of course, was long before the advent of DNA. The killings went unsolved for years.

There were no suspects and no more murders until the latter part of 1974 and into 1975. The bodies of dead transients then began to show up once again in the same Skid Row areas, all with their throats slashed. An investigative task force was formed that included Robbery/Homicide detectives as well as detectives from the LAPD's Central Division. Lange was one of the Central Division cops who showed up early one morning in December of 1974 behind the main downtown Los Angeles Public Library on East Fifth Street, where the latest victim had been found.

The as-yet-unidentified transient was lying in a supine position with his head somewhat propped up against a cement pillar. His neck had clearly been slashed, and his head nearly severed from his torso. The head was hanging off to one side and barely connected with a flap of skin.

In an interesting and strange coincidence, coordinating the operation from the office that day was the Central Division watch commander, Sergeant II Charlie Vaughn. Present at the crime scene and in charge of the uniformed personnel was Sergeant Mike Greenwood. Ironically, the suspect was later identified as Vaughn Greenwood.

Eleven murders and one attempted murder were eventually solved following a foot chase of Greenwood through the Hollywood Hills, after he ran from the home of actor Burt Reynolds. This followed a burglary and hatchet attack at the home involving not Reynolds, but a neighbor. Greenwood was later convicted of the murders and a Hollywood crime spree.

Other cases of the serial killer era throughout the greater Los Angeles area included the following:

The Manson Murders	Multiple suspects	9 victims
The Trash Bag Killer	Patrick Kearney	32 victims
The Hillside Stranglers	Angelo Buono, Kenneth Bianci	12 victims
The Skid Row Stabber	Bobby Joe Maxwell	11 victims
The Freeway Strangler	William Bonin	30+ victims
The Toolbox Killers	Lawrence Bittaker, Roy Norris	5 victims
The Sunset Strip Killers	Douglas Clark, Carol Bundy	5 victims
The Old Lady Killer n/a	Brandon Tholmer	34 victims
	William Bradford	2 known victims;
The Night Stalker		suspected of 50 others
The Skid Row Slayer	Richard Ramirez	13 victims; 5 attempts
The Koreatown Slasher	Michael Player	10 victims
The Westside Rapist/Killer	Joseph Danks	6 victims
	John Floyd Thomas Jr.	7 known victims; 10/15
The Southside Slayers		more suspected.
	Louis Crane, William Seibert,	100+ victims
The Grim Sleeper	Michael Hughes, Chester Turner	" "
	Lonnie Franklin Jr.	" "

All cases were solved and cleared with the exception of those labeled *suspected*. Here, there was a strong belief that these murders were committed by the named suspects; however, the physical evidence was not there to directly implicate them and justify a criminal filing.

———•———

It wasn't long after the Holmes trial and his incarceration for failing to testify in front of the grand jury that Souza and Lange split up temporarily to continue with their involvement in other cases. Souza re-joined well-known homicide cop Detective John "Jigsaw" St. John to continue the investigation of the 1979–1980 Freeway Strangler case against suspect William Bonin. (St. John was the senior man on the entire LAPD and had actually joined the police department three years before Souza was born.) Lange went back to working the Skid Row Stabber case and was preparing for trial. He imagined most folks, including some in law enforcement, didn't realize that when an arrest was made in a high-profile case, especially a serial killer case, it did not signal the end of that investigation. It was usually just the beginning of a long journey into a search for additional evidence and background checks on the suspects and witnesses, as well as the victims.

Souza and St. John were investigating the Freeway Strangler case, involving a suspect who had been picking up young male victims, overpowering them in his van, and sodomizing and then strangling them, sometimes with their own T-shirts. Their brutalized bodies were then dumped along various Los Angeles and Orange County freeways. There were at least twenty-one victims at that point. Other law enforcement agencies were also involved and conducting their own independent investigations. This type of situation had both positive and negative implications. Here again was an example of the flaw in most police investigations: a lack of communication.

No viable suspects had been identified, and detectives from several jurisdictions were taking tremendous heat from their departments and citizens as the body count continued to rise. Personalities and egos of some detectives from the various departments were affecting their investigations. There was also a certain amount of jealousy toward St. John following *Jigsaw John*, a somewhat popular but short-lived television series highlighting John's career, in which the actor Jack Warden portrayed the title character. The obvious connotation was that John solved murder cases much like one would solve jigsaw puzzles by putting the pieces together.

Bob Souza had been partnered with John because of his investigative experiences with the original Westside Rapist Killer task force of the time. The case had involved more than forty elderly female victims who had been assaulted in six geographical areas over a wide period of time, several of whom were murdered. A handful of other suspects were eventually identified and prosecuted in that case. While John Thomas Jr. was ultimately convicted of seven murders, other suspects were arrested for the brutal rapes.) As to addressing a few sensitive police egos, Souza possessed a strong personality and was a good communicator who could help soothe the personality clashes and coordinate the complexities of the case.

St. John and Souza had interviewed a teenage subject who was in custody at MacLaren Hall, a juvenile detention center. The young man told the detectives he had been hanging out with an older man who drove a green van. He also told them the man kept several news clippings about the Freeway Strangler case in the glove box of his van. He knew the man as Bill Bonin and further stated he had had sex with him. That information more than peaked the investigators' interest because Bonin's name had come up earlier when he was identified as a mentally disordered sex offender (MDSO). He had been discounted as a suspect after a short surveillance by the Orange County Sheriff's Office proved unsuccessful. At that point Souza and St. John realized they had a very strong suspect in the Freeway Strangler case.

William Bonin was located at his home in Downey, a small town located southeast of Los Angeles. The LAPD surveillance unit (SIS) was immediately notified and went to work. This was to be a round-the-clock operation for the unit.

On the fourth day of surveillance, June 11, 1980, Bonin was observed by SIS picking up a young male hitchhiker in West Los Angeles. The two were followed to the rear of an unoccupied business. Both were seen moving into the rear of the van. After several minutes one of the undercover detectives crawled beneath the van in an attempt to get an "overhear" of any discussion inside. He heard what appeared to be grunting and thumping noises and picked up the odor of what he believed to be human feces. Fearing for the safety of the hitchhiker, the detective signaled the rest of the unit, and the van was set upon within seconds. Bonin was caught in the act of strangling the youth while sodomizing him. The detective's quick actions no doubt saved the young man's life.

William Bonin was convicted on numerous counts of murder and sentenced to death. Fourteen years later, Souza, then retired, was invited as a special guest of the warden of San Quentin Prison to witness the execution of William Bonin, the Freeway Strangler. He was the first condemned killer to be administered a lethal injection in California.

On February 23, 1996, as Bonin stared out through the glass enclosure at the small gathering of witnesses, the lethal drugs were injected into his arm. As Souza looked at him through the glass and mouthed the same words he had to Amnon Bachsihan several years before, Bill Bonin twitched and closed his eyes for the last time.

Serial killer cases sometimes took years, if not decades, to resolve. The Skid Row Stabber murders occurred in 1978 and 1979. The suspect, Bobby Joe Maxwell, was convicted years after the murder counts were filed and sentenced to life in prison without the possibility of parole (LWOP). For decades the defense petitioned for a retrial because a so-called jailhouse informant had been called as a witness. In the late 1990s, the case went all the way to the California Ninth Circuit Court of Appeals.

The Ninth Circuit, without the benefit of any investigation or hearing, ruled that Maxwell should be retried because the jailhouse informant was the prime factor in the conviction. That was clearly not the case. It was an assumption by the court. A simple inquiry of the principals and the jurors would have revealed that they put no stock in the credibility of that informant and only convicted Maxwell on two of the eleven counts of murder he had been charged with. Without the informant testimony, Maxwell would have very possibly been convicted on all the counts.

Much to their credit, the Los Angeles County District Attorney's Office appealed the ruling, and the case went all the way to the US Supreme Court in 2010, thirty-two years later. Even though the Supreme Court refused to take up the matter, however, two of the justices wrote opinions stating that the conviction was appropriate. A third, Justice Sonia Sotomayor, said it was not and Maxwell should be retried or released.

At the time this occurred, Lange had been retired for several years but was subpoenaed to testify in front of the Los Angeles County Grand Jury. The Los Angeles District Attorney indicted Maxwell on an *additional* three counts of murder and robbery! The defense went ballistic. In the summer of 2017, Lange testified at an evidentiary hearing and awaits a new trial, thirty-eight years in the making!

The Skid Row Stabber and Hillside Strangler cases were investigated concurrently. In the Strangler case, young women were being kidnapped throughout Los Angeles County, sexually brutalized, strangled, and dumped in various remote, hilly areas. When things heated up considerably in the Los Angeles area due to heavy media exposure and increased police activity, the killers moved north to Bremerton, Washington, where two more female victims met the same fate.

For whatever the reason, there had always been an unwritten rule in law enforcement that one keeps his or her criminal investigations and evidence close to the vest. As stated earlier, this has its advantages and disadvantages. While cops want to protect the integrity of their cases for all the obvious reasons, they also don't want to shut out the possibility that the suspect or suspects have moved on to different jurisdictions and continued to dispatch victims. Here, communication with other police agencies was vital.

Well into the Hillside Strangler case, three separate law enforcement agencies were looking at one individual as a strong suspect in the killings. This person had been a neighbor of a Hillside victim in one jurisdiction and was being watched closely. He had also been under surveillance in another jurisdiction and was considered a viable suspect by a third agency. The problem was that none of the agencies knew that the others were also looking at him as a potential suspect, because there was no intelligence sharing. That person was Kenneth Bianchi. He and his cousin Angelo Buono were eventually arrested and charged with the murders.

During the trial of Buono and Bianchi, the Los Angeles District Attorney's Office filed a motion to dismiss for lack of evidence. This was highly unusual, in that the DA's office had filed the criminal case to begin with. One would expect a motion of that type to be filed by the defense, not the prosecution. The trial judge in the matter, Ronald George, denied the motion and ordered that the case go to trial. His unprecedented decision was enthusiastically received by RHD homicide detective Bob Grogan and other members of the Hillside Strangler Task Force. The attorney general's office tried and convicted both defendants on all counts. Judge George was eventually appointed to the California Supreme Court and later retired as its chief justice.

The multitude of serial killer cases was a phenomenon never before experienced by the Homicide Special Section and perhaps by any other known homicide unit. These cases had generated an international law enforcement following. Detectives learned much, sometimes the hard way, just by grappling their way along. Left to their own devices, they handled things well. It just took the bureaucracy a while to catch on and then catch up.

It is important to mention here that the Homicide Special Section (HSS) was not the only Robbery/Homicide Division entity to be involved in the high volume of notable cases. The detectives of the Major Crimes Section, under the leadership of Lieutenant Ed Henderson, were also up to their necks in high profile cases. In addition to their primary responsibility of investigating crimes against Los Angeles police officers (including murder, of which there were several) the unit also assisted in many of the aforementioned cases.

During this period in Los Angeles the murder rates were at all time highs. St. John and Souza were invited to lecture at a tri-county law enforcement seminar in the Phoenix area. During a break a twenty year veteran of the Phoenix police department approached Souza at the dais. He said, "You know, you guys handle more homicides in a weekend than we do in a career…"

Positive technical advances in police investigation were on the way in. Policing and high-profile cases today are handled more methodically because of these advances. With all of this should come high quality candidates and fortunately this is generally the case. However, there are times when some people are retained to fill a politically correct agenda. If true, this serves no one but the killers.

Will there be mistakes? Always! Will there be times when some cops disgrace the badge? Yes! Sad but true, the various police departments in the United States are forced to hire from the human race. Remember, *Robocop* was only a movie. With all of this said, imagery cannot be the prime factor in determining a department's effectiveness, it must be performance and results.

Politics and policing never mix well. Most politicians prefer to stay clear of high profile cases because they don't wish to upset the status quo. If they were to take a stand one way or the other they may well risk up-setting their constituencies. Or, they may interfere with an investigation unknowingly and harm the efforts of law enforcement. Such was the case of Richard Ramirez.

In August of 1985, after terrorizing greater Los Angeles with several months of "hot prowl" murder, rape, and torture, Richard Ramirez, a.k.a. the Night Stalker, traveled north to San Francisco. There, the crime spree continued. Following similar attacks in the Bay Area, San Francisco police, the Los Angeles Police Department, and the Los Angeles Sheriff's Department task force teamed up to coordinate their efforts. The San Francisco cops briefed their mayor, Dianne Feinstein, later to be Senator Feinstein, regarding their investigation and the evidence. For reasons known only to a politician, Feinstein felt the need to hold a press conference irrespective of the sensitive nature and status of the case.

Note: As opposed to a burglary, a hot prowl case is one in which the suspect forcibly enters a residence knowing full well it is occupied. His intention is not strictly to steal but to create mayhem. The Night Stalker case had police officers sleeping with their guns beneath their pillows.

During the affair Feinstein stated publicly that police were closing in on the killer, had a "footprint" that was evidence from a crime scene, and had also identified a handgun belonging to the as-yet-unidentified killer.

Upon hearing of the release of this information to the media the San Francisco police, Los Angeles sheriffs and LAPD homicide cops were outraged. Releasing that kind of evidence to the public could have undermined their investigation. This was the biggest crime story in the state at the time, and now crucial evidence had been revealed to the media, to the public, and more importantly, to any potential suspect.

Sometime later, while suspect Ramirez was being interviewed by lead investigator Los Angeles County Sheriff's Lieutenant Gil Carillo, Ramirez stated he had actually watched Feinstein's press conference. Shortly thereafter, he had proceeded to the Golden Gate Bridge and tossed his Alva athletic shoes and small-caliber handgun over the side and into the San Francisco Bay.

Cops found themselves asking whether the media was a help or a hindrance. Depending on the case, both were possible. Police departments operated under the theory that the media and the public had a basic right to know about criminal activity and police action, but not at the expense of the evidence and the particular case. The media should always be entitled to reasonable access; however, the first consideration has to be the protection of the crime scene or evidence from compromise. This would also include potential testimonial evidence from witnesses.

Note: The media has a job to do, and there is a tremendous amount of competition for stories. The news cycle is continuous. Today's reporting is much different than it was in years past. In the minds of some, it is not just a news story anymore but a story that needs to have conflict. It is basic Creative Writing 101: a story is not a story without conflict. In many cases, facts are not even considered newsworthy. The media believes it is entitled to all information and should make its own call on relevance. Readers will often see a prosecution case pitted against a defense case and built up to advance a perceived conflict.

Detectives involved in handling a reported-on active police investigation have seen "news stories" wherein they couldn't understand what was being written about their own investigation. On the other hand, certain reporting may also advance an investigation in a positive manner.

There may be times when a ruse can be employed to draw out information. There are usually some false confessions in any high-profile case. Persons can be eliminated as suspects or witnesses after they have attempted to involve themselves through false statements that can be disproven with a ruse. While a ruse is not considered a "lie," there may be a fine line. Of utmost import here is that there is crucial information, referred to as investigative keys that cannot be revealed. It should be known only to the investigators and the perpetrator.

It is never wise to make an enemy of the media as a whole. There are always opinionated types and zealots poking around any big case. Most have agendas, and they are not usually to the advantage of law enforcement. An investigation cannot be driven by inaccurate reporting and innuendo.

A classic example is the Southside Slayer case. In the mid-1980s, the RHD Homicide Special Section was assigned to look into approximately one hundred murders that had taken place over a ten-year time span in South Central Los Angeles. The victims were primarily black prostitutes who had met brutal death through strangulation, blunt force trauma, and stabbing. The vast majority were also addicted to all manner of drugs. The unit formed a task force of several detectives and approximately two dozen Metro Division officers supervised by Lange. The effort lasted nearly three years.

Some of the initial investigation included background and statistical inquiries. This included probes into many major cities of the industrialized world. The first big surprise was that the task force could not find one large city that did not have a problem with prostitutes being murdered. In fact, murders involving prostitutes were among the more common types reported anywhere. Drugs were also at the core of the majority of these cases.

The media quickly caught on to the mission of the task force. Protesters would show up in front of Parker Center and complain that the LAPD was not doing enough to solve the cases and had ignored these murders for years because the victims were prostitutes who lived in poverty and were drug addicts. Never mind that this was the very reason for the task force in the first place.

The unit was running undercover operations throughout the affected area, usually at night. Three of the undercover operators were women. All had been involved in shootings when things got out of hand, pointing up the dangers of the operation. The entire operation was proactive from a law-enforcement perspective. Undercover officers were making several felony arrests every night. While crime did go down in the area, it took some time before arrests were made for any of the murders.

There were two separate arrests in the killings over the months, and some seven murders were solved initially. One of the suspects, Louis Crane, was charged with five counts of murder and convicted. This was largely due to the outstanding work done by Detective Vic Pietrantoni, Lange's last partner on the LAPD. A second suspect, William Seibert, fled the Los Angeles area and was later arrested in Alabama after murdering a family of four. He had also killed a lone prostitute while moving through Ohio.

As detectives delved deeper into the various cases, they discovered that all manner of suspects were involved. It was not just one serial killer, as the media had reported throughout. The investigation revealed that many victims had been killed by copycats, pimps, other prostitutes, drug dealers, and "tricks." Although some had died at the hands of a serial killer or killers, many others had not.

Of course, if there was a serial killer, then the press would have to give that killer a name. And so, the Southside Slayer was born. No matter how many times it was explained that there were other suspects committing the murders, it didn't matter to the conflict-crazy media. It was the Southside Slayer prowling the streets at night causing death and destruction. That certainly looks much more alluring in print.

Well into the 1990s, with the implementation of DNA technology, several dozen of these cases were solved. Four additional suspects were identified. All were convicted...and the Southside Slayer was still out there.

As previously alluded to, there were also those times when the media proved to be an asset to law enforcement, as illustrated in the summer of 1969.

The house at 10050 Cielo Drive was but a few short miles southwest of 8763 Wonderland Avenue, across the Hollywood Hills. On the night of August 8, 1969, Charles Manson sent four of his murdering disciples to the home of actress Sharon Tate and slaughtered her, her unborn child, and four houseguests.

As the killers fled north on Benedict Canyon Drive, they stopped briefly along the side of the road to discard their bloody clothing down an embankment. Tracing what he believed to be the murderers' path, an astute young reporter from a local television network affiliate found the items. He then notified a somewhat-chagrined LAPD of his find.

Note: A handgun used in the murders had also been found by a local resident after it had been tossed down a hillside off of nearby Beverly Glen Boulevard.

Nineteen

It hadn't been all that long since Ed Nash walked out of federal court in Los Angeles, acquitted of arson-for-hire charges. The time had now come for him to walk into the Los Angeles Superior Court building two blocks up on Temple Street. Now it was about the warrants and the drugs.

Sometime earlier, the LAPD narcotics cops had served a third search warrant at the Nash residence and had come up with another big score. Lange and Souza had joined them. Nash was becoming very tired of seeing the two detectives as unwanted "guests" in his home. The same no-knock entry was applied, and the home was again searched thoroughly and pretty much trashed. Nash and his dope, money, and firearms had been carted off once again. At that time there were no pleadings, no comments by Nash. By now the operation was all routine stuff.

The judge in the current matter was the Honorable Everett Ricks. Judge Ricks had a reputation as a bit of a curmudgeon. He was known to go off on the defense or the prosecution without notice but with plenty of fervor. He was not a patient man.

The three search warrants and the evidence gleaned from them had been consolidated into one case and were to be presented together in one trial. Ron Coen was prosecuting the cases as he was handling all criminal matters regarding Ed Nash for the DA's office. As usual, Nash was in a fog and looked as trashed as his pad during warrant service.

Late one morning, during a break in the trial, Souza and Lange were sitting outside the courtroom at the end of a deserted corridor. Nash and a couple of his attorneys exited the courtroom. Nash was clearly agitated, which was not hard to understand under the circumstances. He spotted the detectives down the hallway and, brushing off obvious pleas from the lawyers, walked briskly toward them.

As Nash approached, he was already talking and sputtering on about Lange and Souza not being dope cops. They were homicide cops; why were they bothering with him? Why did they care? He wanted to know, "What can we do? How do we make this go away? What do you want? How much? Tell me—five hundred thousand?"

Note: This is not verbatim, but very close.

The cops were nonchalant and dismissive of Nash. He turned and stormed away in a huff. Picking up on at least some of this conversation, the two lawyers grimaced. They were not pleased their client had just attempted to bribe two LAPD homicide cops right in front of them.

At the lunch break, the detectives were once again up in Ron Coen's office, this time discussing the "offer." They'd known since the beginning that this was how Nash operated. This was no doubt one reason he had survived in his nasty little world of drugs, depravity, and destruction. But Lange and Souza looked at this differently. Would this guy really roll the dice with the detectives considering all the publicity around the case, or would he perhaps try to turn the tables and set up the cops?

Coen and the detectives believed Nash might have been thinking they would wire themselves up and return to him with an acceptance of his offer. They would then have him on tape attempting to bribe a public official. That would be all well and good until he turned the tables and denied any offer to them and accused the cops of soliciting a bribe. Since it would be on tape, it would no doubt be discoverable, and the defense would have a field day going after the dirty detectives. They would own Lange and Souza at the trial.

A worst-case scenario would be Nash concealing a recording device on his person and then having the detectives come back to him to discuss the offer. Under these circumstances Nash could easily make it appear that the detectives had initiated the bribe. He was just that devious and crafty. After some thoughtful consultation, Lange and Souza decided to scrap the entire affair, at least for a time. There were enough irons in the fire at that point. They did not want to throw gas in on top of an already-burning fire. Coen was in accord.

———————

On November 6, 1982, Ed Nash was convicted on seven counts of illegal possession of a controlled substance for sale. Sentencing was set for later in the month. Things were not looking overly advantageous for Nash. That evening, Ron Coen received a phone call from the Los Angeles County jail. Nash wanted to speak with Coen about the Wonderland murders! With some apprehension, Coen and DA Investigator Diane Egan drove over to the facility and met with Nash in a visiting attorney's room.

Once they were seated, Nash began to once again complain that he was a businessman and did not understand his predicament. Coen got right to the point and asked Nash just what it was that he wished to discuss. Nash said he knew who one of the killers was: "That biker guy, David Lind." When asked how he knew that, he related that people told him such things. He just knew them to be true. Coen asked if there was any evidence. "Not really," Nash responded.

Ready to leave, Coen and Egan stood up. Coen stated something to the effect that he had more important things to do, such as "locking up crooks like you." They then walked from the room to a barrage of profanity-laden expletives and proceeded down the hall.

On November 22, 1982, Judge Ricks sentenced Ed Nash to the maximum allowed by law, eight years. There were also fines levied of more than $100,000. Nash was remanded to custody. Judge Ricks had apparently bought into the prosecution's argument that Ed Nash needed a long separation from society and his many victims at government expense.

In spite of Nash's conviction and relatively long sentence, the investigation of the Wonderland murders and the other cases continued. The only thing missing was that Lange and Souza wouldn't be dropping in on Nash's home again anytime soon. Diles was also away, doing time for the assault on the sheriff's deputies during the July 10, 1981 warrant service. With Nash out of the way, at least temporarily, it was an opportune time to do some follow-up with a few of the players.

———

Tracy McCourt was out of jail, at least for the time being. Souza and Lange thought they'd drop in unexpectedly, just to let Tracy know they were still around and interested in him. When he opened the door at his mother's home just off Lankershim Boulevard in North Hollywood one night and saw the detectives, he looked as though he was going to be sick to his stomach. There was that glint of bewilderment, then a little defensiveness. He finally settled down after the detectives told him to light up a joint if he felt more comfortable. He did. Souza and Lange produced a six-pack of beer for themselves that guaranteed they would be spending some quality time with McCourt, if there was any such thing under the circumstances.

When witnesses want to play games with detectives, the key is to keep them off balance. They should never know when detectives might show up or what they may have on their minds. One moment, Souza and Lange could be accommodating, the next moment intimidating. A witness like McCourt would always have something to say. It became a matter of separating the wheat from the chaff.

That night, there was nothing but chaff. McCourt would do for McCourt whatever he felt was good for McCourt. He was still afraid of the dark, even though Nash was miles away in a jail cell. McCourt would be utilized later in trial to corroborate David Lind. Without question Nash and his folks would much rather have had him completely out of the picture.

After leaving McCourt's place, the detectives dropped in at the North Hollywood station to check the office for messages and call home. It was a habit both Lange and Souza had picked up years earlier when working all hours of the night and not sure when they'd return home. Lange's phone at home rang several times without a pickup. It was after 8:30 p.m. He became concerned why no one was answering. He phoned again ten minutes later and still no answer. Lange's mind was racing to places he didn't want it to. Someone had fired a shot one night recently through the rear sliding-glass door at the home of Detective John Helvin, and he'd been working with Lange and Souza on the Wonderland case.

Even with Ed Nash safely ensconced in state prison, he and his minions were still playing mind games with a bunch of people, the cops included. The thugs who hung with Nash were not known for their altruism, nor were they out to improve the human condition.

Lange told his partner he was concerned that nobody was picking up the phone at his home. He left North Hollywood Station, jumped on the freeway, and was home in less than thirty minutes. Hurrying into the house, he discovered his wife was upstairs, putting their young daughter to bed. Shaking her head, she reminded him that she had been at a friend's house visiting earlier in the evening. It wasn't too long after that that Lange purchased some fairly new telephone technology, an answering machine. Even after that incident, the answering machine didn't solve everything. Both detectives were nervous about their families. On another night Lange went into overdrive when he continued to get a busy signal after 9:00 p.m. When he reached home, he discovered that the receiver had somehow been knocked off the hook.

Souza, too, had discussed an escape plan and advised his wife, Sharon, and his sons to be observant and report any strangers around their property. Cops didn't worry much about themselves, but their families were always a concern.

When Bob Souza was working the Bonin case, he became increasingly concerned as the victim toll rose. Sean, his oldest teenage son, had talked about hitchhiking to the beach with his friends. At the time Souza lived within a few miles of one of Bill Bonin's victim dump spots near two intersecting freeways. He told his son in no uncertain terms that he would be more than happy to drive him and his pals to the beach whenever they wanted to go.

Twenty

DEN OF SNAKES

*I*t was the summer of 1983, and the serpents were beginning to stir in their dens.

Captain Jim "Doc" Docherty was the commanding officer of the LAPD Administrative Vice Division. Doc was a bright, well-liked, common-sense captain known department-wide as a straight shooter. He was one of three captains in the entire department who reported directly to the Chief of Police, Daryl Gates. Two of his detectives—Tom Blake, whom Souza and Lange had been dealing with, and his partner, Joe Salce—were called into Doc's office. Blake was a senior detective in the division who, of course, had an informant by the name of John Holmes. Salce was new to the division with little investigative experience. Docherty told his men the three of them were expected at the federal building forthwith and were to meet with a federal agent from the Bureau of Alcohol, Tobacco, and Firearms assigned to the US Attorney's Organized Crime Strike Force.

Docherty told his guys that the agent, Henry Hoskins, had "very sensitive" information to share on the Laurel Canyon murder case. Hearing that, Blake responded that that was a Robbery/Homicide Division case. Docherty nodded and explained that the ATF's Hoskins believed Bob Souza, his brother Glenn Souza, and Tom Lange were in cahoots with Ed Nash and organized

195

crime. Docherty also mentioned that Hoskins felt the detectives were running cover for Nash on the Laurel Canyon murder investigation.

Docherty advised his men that the department had initiated a so-called chief's special investigation to be run directly under the authority of the chief of police. The entire investigation would be conducted in a highly confidential manner.

Arriving shortly, the three men were met by Hoskins. Some pleasantries were exchanged, and they were escorted to his office. It was the same office Souza and Lange had been in eighteen months earlier on a follow-up meeting concurrent with Hoskins's original visit. This conversation was a bit more sensitive.

Despite Hoskins's semi-gracious introduction, Docherty got right to the point and asked what they could do for him. In his deep, slow southern drawl, Hoskins explained how he had talked to Lange and Souza on several occasions and provided them with solid leads on the killers involved in the Laurel Canyon murders. He went on to say that none of this "valuable information" had been followed up on. Hoskins awaited a concerned response from Docherty. It didn't come.

Docherty urged Hoskins to go on. Hoskins then told the vice cops he had received a call from a source, a private investigator in Arizona. The so-called source told Hoskins he had seen Glenn Souza, brother of Bob Souza, at a cocktail party. The PI related that the older Souza appeared "very close" to Ed Nash, who was also at the party. Hoskins then stated he had informants within the Nash organization who corroborated his information. He also said Nash "owned a lot of LAPD cops."

Blake asked Hoskins whether or not he had anything concrete to back up what he was saying. Hoskins related that he had an informant by the name of Jerry Van Hoorelbeke who was in federal custody with keep-away status. He said Van Hoorelbeke also had good information on where the murder weapons were and who drove the killers and John Holmes over to the Wonderland house to commit the murders.

When asked who the driver was, Hoskins stated it was Dottie Glickman, wife of Hal Glickman. He went on to discuss the Glickman/Nash "business" relationship. He then stated that Hal Glickman had told him, "Lange got some shit-bird biker a gun permit" and introduced him to Glickman as an LA cop. Hoskins then gave Docherty and his detectives contact information for the Glickmans and Van Hoorelbeke, probably ensuring in his mind that the cops would interview them.

After the exchange Hoskins pressed Doc, wanting to know what he would do with this information. Docherty told Hoskins they would look into the matter. Hoskins again pressed him regarding what would happen after that. Docherty told Hoskins there were procedures in place, and if anything was found, they would take appropriate action. Hoskins asked if they would inform him of any results. Standing up to leave, Tom Blake told Hoskins the release of any information would be strictly up to the chief of police.

The following day, Captain Docherty met with Chief Daryl Gates, and the special investigation into alleged corruption by the homicide investigators in the Laurel Canyon murder case was officially underway.

Note: Sometime later, Lange and Souza wondered if anyone at the time considered the fact that this special investigation, regardless of the outcome, would be discoverable by the defense team in any upcoming trial, unless the courts ruled otherwise. Additionally, did the question ever arise that these allegations could have been a setup to derail the entire investigation while also implicating Dottie Glickman after she went against her former husband and Nash?

Unaware of any of this wholesale BS, Souza and Lange plodded along on their quadruple murder investigation with the sword of Damocles hanging over them.

They learned later that the Robbery/Homicide Division's Captain Bill Cobb and Lieutenant Ron Lewis had been brought into the fold and made aware of the investigation out of the chief's office. Additionally, Homicide Special detectives John Helvin and Jack Holder had also become a part of the probe. They would be discreetly checking into Souza and Lange's murder books for log entries, persons interviewed, and dates and times of various activities. The entire affair would be conducted confidentially, with all information gleaned to go directly to the office of the chief of police through his chief of staff, Commander Thomas R. Windham. Everyone had been admonished and briefed, except Lange and Souza, the primary detectives on the case.

Note: As leaks were always commonplace in major investigations it was astonishing that Lange and Souza never had any idea this investigation was ongoing.

Blake and Salce, the investigators investigating the investigators, met with Hoskins's "source" in Phoenix. He was a private eye and former Las Vegas police officer. He was asked about the Glenn Souza meeting with Nash at the Phoenix cocktail party. The source stated that a so-called local mob affiliate had given him the information, but he refused to reveal his name because he was a confidential informant. He had no information regarding the supposed contact with Nash. He also related that he had a good snitch the vice detectives could talk to. His name was Jerry Van Hoorelbeke. The detectives were beginning to realize that Jerry Van was moving around pretty good for a federal prisoner locked up in San Diego.

Note: Additionally, had the information regarding Glenn Souza's meeting with Nash in Phoenix been researched thoroughly, the investigators would have learned that Glenn Souza was 3,500 miles away in Hawaii with his wife at the time.

Later, a background check of the Phoenix private investigator revealed he was, indeed, a former Las Vegas cop. What he failed to mention was the fact that he had been fired for a number of questionable activities. Whenever he showed up in Vegas, he was usually under surveillance by local law enforcement.

In the middle of all their running around (sometimes running in place), Blake and Salce received information that the targets of their internal investigation, Lange and Souza, had a meeting with a known local organized crime figure at a Hollywood restaurant called Musso and Franks. Apparently, no other "intelligence" accompanied the communiqué. The vice cops assumed where there was smoke, they would find fire. Recapping the entire ordeal later reminded Lange of a red flag flapping in the breeze in a bullring … without the bull.

As previously alluded to, Souza and Lange were, indeed, having lunch with a local crook, a fence by the name of William Vlick, a.k.a. Rico. To anyone watching, the three seemed to be getting along well while they enjoyed a leisurely lunch. The meeting might have appeared to have nefarious undertones in the world of organized crime thugs, but in reality it was a meeting with a potential witness in a quadruple murder investigation.

Souza had logged the meeting into the detectives' murder book with Vlick's name, which would seem to eliminate the possibility that the detectives were up to no good. Had the vice cops gone a step further, they might have found that Lange and Souza were still searching for that "angel in hell."

The point of lunch with Bill Vlick at Musso and Frank's was that the detectives were investigating an organized crime situation, in this case, murder. Would it be reasonable to assume they might interview organized crime figures? And did it make sense to do this in a public setting and then document their lunch meeting in their official log if they were lying with dogs? Is it also reasonable to do this over lunch when the meeting had been set up by Vlick? No one bothered to check into these details or follow up with Lange or Souza.

Next up for Salce and Blake was Hal Glickman. It was apparent to the two detectives that Glickman knew who they were and what their purpose was in interviewing him relative to some type of an internal investigation. Glickman made the point that he was in prison at the time of the murders and then gave up information that he had not given Lange and Souza during the earlier interview in his feces-laden home.

Glickman stated to Blake and Salce that his estranged wife, Dottie, drove the killers to the Wonderland location at the time of the murders. The car was registered to him and was eventually repossessed. Also, Dottie bilked his bail bond business out of some $240,000, and that money had been given to Ed Nash. He further related that Dottie had told him the killers were Nash, Sam Diles, John Holmes, and a guy named Buster. Two wristwatches had been taken from victims Barbara Richardson and Joy Miller and given to Jamie McGuan. Hal claimed Dottie stole one of them from McGuan later.

Note: There was never any evidence that wristwatches had been taken from the female victims at the time of the killings.

He also mentioned other probable witnesses: Diana Markworth and Desiree Jones, two other addicts who often visited the Nash house. Glickman told Blake and Salce that Dominic Fragomeli, the Starwood employee, had been given a hot shot at the behest of Nash while at the Dona Lola home.

Note: Both women were located and interviewed. Neither one related anything of relevance other than their reliance on their narcotics habits.

Glickman further stated that Henry Hoskins from the ATF also had this information and that Hoskins had given it to Lange and Souza. (At that point it was clear to Salce and Blake that Hoskins was sharing information with Glickman). He said Dottie, Nash, and John Holmes had gone to breakfast together the morning of the murders. He included that Souza and Lange had photos of the vehicle involved, a maroon Lincoln, driven by Dottie to Wonderland with the killers inside.

Note: Detectives never had photos of any involved vehicle. Also, Dottie Glickman had told Lange and Souza that she and Holmes went to breakfast alone, not with Nash.

Glickman believed Lange and Souza were holding back this information and that Hoskins could have solved the murders on his own with what he knew. For reasons unknown, Glickman was also aware that Los Angeles County Sheriff's narcotics deputies had the Wonderland location under surveillance just prior to the murders.

Note: Of particular interest here is why a federal agent investigating an organized crime figure like Nash would share this type of information with a known felon just out of prison for attempting to bribe a federal judge. It was common knowledge that Glickman had an extensive criminal record and was clearly associated with the very organized crime figure Hoskins was supposed to be investigating.

Hal Glickman continued to relate information he assured them had been given to him by Dottie Glickman while he was still in prison prior to the murders. He said Dottie told him there would be a "bloodbath" and then stated there was an additional suspect by the name of "Johnny," a so-called muscle man for Nash. Glickman described him as white, but he appeared to be an Arab. Additionally, Glickman told Blake and Salce that Lange and Souza had obtained a concealed weapons permit from Kern County, California, for Dottie's biker boyfriend, Terry Guinn.

Note: According to their official record, by this point Salce and Blake were beginning to believe Glickman had been coached on this influx of information. Regarding any type of a gun permit being issued by RHD detectives to Guinn, it did not and could not occur under any circumstances. For whatever the reason, the vice cops were beginning to view the entire Glickman situation as a setup.

Days later, Blake and a third Ad Vice investigator, Sergeant Joe Ganley, drove to the Federal Detention Center in San Diego to interview Jerry Van Hoorelbeke. The way had been cleared by Henry Hoskins, since Van Hoorelbeke was his informant.

Note: Clearance had never been required when Souza and Lange had gone to San Diego to interview Van Hoorelbeke.

Jerry Van told the vice cops that Hal Glickman, a close associate of Nash, had good information regarding the Wonderland murders. He said Dottie Glickman drove the killers to and from the Wonderland home the day of the murders. According to Jerry Van, the murder suspects were Greg Diles, Sam Diles, and John Holmes. He further related that the two homicide cops handling the case, Lange and Souza, knew this but were covering for Ed Nash.

Blake and Ganley began to press Van Hoorelbeke; he had outlived his usefulness as a federal snitch, and they all knew it. Asked who had put him up to this interview, he told them Henry Hoskins said if he cooperated with them, he might get consideration on his federal sentence. Hoskins had intimated to him that Gannon and Blake were trying to make a case of corruption against Souza and Lange, and he might be a factor in the investigation.

For Blake and Salce, it was back to Hal Glickman to follow up on what Van Hoorelbeke had to say. Glickman was more defensive during the second meeting. He was asked why he thought Hoskins could solve the murders with the information provided. Glickman said he got all his information from Dottie, his wife, and he apparently believed all she had to say. (Except the part about her denying she looted his bail bond business!)

Glickman went on to add that he had seen "vice cops" in Nash's bedroom in the past. Also, Greg Diles knew too much about the Nash operation and therefore would remain close to Nash. He then said Paul Kelly was owed money by the Wonderland crew. Asked how he knew this, he stated that being in the bail bond business, he had heard certain things. The hodgepodge of nonsensical responses was enough to tell the interviewers that something was beginning to reek.

In a follow-up meeting with Hoskins, Salce and Blake attempted to fill in a few blanks. Hoskins said he believed that Fat Howard Cook had set up the robbery at Nash's place, not the Wonderland gang. He further stated that Hal Glickman owned a motor home Hoskins believed might have been used in the murders in some way. He had also heard that "Johnny" now had the vehicle. Hoskins insisted he still believed Souza and Lange were covering up the murders for Nash and that he had met with them on several occasions with important information that was never acted upon. The vice investigators never pressed Hoskins on just how, he would know that.

Well into their internal investigation of Lange and Souza, Captain Docherty's men received additional information from the Hoskins/Glickman camp that there was also a North Hollywood Division detective supervisor who they believed was actually the godfather of Ed Nash's children.

Detective III Al Gastaldo was a nearly thirty-year veteran of the LAPD with an unblemished record and a reputation as one of the finest detective supervisors in the entire department. Why anyone would target him is unknown; however, he did work out of the North Hollywood detective bureau, which initially investigated the Dominic Fragomeli over-dose at the home of Ed Nash.

Of course, the allegation that Gastaldo was the godfather of Nash's kids or even had any connection to the Nash family was untrue and ridiculous on its face. This was clearly just another shot at the cops for going after Nash as a suspect in the Wonderland murders.

Incredibly, later on, after the nonsense regarding Gastaldo had begun to fall apart, there was another allegation that Glenn Souza, the retired LAPD detective and brother of one of the primary case detectives, Bob Souza, was also a godfather to Nash's children. By now, things were becoming almost comical. This was obviously not true but further served to stymie the investigative efforts of Lange and Souza and their case.

Note: Al Gastaldo was a reserved and sensitive man who took the godfather accusation to heart. But it never stopped him from being one of the more revered detective supervisors in the department. Glenn Souza and his brother, Bob, took the matter in stride. Both were well versed in the way of the streets and phony accusations by the lower forms of human life they had dealt with throughout their careers.

Later, when Salce and Blake met with Captain Docherty after being led down one rabbit hole after another, they were in agreement that all these folks were working off the same script, a script apparently written by Henry Hoskins for Ed Nash. Salce and Blake believed they were all liars, but their motivation was not yet clear. Had Lange and Souza been aware of the internal investigation at the time, they could have enlightened the investigators and exposed Nash's den of snakes for what they were.

U naware of the subversive probing involving them, Souza and Lange continued to move along with the investigation of the Wonderland murders. In what little spare time they had, they also dug into the upcoming Freeway Strangler and Skid Row Stabber trials. At this point they were also up to their necks in the highly emotional Dorothy Mae arson murders, which involved twenty-five victims. They had also recently picked up the murder of Hollywood character actor Frank Christi. None of the cases assigned to them would be an easy fix. Their current caseload involved the murders of more than sixty people that they knew of.

F rank Christi's body was found in the driveway of his Hollywood Hills home on July 9, 1982. He had been shot to death with two different weapons. Christi was known for playing the badass tough guy in several television productions and had a small part in the movie *The Godfather*. In delving into his background, Lange and Souza discovered his real-life escapades mirrored those of his TV persona in many ways. He still tried to be the tough guy in real life. That was until July 9 of 1982.

Three separate motives were considered during the investigation, but the one that stood out was the well-worn and familiar love triangle. There was also a murder-for-hire angle and a lying-in-wait scenario. The case took a number of years to put together. After Souza's retirement, Lange was joined in this effort by Detective Enoch "Mac" McClain. He became instrumental in identifying the suspects and solving the Christi case. Mac would later become a factor in the Wonderland murder investigation as well.

In the Christi case, three suspects were eventually arrested, two out of state and a third in Ventura, California. All were convicted of the murder. The driver of the getaway car was dying of cancer when Lange and McClain obtained a deathbed confession that implicated the others. A fourth suspect, the third party in the love triangle was tried for the murder on three occasions. All three juries were hung, and he walked.

When investigating murders, life's real coincidences and twists and turns kept the game interesting. Frank Christi had a friend by the name of Frank Salitieri. He was an attorney who had handled Christi's divorce and was also a movie producer (*Blacula*, 1972). Salitieri was brutally murdered in his home just a few miles from Christi's home within forty-eight hours of Christi's death. Additionally, Hollywood actor and Christi friend Vic Morrow was tragically killed in a freak helicopter accident on the set of the *Twilight Zone* movie in Indian Dunes, California, two weeks to the day of the Christi murder. Vic Morrow's tragic accidental death was in no way connected to the two murders.

Twenty-One

THE AFTERMATH

Captain Jim Docherty and his team had interviewed and re-interviewed everyone they could, regarding the internal investigation of RHD detectives Tom Lange and Bob Souza. The inquiry had been launched subsequent to the somewhat peculiar accusations made by a federal agent. They were unable to substantiate any malfeasance on the part of Souza, Lange, or Souza's older brother Glenn.

In order to complete the inquiry on Dottie Glickman and her common-law husband, Terry Guinn, Detectives Blake and Salce decided to seek and then serve a search warrant at the couple's residence in Bakersfield. The basis for the warrant was to further the investigation of the grand theft report and the allegation that Dottie had looted Hal Glickman's bail bond business while he was in prison (if indeed a crime had been committed at all). The items to search for included jewelry and various documents that, according to the crime report, had been removed from the safe at the business located in downtown Los Angeles near the LA county jail.

The warrant was served, and both Dottie Glickman and Guinn were arrested on probable cause for grand theft and interviewed. It was felt at the time that if there was any validity in what Hal Glickman had to say regarding Hoskins, the Wonderland investigation, and what Dottie purportedly told him, it would go to the credibility or lack thereof of Hoskins and Glickman. Another interview with Dottie Glickman with possible felony charges of grand theft hanging over her might aid in getting to the truth of the matter. About all that was gleaned from Dottie during the interview was that she was currently in a twelve-step program to beat her addiction to cocaine. Appearing truthful, she denied all Hal Glickman's assertions. She was also adamant that she wished to break away from husband Hal and Ed Nash forever. No evidence regarding the grand theft or evidence of narcotics use was recovered from the home.

Prosecutor Ron Coen from the LA District Attorney's Office was finally informed of the LAPD "special" internal investigation of his two detectives and what it had produced to date. He was told of the accusations of Hoskins, Glickman, Van Hoorelbeke, and the Phoenix private investigator with his phantom informant as they related to Lange and Souza. Coen was incredulous when he heard that the detectives had been accused by a federal agent, involved only peripherally in the matter, of being complicit in covering for any crook involved in anything, especially murder. Coen was not surprised to find out there was no truth to the allegations. However, he was concerned about the part the internal investigation would play in a trial once it became discoverable.

In the fall of 1983, all the dust recently raised over the Wonderland case seemed to settle. There was nothing relative to the Laurel Canyon murders or the other cases Lange and Souza were working that needed immediate attention. Consequently, Lange had taken a couple of weeks off. The LAPD's administrative policy being what it was at the time, Lange needed to use his vacation time or lose it. There were also times when detectives were directed to take time off that they had accumulated from working large amounts of overtime. Those hours were also time sensitive. Paid overtime was never a sure thing.

Lange was at home when the phone rang in the early evening. It was his partner, Bob Souza. Lange knew Souza would not call him while he was on vacation unless it was something of real importance. Vacations were meant to be sacred, but they never really were to homicide cops. Lange was greeted with "I hope you're sitting down!"

Lange could think of only one word: "Shit!"

Souza was angry. He spelled out what he had just discovered. For the past several weeks, he and Lange had been the targets of a special investigation out of the chief of police's office. They had been accused of conspiring with organized crime figures to cover up the case against Ed Nash. Souza went on to tell Lange he had come in to their office to log a phone call he had received about their Wonderland case the night before. He said the entire Wonderland case file, including all four volumes of the murder book, were missing. Lange listened intently. Souza said he searched all the shelves and cabinets assigned to Homicide Special teams, and the files were nowhere to be found. He then explained that Captain Cobb was still in his office. Half panic stricken and very concerned about the lack of security in the office that the detectives had been complaining about, Souza had to tell Cobb about the missing files.

When Souza entered the captain's office, he saw Cobb with his feet up on his desk, reading a report. Cobb acknowledged his presence and told him to find a chair. Without waiting for an inquiry from Souza, Cobb explained to him that all the Wonderland case files were in the hands of Detectives John Helvin and Jack Holder.

Lange interrupted on the phone: "So what in the hell were Helvin and his partner doing with our case?"

Souza said, "It gets better." He explained to Lange that their own people had been assigned along with Administrative Vice Division to investigate them for corruption!

Unable to even think straight for a moment Lange blurted out, "Who? Who accused us of corruption?"

Souza said, "Hoskins! The same fucking federal agent who was sucking up to us for information about Nash and our case."

The two stayed on the phone for several minutes, discussing the internal investigation with all the twists and turns the case had taken. They discussed Hoskins, the Fed who was frustrated with them for not taking him into their confidence and sharing pertinent information on their case.

Souza went on to say that Hoskins had accused the detectives of covering for Nash and generally being in bed with organized crime. It smacked Lange right between the eyes. All the intelligence reports and affidavits beneath Nash's bed! Who could have supplied them to Nash? Perhaps one dirty Fed?

Continuing, Souza said, "We've been exonerated, but that doesn't mean shit to me." They went on to discuss just how the special investigation would affect the criminal investigation. Was it discoverable? What would the media do with it if it got out?

Lange: "Has anyone considered that this might derail the entire investigation? If the department had the slightest hint that we were corrupt cops, why didn't they confront us directly?"

Souza: "Plus, we were under surveillance."

Lange: "Yeah. But so what? We're not doing anything wrong."

Souza: "You think maybe that's why no one wanted us to confront Nash directly?"

By the end of their conversation, the blood temperature of both detectives was at the boiling point. There were many more questions on the detectives' minds. They doubted they would ever get all the answers. Lange hung up. His stomach was churning. How would he explain this to his wife? Souza left the office and stopped halfway home at a cop watering hole to settle down.

When Lange returned from his vacation a day or two early, the two detectives sat down in private, attempting to figure out exactly what had occurred regarding the ball-busting news. They decided to consult with their department's union, the Los Angeles Police Protective League, about retaining an attorney. Their situation not only put the investigation in jeopardy, but could affect their careers as well.

Note: From this point on, the detectives were represented by legal counsel. For them not to have sought legal advice at this point would have been foolish.

A short time later, they discovered that Tom Blake, their contact at Ad-Vice, had also been a part of the team investigating them. It appeared that the part about one of their murder suspects (John Holmes) being a long-time informant for Blake must have passed someone by. Blake was the guy who had seemed to balk when Lange and Souza initially asked for his assistance in locating Holmes…his informant.

It was some months later that Souza and Lange learned just how deeply federal agent Hoskins had been into disrupting the Wonderland investigation. Not only had he been consorting with the likes of Hal Glickman and federal prisoner Jerry Van Hoorelbeke, it was also highly probable that his treachery extended to the fiasco in Phoenix with the phony informant.

The intradepartmental correspondence was dated November 1, 1983; originated from the Chief of Staff, Office of the Chief of Police; and was authored by Commander Thomas R. Windham, Chief of Staff. It was sent to the commanding officer of the Operations-Headquarters Bureau as well as Chief Daryl Gates. The summation line simply reads, "I have completed a review of a Robbery-Homicide Division investigation of which you are aware. My review revealed no indications of previously suggested improprieties." The very last page of the rather extensive internal investigative file reads: "Conclusion. This reviewer could find no indication that Souza and Lang [sic] were involved in covering up the Wonderland murders." There was no apology; however, none was ever expected. There were no explanations and no written justification for the investigation. Lange and Souza believed the extensive internal investigative report would not play well and would be a clear hindrance if the detectives ever ended up in trial with Ed Nash as a murder suspect.

Eventually, the detectives wound up at the Protective League offices with one of their attorneys to mull over the somewhat vague findings of the reviewer, void of any specifics.

Note: Lange and Souza would later acquire copies of the entire internal investigation.

So incensed were the detectives that they decided to go after Henry Hoskins civilly for defamation of character and damaging their careers. However, after researching the case, the League's attorney gave them the bad news. They had no recourse since all federal agents enjoyed immunity when engaged in official duties. Lange and Souza thought that if what Hoskins had been doing was considered "official duties," then there was a huge credibility gap in federal law enforcement and the way they did business.

Some years after the internal investigation was concluded, Lange was approached by internal affairs investigators from the Bureau of Alcohol, Tobacco, and Firearms. They wanted to interview him regarding one of their employees, Henry Hoskins. The investigators told Lange there were questions about Hoskins's activities throughout his stint with the Organized Crime Strike Force and his association with certain organized crime figures, including one Adel Nasrallah a.k.a. Ed Nash.

It was get-back time, and Lange told them to take all the time they needed with him. After a couple of hours discussing everything "Nash and Hoskins" in depth, Lange walked away from the interview thinking that while these guys knew everything, they couldn't prove anything. However, perhaps one day, there would be a reckoning.

Shortly thereafter, Henry Hoskins resigned his position with ATF. The question lingered in the minds of Souza and Lange whether he parted ways with the Feds because he was given an opportunity to leave as a way out of the scandal. Of course, that's where they would have put their money. In the LAPD, when a cop was caught with his pants down, it was called "retiring in lieu of disciplinary action."

Hoskins ended up in Las Vegas, working in a security capacity for a local hotel. A few months later, he wound up back in Los Angeles. He obtained a California private investigator's license and hung out a shingle for H&H Investigations at 6904 Hollywood Boulevard in Hollywood. His new business address was the former Seven Seas Restaurant, reopened as Club Hollywood. It was owned by Ed Nash and run by Hal Glickman.

Lange and Souza continued to receive circumstantial information from witnesses on the Wonderland case, and it seemed like the detectives were forever reopening the several volumes of the murder book and chasing down new leads while re-checking old ones.

New background information from the LA County Sheriff's Narcotics Division revealed that "Johnny," mentioned previously in the investigation, was in fact one Hovsep Boyadjian, a recent arrival from the Soviet Union. The original info providing the nickname as that of a possible suspect had been offered by Dottie Glickman. He had been arrested in 1983 by LAPD Ad Vice and at the time was in possession of a San Francisco police badge similar to the one David Lind had at the time of the Nash robbery. Johnny was known to be a close Nash associate.

Boyadjian was also close to one Joe Mikaelian, owner of an auto body shop in North Hollywood. Both men were well known as thugs and more muscle for Ed Nash. They were also considered as suspects in the Wonderland killings but could not be connected to those crimes. Mikaelian had also been indicted with Nash by the US Organized Crime Strike Force on arson-for-hire charges in the late 1970s.

When the time came, Lange and Souza approached Boyadjian and requested he give the detectives an audience. Instead, he gave Lange and Souza a little less than the time of day. As for Mikaelian, he was represented by local attorney Ted Flier. In meeting with Mikaelian and the attorney, detectives were hopeful Mikaelian would at least give a statement. They figured they would get something since Flier had invited them into his office, knowing full well why they were there. But it was not to be. Mikaelian let his lawyer do all the talking while he sat there, grinning and making obscene gestures in the detectives' direction. Mikaelian reminded them of the dopey kid everyone knew in grade school who was always playing grabass. The only difference was that Mikaelian lacked the intellect of the grade school kid.

Meanwhile, things appeared to be going sideways in the courts. On August 30, 1984, Ed Nash's newest attorney, Paul Caruso, appeared with his client in Judge Everett Ricks's courtroom. Caruso had filed a motion requesting that Nash be released from Folsom Prison early because he had a sinus tumor, for which he had been treated in the past. According to Caruso, doctors had indicated Nash needed surgery. Caruso dug up a doctor, one S. M. El-Farra, who stated that, in his professional opinion, Nash could not get proper medical care while incarcerated.

DA Ron Coen, speaking on behalf of the prosecution, was not having any part of it. He countered with the fact that inmates from the California prison system are afforded world-class medical treatment at various facilities under certain situations that can be dictated by the courts. This would include the prestigious Stanford University Medical Center, a highly respected medical institution located not far from the prison.

Judge Ricks was not overly receptive to Ron Coen's rebuttal. Ricks resentenced Nash to four years instead of the original eight years, and with a whack of his gavel, Ed Nash was out and about after serving less than two years of his original sentence. To no one's surprise, Nash never got the surgery.

Later, things went south for Judge Ricks as well. He ended up having his own problem with cocaine addiction. He resigned from the bench and was later arrested for petty theft. Then things got really messy. There was talk of a $100,000 payoff for the Nash prison sentence reduction by none other than Hal Glickman years later. Ricks died in 1993. Some say it was the cocaine habit he was alleged to have that ended his life.

———

One morning soon after Nash's release, Lange was summoned to the courtroom of Judge David Aisenson, once described in an ABC television news special as the most incompetent judge in Los Angeles County. This time, it was the Skid Row Stabber case. The suspect, Bobby Joe Maxwell, was represented by Los Angeles attorney Fred Alschuler. Mr. Alschuler appeared nearly apoplectic as he ranted and raved to Judge Aisenson, accusing Lange of withholding evidence in the case and obstructing justice. Since Lange was accustomed to such nonsense from defense lawyers, he sat through the tirade and waited for his opportunity. Lange was not concerned because he had not ever knowingly withheld any evidence in his investigations on any case.

When Alschuler had finished, much to Lange's chagrin, the good judge had him stand up in court while he advised Lange of his constitutional (Miranda) rights. The judge actually remanded Lange and sent him to the jury box while he decided what to do.

He advised Lange to make a phone call to his commanding officer and have him consult an attorney. Somewhat bewildered, Lange went through the motions, using the court clerk's phone. The judge had taken what Alschuler said at face value with no evidence presented since there was none to present. Lange called his commanding officer who in turn phoned the LA City Attorney's Office, who then dispatched a legal representative.

After a bit of legal mumbo jumbo here and there, somehow cooler heads prevailed, and Lange was soon released and left the courtroom shaking his head.

Note: No further action was ever taken or contemplated because there was no basis for the accusations to begin with.

Twenty-Two

Ups and Downs

Late in 1985, Lange and Souza were in the office working on a number of items and preparing for a couple of trials. Their boss, Lieutenant Ron Lewis, approached his team and told them there was a female inmate, a former nurse, in an Iowa prison admitting to a number of infant deaths in the Los Angeles area. Initial inquiries had failed to come up with anything related to this mode of death (infanticide); however, he felt that a follow-up was required with this inmate to check out her veracity and determine whether or not a crime had been committed. A case of that nature fell under the purview of the Homicide Special Section and for obvious reasons could become a very sensitive matter. Ron's demeanor said, "We need this now."

Bob Souza had had enough. It seemed to him that he and Lange had been given all the challenging and emotional cases lately. He'd had enough of the years of call-outs, the long hours, the image concerns from the brass, the phony allegations of police misconduct, the bad managerial decision-making, and just plain having to deal with bad people. Souza was seated with the lieutenant standing over him. Lange was across the table, also seated. Souza said to Lewis, "Ron, we're not taking that case." He felt he was speaking for the team since he was the senior partner.

Lewis looked to Lange for backup, but it didn't come. Lange was as surprised at Souza's refusal as Lewis. Souza had always accepted what was thrown at them. Murder was an ugly business, and nobody realized it more than he.

"What the fuck is wrong with the rest of the teams?" Souza shot at Lewis. "Tom and I get stuck with every bullshit case that comes down the pike."

Lewis shot back, "They're all busy, Bob. I need you guys to take it."

Souza didn't budge. "We're not dealing with some wacko bitch claiming she killed babies."

Lange knew his partner dreaded cases involving children and recalled the horrific Dorothy Mae fire they had handled, in which most of the twenty-five victims were women and children. Souza had stood the postmortem exams of more than two dozen people who had succumbed to the flames and were burned beyond recognition.

Taken aback, Ron looked at Lange and simply said, "I need you for this one…soon." Perplexed, he turned and walked back to his desk.

Souza turned to Lange after Lewis walked away and said, "I'm outta here. You might not see me here again." He grabbed his suit jacket off the coat rack and walked out of the squad room.

Lange had heard disgruntled cops spout off about leaving before, and the last time it happened, Frank Tomlinson hadn't come back.

Souza went home. Later, Lange made sure his time was covered administratively on the books. With this, Lieutenant Lewis knew that Souza was serious and wouldn't be returning.

Within a few days, Souza saw his doctor as he was having trouble sleeping, and his heart was racing even at rest in bed. He hadn't been feeling well and suspected something was wrong. A complete physical exam revealed that his blood pressure was extremely high, and he was immediately put on medication. Soon after, his cardiologist ordered him officially off duty (and off the books) to alleviate stress and control his blood pressure. He would never return. Lange had now lost two very experienced and talented partners to the Wonderland case.

Souza had bad reactions to the blood pressure medication, so he was taken off of it and put on a rigorous exercise program involving long walks in the hills above his home. He was also put on a heart-healthy diet, which he would have been unable to sustain while working murder cases. He went on to work in real estate development and teamed up with a neighbor to build custom homes in Southern California beach communities. Souza had gotten a real estate broker's license while on the police department and once retired from police work, he had planned to use it.

He and his neighbor both sold their homes in Glendora, a pleasant bedroom community east of the city. They opened up shop in San Clemente and soon had clients wanting to build ocean-view homes in a guarded and gated community. Lange stayed in touch with Souza and was happy he had found a life away from the streets of Los Angeles. Lange once told Souza over lunch on the San Clemente Pier that he wasn't ready to hang it up yet. Souza told him he knew Tom had always liked the work more than he himself did and that he should stick with it.

Souza's departure from the police department treated him well. He had lost forty pounds, his blood pressure was back to normal, and life was good. He had gone from death and destruction to sunshine and creativity. Souza often met with former partners and friends on the police department at the beach or on the sailboat he had recently purchased. He marveled at how they stayed in suits and ties, checking their watches and pagers every few minutes. It was a life he didn't miss.

As the economy shifted, Souza moved from one pursuit to another, never really retiring. He was a member of the Writers Guild and wrote for television and movies from time to time. When the money was right, he worked for various security firms, handling some fairly healthy accounts. One firm called on him whenever Dodi Fayed was in town to serve as his personal bodyguard. The Fayed family managed finances for the Sultan of Brunei, the wealthiest man in the world before Bill Gates.

Dodi was involved in filmmaking long before he hooked up with Princess Diana. He told Souza one evening that he had been looking for a home in Los Angeles that had some Hollywood history. Souza's brother, Glenn, had retired and was working full time for Paramount Pictures producer Robert

Evans of *The Godfather* and *Chinatown* fame. Evans was interested in selling his luxurious Bel Air home at the time, and there was no home in Los Angeles with more history than Evans's place. Bob managed to get a pocket listing from Evans (nothing in writing), and he agreed to a commission. The deal never came about, but the story was featured in a movie entitled *Hollywood Homicide* that Souza co-wrote with screenwriter-director Ron Shelton.

As for the possible infanticide suspect, Lange ended up flying back east and wasting three days of travel and nonsense conversing with a very confused, agitated, and psychologically unsettled woman. There was never evidence that any crime had occurred in Los Angeles involving the former nurse; however, Lange felt she was probably exactly where she should have been, away from a sane and settled society.

———

On December 31, 1985, Nash "houseguest" Jamie McGuan was the subject of a police investigation in the city of Torrance, California. It was 6:00 a.m., and officers had been dispatched to a busy intersection where a young woman was jumping up and down on the hoods of several vehicles. When the officers arrived, they approached Jamie, whom they later described as "extremely agitated, tense, and extremely paranoid." She was pointing and yelling at various people, then broke and ran into the intersection, where she was nearly hit by a passing car. Officers finally tackled the young woman on a median as she resisted, kicking and screaming. Seconds later, she stopped breathing. The officers started mouth-to-mouth resuscitation and called for an ambulance. She was transported unconscious to a local hospital.

McGuan remained in a coma and on life support until January 5, 1986. At 6:28 p.m. on that day, she was removed from life support and declared dead. Death was later attributed to severe narcotic intoxication. McGuan certainly would have been an important potential witness in any subsequent criminal trial, but to Lange, she was always just another victim of Ed Nash. She was twenty-five years old.

Shortly after McGuan's death, Ron Coen was enrobed as a municipal court judge, a tremendous achievement for the former prosecutor. Lange admired Coen both personally and professionally. It was clearly a dark period for the district attorney's office and the cops as well to lose him as a prosecutor. Coen went on to the Superior Court of Los Angeles County, where he remains to this day. Judge Coen has always enjoyed a solid reputation as one of the finest and most respected jurists in the County of Los Angeles.

A few years back, Lange attended a funeral reception for a friend at a private residence and noted a man there who seemed a little too young to be Ron Coen yet could have passed as his double. Later, the young man approached Lange and introduced himself as Ron Coen's son. He had the looks, the voice, the demeanor, and the whole package. Incredible! His occupation: a Los Angeles County deputy district attorney.

Pornographic film maker Bill Amerson seemed to have his hands full with John Holmes. He was simply not performing like the old John Holmes. Because of his drug use, Holmes was eventually dumped by Amerson. But that was just business; Amerson still supported Holmes in public and in the media. He told anyone who would listen that Holmes had dropped by the Wonderland house only after the murders had occurred. He blamed Fat Howard Cook and Paul Kelly for all the butchery.

Meanwhile, Ed Nash had been released from prison, and John Holmes had a new girlfriend. Lori Rose a.k.a. Maria Lee Gardner, twenty-four, had been "in the business" for a spell and was known professionally as Misty Dawn. She and John hooked up for a time and eventually married. Holmes continued to find some work in the industry, but the drugs still ruled the roost. By all appearances it seemed Holmes and Laurie just wanted to lead a low-profile life, at least for the time being.

Holmes was not the only one who had picked up a new partner. In 1986 Lange was working alone on the Wonderland case, as well as other, older murders he had been assigned. The suits up on the sixth floor at Parker Center decided to put together a task force in an attempt to solve some one hundred murders of prostitutes in South Central Los Angeles that spanned a period of approximately ten years. Lange was tasked with overseeing the field investigative process. Some two dozen Metro Division officers were assigned, and the investigation was expected to last a considerable amount of time. Among the Metro officers on loan was Enoch "Mac" McClain.

Lange had previously met McClain when he was a part of the security detail from the Metro Division. He was also on light duty status because of a back injury suffered in an on-duty traffic accident. Therefore, he would be spending much of his time in the office doing background investigations on possible suspects and witnesses. He was a quiet man with a very deceptive, but genuine, sense of humor. He was an impeccable dresser and without a doubt was born to be a cop.

Realizing he would be spending quite a bit of time with Mac and would depend on him for many things, Lange felt he should get to know just who the guy was.

Lange was used to sizing people up and went to work on Mac. The two discussed all the usual background stuff, and within a few minutes, Lange discovered Mac had been in the US Marines. Lange then found out they were in the Corps at the same time. Then there was the realization that they were both in combat infantry units of the Third Marine Division in Vietnam at the same time. From that instant on, the two bonded.

A new captain was also heading up the Robbery/Homicide Division: the popular and legendary William O. Gartland. He refused to be called "Captain" or "Bill"; he was "WOG." WOG was also a welcome and refreshing change for the division. He was genuinely old school with a sense of humor as dry as the Mojave Desert in August.

The task force investigation on prostitute murders dragged on through 1986 and 1987 and into 1988. The unit solved a handful of the murders as well as several unrelated felony cases. Throughout this time, Lange was still at work on the Wonderland investigation, and from time to time, he needed a partner. Mac was always more than happy to get involved. Lange also stayed on top of the Frank Christi case, bringing Mac along on various interviews and follow-ups so he could become familiar with it. McClain was inquisitive and persistent and always knew the next question to ask. His investigative abilities came naturally. Lange began to view him as a regular partner and did not want him to return to Metro Division. Lange immersed him in anything that came up to make him invaluable to the division and keep him from being sent back to light duty status and a desk assignment. In Lange's mind, that would have been an incredible waste of talent.

When the Southside task force mission was wrapped up, everyone returned to their old assignments at Metro. That is, everyone except McClain. Since he was still on light duty and unable to perform in the field, RHD got no heat from his bosses at Metro. However, WOG had a problem justifying the retention of McClain in view of his light duty status. He could not convince the brass to bring him in permanently. Lange, playing the salesman, explained to WOG that Mac was so steeped in Wonderland and the Christi case that he could not afford to let him go. WOG was hesitant, but he managed to pull a few strings, and Mac would remain, at least for a time. Lange had managed to take on partner number three in the Wonderland saga.

———•———

Meanwhile, over at the district attorney's office, two new prosecutors were assigned to the Wonderland case. Dale Davidson and Carole Najera had been boning up on the case for several weeks and were more than happy to sink their teeth into it. Both prosecutors were bright and aggressive. Neither of them brooked any nonsense. Davidson was a senior prosecutor with a good amount of experience. Najera was much newer but talented. She was also married to a Los Angeles County sheriff and had two brothers who were LAPD cops.

One of them, Joe Najera, was assigned to Robbery/Homicide Division, Robbery Special Section. Also joining the new Wonderland group was senior administrative aide for the prosecutor's office Patti Jo Fairbanks. Every successful operation needed a go-to person who was capable of handling damn near anything. That was where Patti Jo came in.

With Mac McClain fairly well ensconced in the unit, the detectives were getting back into the Laurel Canyon murders. Since it had been a while, they wanted to make contact with John Holmes. As far as Ad Vice and Holmes were concerned the one time snitch was officially "out of pocket!" However, sometimes it paid to allow a little time to pass. Things had a way of evolving; tongues sometimes loosened. Lange knew one way to contact Holmes would be through Bill Amerson, a guy who was not necessarily enamored with law enforcement. In regards to Holmes, Lange figured, "Once a snitch, always a snitch."

In late February of 1988, Mac and Lange drove to the address in the San Fernando Valley they had for Amerson. There was a car in the driveway but no response at the door after several very audible knocks. A little banter between Lange and Mac at the door would make anyone listening inside believe the callers thought no one was home and they would have to return later. The detectives left and drove around the block. Then they took up a vantage point down the street that afforded them a view of the front of the home. Lange and Mac had a little time to kill, and sometimes those things paid off.

Approximately twenty minutes passed. As the sun was setting, Bill Amerson walked out the front door and strode to his car. Lange drove forward and stopped in the street, blocking Amerson's car in the driveway. The detectives exited and walked toward him. Introductions were not needed.

Amerson gruffly asked what their business was, and Lange inquired about Holmes. Amerson explained that he and Holmes no longer worked together. He also said Holmes was very sick. He believed Holmes had contracted AIDS. He told Lange and Mac that Holmes was at the Sepulveda Veterans Hospital in the western part of the San Fernando Valley. Amerson claimed he got the info from Holmes's new wife, Lori.

Taking a stab at the obvious, Lange asked Amerson if John had ever discussed with him what happened up on Wonderland the night of the murders. Amerson's response was curt: "Nothing!" The accompanying glare signaled to the detectives that they had just heard everything Bill Amerson was ever going to say on the subject.

A call to the security folks over at the Sepulveda Veteran's Hospital verified that John Curtis Holmes was, indeed, a patient. According to security, the only visitors he'd had during his brief stay were his wife and half brother. The detectives were now certain Holmes would be overjoyed to get a couple more visitors.

The following day, McClain and Lange drove over to Sepulveda. The hospital itself looked to be in sad shape. Being veterans themselves, Lange and Mac didn't have a high opinion of the facility. It was old and much in need of up grading, not to mention a good scrub down fore and aft. The interior reeked of urine and looked like a dog pound for humans. Lange and Mac had both gotten through Nam without any major damage, and to think of those who hadn't ending up in a place like that was unnerving.

They found Holmes in a small single room at the end of a large ward. He was in bed. Lori was there with him. Lange and Mac later agreed they had seen dead people who looked better. Holmes was emaciated with scraggily hair and beard. His fingernails were exceptionally long. His face, hands, and arms exhibited various ulcerated splotches. He didn't look like he weighed a hundred pounds.

Since Holmes had apparently known the cops were coming, the introductions were minimal. It was a simple "Hey, guys!" Lange then introduced Mac as his new partner.

Lange did the talking and asked how Holmes was feeling. The first complaint he had was that his fingernails hurt. Then he told them he needed a smoke but couldn't do it in the room. He asked if they'd go outside with him, and the detectives consented. Lange and Mac watched Lori help him into a wheelchair by the side of the bed. Both cops then realized he was no longer able to walk. Lori then rolled him outside and he lit up. Nirvana!

It was small talk for a very short time. Lange got right to the point and told him the obvious: his race had been run. Holmes acknowledged this. Lange said that he wasn't breaking any news discussing the seriousness of his condition. The cops were then treated to a breakdown of Holmes's acting career and the Johnny Wadd persona he was known for. Holmes said he had always equated his role as the porn private eye to real-life detectives. He rattled on about how he was representing all cops, especially the LAPD, when he shot those flicks. It was actually a little sad, but then he began to do what he always did: talk out both sides of his mouth.

He carried on about how bad he felt because of the way things turned out. While he wanted to help the detectives in their investigation, he needed to think things through first. He then said he was very tired and needed to rest. He told the detectives to come back and he'd have everything written down for them. He said if he was not around, he'd give the info to Lori for the detectives. It never happened.

A couple of weeks passed. It was March 13, 1988, and John Holmes was dead. He went out the same way he came in, the same way he lived—lying right to the end.

Note: There was a bit of an ironic postscript to the death of John Holmes. If he had been convicted of the Wonderland murders, he would no doubt have lived for many years, although he would have been incarcerated. He had contracted AIDS after he was acquitted, when he resumed his career performing in the porn industry.

Lange later called his old partner Bob Souza to bring him up to speed on Holmes and the Wonderland case. Souza told him Holmes's death was poetic justice, and the retired detective had little empathy for the porn star. Souza was busy with his new pursuits, but he always appreciated Lange's sporadic updates. He invited Tom and Mac down to the beach for lunch. They planned to get together soon.

In mid-1988 Lange and McClain were in the office, still plugging away on cases when Lange picked up a call from an LA sheriff's deputy at the Los Angeles Central Men's Jail. The deputy wanted to know if he was familiar with a guy by the name of Scott Thorson. Recalling the late performer Liberace's gay boyfriend whom he'd interviewed early on, Lange told the deputy he did know Thorson. The deputy told Lange that Thorson wanted to talk to him regarding the Wonderland murders. It had been some seven years since Lange had spoken to Thorson, who had been heavily dependent on Ed Nash to support his drug habit. He was reluctant to talk back then, but things could change over time.

It was a five minute ride over to the county jail, and Lange and Mac were there within the hour. They signed in and were directed to an isolated attorney's conference room to wait for Thorson. When it came to interviewing witnesses in the county jail, detectives never wanted to meet them with the general population looking on or even make their presence known if possible. The witness, or informant, would without a doubt develop a so-called snitch jacket, and the detective might never see that person alive again.

When Thorson entered, he looked like he had spent the last few years in a concentration camp. He was gaunt and appeared ready to come apart. Lange figured he was drug sick. He asked for a smoke.

"We don't smoke!" Lange shot back. "What do you want?" The detectives' message was simple. We have no time for bullshit.

Scott apologized for not being "straight" with detectives back in '81. He claimed he had "some trouble" then and was unable to level with the cops. Thorson also claimed Ed Nash and his bunch terrified him.

Lange was in a testy mood. "Fine, now tell us what you want."

Thorson explained he had been at Nash's home on the night of the murders. He'd been heavily drugged up throughout most of the day. He said Greg Diles was there and had brought John Holmes in and beaten him up, trying to get information on the robbery at Nash's. Thorson went on to say that Holmes was crying and eventually admitted to Nash that he had set up the robbery. According to Thorson, it was shortly after this that Diles put Thorson into a room and told him to stay there. Later, while in the room, Thorson had heard others enter. He then heard Nash yelling and shouting something to the effect of "I want them tonight. I want you to kill them all!" Thorson believed Nash was ordering the murders in retaliation for the robbery at his home.

He further told the detectives that besides John Holmes, there was a guy there by the name of "Johnny," who was Armenian or of Middle Eastern descent. Thorson then said there was "another guy" with Johnny, whom he did not know and could not identify. Scott was thrashed but looked somewhat relieved and, of course, hopeful that Lange and Mac could do something for him once he testified. Lange told Thorson they didn't know if the case would even go to trial, but his statement and possible testimony would be considered.

By late in the year, Nash had put his home in Studio City on the market and was living in a condominium in the western San Fernando Valley. He was probably tired of all the surveillance on Dona Lola Place and getting his windows busted out and his house trashed by tenacious cops. Or maybe he just wanted to downsize. Some of his business dealings had been minimized, and apparently, he had had a meltdown with Hal Glickman regarding the Club Hollywood property. Hal, operating the spot, hadn't been paying Ed the rent on the place in a timely manner or at all.

It also looked like Greg Diles might have been demoted as he was then parking cars at the club. According to others, he was also usually available as some extra muscle around the club when needed.

Meanwhile, Fat Howard Cook was having his own problems. On September 22, 1988, he reported that he had been the victim of a burglary. Apparently, anyone can be a victim. He said someone had absconded with "eight various types of fur coats, a red-fox bedspread, a handgun, and jewelry" with a combined value of $494,050. At least that's what was written in the burglary report.

It was certainly a wonder how Howard could have possibly ended up with eight fur coats. But that was the insurance company's problem, as was Howard.

Twenty-Three

READY FOR EDDIE

There had been an uptick of activity in the Wonderland case, and Deputy District Attorney Dale Davidson felt the time was right to make a move and arrest Nash and Diles for the four murders and one attempted murder. With Scott Thorson's statement regarding the night prior to the murders at Nash's house locked in about as much as possible and with everything else in place, the prosecution team was ready to make their move. Nash was under constant surveillance by the Special Investigation Section as he motored to and from his new digs at the San Fernando Valley condo. Greg Diles was less of a flight risk for a number of reasons and would be easy to nail once the arrest warrants had been cleared for both him and Nash. As of late, Diles was either home at his mother's place in south Los Angeles or parking cars at Nash's Club Hollywood managed by Hal Glickman.

Lange, Mac, and the prosecutors felt that although they had been keeping things pretty close to the vest evidence-wise, witnesses included, they did not want to take the chance that something had blown Nash's way and watch him split for the airport. It had happened before. Therefore, SIS again had strict orders. Should Nash end up at LA International Airport or any other air strip, they would immediately affect a probable-cause arrest. However, once

226

the actual arrest warrants were processed and signed by a magistrate, detectives would immediately move on both men.

It was September 7, 1988, more than seven years since the Wonderland murders. A quick drive-by at Club Hollywood revealed that Diles had arrived at about 10:00 a.m. and settled in for the day. Nash had gone out alone in his gray Lincoln, made a couple of local stops then returned home early in the afternoon. Lange was at the district attorney's office with Davidson and Patti Jo Fairbanks. Mac was monitoring SIS movements over the phone and staying in touch.

It was easier for the cops to take down potentially armed suspects out in the street than inside a dwelling. The street approach eliminated a possible barricaded suspect scenario or even a possible suicide situation. That's where the detectives hoped Nash would be once the warrants were signed. Here, plain common sense and experience dictated they should assume the suspects would be armed until the arresting officers knew better.

Time dragged on as Lange and McClain both considered all the possible scenarios that could go sideways under the circumstances. Meanwhile Davidson had found some kind of a flaw in one of the affidavits. That delayed the process. It was sent over to Patti Jo. It looked like a quick fix before the document was hand carried down to court for a judge's signature. Lange called Mac to fill him in on the minor glitch. Mac told Lange Nash was once again on the move.

Nash appeared to be on his way home just as the signatures from the court were obtained. Lange called Mac, who in return green lit SIS. Ed Nash was taken down without incident in the middle of the street just blocks from his home. Mac McClain was on his way to Club Hollywood where he would meet up with a couple of units that were already en route to grab up Greg Diles.

Arriving just in front of his backup, Mac pulled up and quickly checked the parking lot for Diles but was unable to spot him. Realizing that Diles had never seen him before, he threw an old jacket on over his shirt and tie, unholstered his gun, and prowled the lot for Diles. Moments later, a backup unit arrived and observed Diles nearby. Within seconds Greg Diles was in handcuffs after being taken down looking up at the business end of a shotgun. And once again, he was laying face down, only this time on the pavement and fully clothed.

When the arrests were announced publicly, the *Los Angeles Times* wanted to get back into the mix and were asking all manner of questions. When Dale Davidson was asked about the arrests, he was quoted as saying in a somewhat tongue-in-cheek manner, "There must be new evidence in the case." He did not go into detail for good reason. The *Times* went on to recount that the now-deceased John Holmes had been acquitted of the murders in 1982. Certainly the prosecution did not need that reminder. It took the media little time to get on to Scott Thorson's involvement in the prosecution's case; however, they would not be interviewing him anytime soon, thanks to the efforts of the district attorney's office. Instead, they were reduced to quoting from Thorson's 1987 book *Behind the Candelabra: My Life with Liberace.*

The book delved into Thorson's relationship with Liberace, which had collapsed because of Scott's cocaine addiction. It also mentioned associations with various underworld types, one of whom he referred to as "Mr. Y." Meanwhile, Nash was acknowledged in the book as someone who was close to Thorson and lent him "support," which was a very interesting term to describe their relationship.

Ed Nash's newest attorney, Paul Caruso, was back at work. He denied Nash had anything to do with the murders and said that the LAPD, in cahoots with the district attorney's office, was attempting to "save face": hence the criminal filings. Caruso stated he was not aware of any new evidence. He argued vigorously for bail, as did Greg Diles's newest attorney, Richard Lasting. The DA's office argued that Nash was a flight risk even though he had surrendered his passport. Prosecutors made the case that there was a risk involved because of Nash's underworld connections. Bail was denied for both defendants. The two men were remanded to custody and sent off to the Los Angeles County Jail.

Ed Nash was placed in high power at the facility. This meant that he was essentially a keep-away, which prevented him from associating with other prisoners. His actions within the facility would also be monitored more extensively than those of other inmates. Greg Diles was booked directly into the general population. Later, this would prove to be a huge mistake with disastrous consequences for many involved.

Ed Nash was once again playing musical chairs—lawyer edition. Soon after his incarceration, he replaced Paul Caruso with well-known Los Angeles attorneys Leslie Abramson and Gerald Chaleff. Abramson had a reputation as a foul mouthed, anti-cop, anti-death penalty lawyer who would push the envelope right to the edge of the table and then deny there was any envelope at all. She was frequently praised by the *Los Angeles Times* for her advocacy work in assisting the downtrodden who had been falsely accused of various crimes by the uncaring and ruthless cops. Coincidentally, her husband was on the editorial staff of that particular newspaper.

Abramson went on to represent the Menendez brothers, who brutally shot- gunned their parents to death in Beverly Hills on August 20, 1989. In that case she was able to hang two juries in two separate trials, claiming that the "boys" had been physically beaten and sexually and mentally abused by their evil parents. All of this while growing up in the concrete jungles of Beverly Hills.

There was talk of malfeasance on her part for altering the notes of a psychiatrist who was a witness in the trial. When asked about this by the judge on the record, she had flipped over her ace in the hole, the Fifth Amendment. Abramson was censored by the State Bar of California. Both brothers were eventually convicted in a third trial and sentenced to life imprisonment without the possibility of parole by Judge Stanley Weisberg, who would not permit cameras in his courtroom, too bad. Lange later thought it might have been a better show than O. J.

Gerald Chaleff, clearly the more deliberative of the two attorneys, would also become a member of the Menendez defense team prior to being replaced after citing various conflicts. He had also represented Kenneth Bianchi, one of two defendants in the Hillside Strangler case, who was eventually convicted of torturing and murdering twelve young women in the late 1970s. This was another case that Lange and Souza's unit had been involved with. Ironically, Chaleff would eventually be appointed as president of the Los Angeles City Police Commission.

Just prior to the preliminary hearing in the Nash/Diles matter on September 23, 1988, Leslie Abramson was quoted in the *Los Angeles Times* as stating she was "seriously underwhelmed" by the prosecutor's case. She then went after various persons who were going to be called as witnesses, citing their predilection for drugs and having various criminal records. Her tactic was a common one for defense attorneys: put the witnesses on trial, not the defendants. The only difference Lange saw was that this was usually done when the witnesses were on the stand, not before they even walked into the courthouse.

———◆———

The preliminary hearing in Los Angeles Municipal Court was held on January 10, 1989, in the courtroom of Judge Marion Obera. The hearing was to determine whether or not there was sufficient cause and evidence for the court to bind Nash and Diles over for trial in the Wonderland murders.

During the hearing Abramson attacked each and every facet of the prosecution's case she could get away with. Much of the preliminary case was presented with police testimony. Because this was a hearing and not a trial, she was prohibited from going to the mat over each individual issue. She also attempted to intimidate civilian witnesses, including Scientific Investigation Division personnel, alluding at times to the prosecution "failures" in the Holmes trial. That tactic actually proved to be fairly successful.

When Scott Thorson was called to the stand, the intimidation tactics backfired. Of course, with Thorson's background and criminal record, his reputation was on the chopping block, and Abramson did everything in her power to impeach everything he had to say. Her ploy didn't work.

Every time Abramson got snide with Thorson, he would get right back in her face. It was so cheeky after a bit that Judge Obera had to intervene from time to time and admonish Thorson. When Abramson asked a question and Thorson didn't like the tenor of that question, he came back at her with another question and not without a certain amount of animosity. The exchanges were courtroom theatrics at their very best.

Abramson was clearly getting flustered in spite of the judge's interventions. Thorson was having no part of her accusations and innuendo. Seated at the defense table, Nash actually appeared sober and attentive. Perhaps the stories about him beating his cocaine habit were genuine. However, he was also fuming. It was unclear whether his anger was directed at Thorson, his attorney, or both. When Thorson got into the story about the robbery at Nash's home, which purportedly motivated the murders, Lange thought the court deputies would have to order body restraints for Nash.

Thorson went on to testify that Nash had once expressed regret to him about the murders at Wonderland—"It got out of hand"—and said Nash "regretted" having sent Diles and Holmes over there. Abramson countered with her argument that Thorson was a pathological liar. She stated she had documentary evidence that Scott Thorson perjured himself in civil court during his palimony suit against entertainer Liberace. Judge Obera denied the defense request to bring that in and held both Nash and Diles to answer for their crimes, binding them over for trial.

At their arraignment in superior court, bail was once again denied for both of them. On February 6, 1989, both men formally pleaded not guilty in Los Angeles Superior Court. Ed Nash had fired both Abramson and Chaleff within hours of the court's preliminary decision. It was only speculation, but the thinking was that if any ass kicking had been done at the preliminary hearing, it was probably done by Scott Thorson.

Note: A few years later, Lange was entering the Los Angeles County Courthouse on Temple Street one afternoon during the O. J. Simpson trial. As he approached the entrance, he observed Jerry Chaleff entering at the same time. Lange walked up and cheerfully greeted him. Chaleff turned toward Lange and once again got that "Oh, shit" look. A couple of media types approached them, as they always did during the trial, and Chaleff moved away from Lange quicker than a man would from a rabid dog. It simply would not look good for a well-known defense attorney of his ilk to be friendly with a homicide cop, or perhaps vice versa.

The murder trials of Ed Nash and Gregory Diles commenced on Monday, March 20, 1989, in Department 120 of the Los Angeles Superior Court, Judge Curtis Rappe presiding. There was to be one trial for both men; however, two different juries would be impaneled to decide the fate of each one separately. It was an unusual arrangement that would take a considerable amount of time to coordinate.

When evidence was presented involving both defendants, both juries would be present to hear it. When evidence was presented involving just one of the defendants, then that particular jury would be the only one present. Lange imagined the court felt that one or the other of the juries might be tainted or conflicted if they heard any evidence inculpating the other suspect. It sounded reasonable on its face, but they were still talking about one incident of mass murder and attempted murder and what led up to it. Clearly, the suspects were connected at the hip in all respects throughout.

The trial did not draw anywhere near the amount of media attention that the Holmes trial had some seven years earlier. Obviously, Holmes, with his sordid past, being put on trial was much more alluring than a couple of unknown thugs and their legal woes tossed into the arena.

Meanwhile, Mac McClain had been communicating with Susie Launius and her family, preparing them for the upcoming trial. Realizing what she was in for, Susie was reticent to travel to Los Angeles and take part in the trial. Mac, of course, had been a part of her security detail and had earned the trust of Launius as well as her family. He proved to be a calming influence on all, taking over the position that Detective Bob Souza once held. That "calming influence" would be instrumental in getting Susie back to Los Angeles to testify.

In her opening statement, Deputy District Attorney Carol Najera aptly described the robbery at Nash's home. She also established the fact that the violent incident led to the revenge killings at Wonderland. She then mentioned the name of each victim and articulated the savage injuries sustained by Susan Launius. Her opening was strong and to the point.

Ed Nash had two new attorneys to replace Chaleff and Abramson. Ed Rucker and Jeff Brody were well-known and highly experienced Los Angeles defense attorneys. Rucker's opening statement was a bit more artistically drawn up than Najera's. It was something about "dark hues of that kind" and "a world of drugs" and that it was "where Mr. Nash had chosen to live."

His client existed in a world "devoid of the value system that we know." He also told the jurors that before the trial had ended, he would name the real killers of the people at Wonderland, and that his client had not been involved.

Counsel to Greg Diles was defense attorney Richard Lasting. Lasting primarily went after Scott Thorson in his opening statement and accused him of fabricating his previous statements concerning what had occurred on Dona Lola Place. The court-appointed lawyer ripped into Thorson, who he stated was guilty of "play for pay" because of robbery and drug charges Thorson had pending with the Los Angeles district attorney.

As usually occurs in a murder trial, among the first witnesses called were law enforcement types. This included the investigating detectives and investigative personnel from the Scientific Investigation Division, which included criminalists, who were responsible for the collection, preservation, and analysis of all evidence.

Lange was called to testify to what he and his partner had discovered at the crime scene in the way of victims and evidence. Lange also introduced the twenty-five minute videotape of the bloody crime scene, in which he had walked through the Wonderland house, describing the brutally beaten victims and various forms of evidence observed and collected. This was the second time the crime scene tape had been used in the murder trial of a suspect in the Wonderland case, the first being during the Holmes trial. It was graphic and clearly showed both juries just how brutal the attacks were. Once again, there were the gasps and other emotional responses from the courtroom.

One of the first civilian prosecution witnesses called by Dale Davidson was David Lind. He was sporting a long gray beard, and while his steely-eyed expressions were still evident, the fierce glares were a thing of the past. In speaking with Lind before he was called to the stand, Patti Jo Fairbanks learned he had married and was now employed … legally.

Clearly, Davidson wanted to lead Lind through his long and violent past history of drug arrests, robbery, assaults, burglary, and anything else he could get in so as not to leave this for the defense attorneys to exploit. Once his sordid past was ingrained in the jury, Davidson had Lind go into detail describing the Nash robbery. Toward the end of his testimony, Lind admitted the Wonderland crew had been "in over our heads" when ripping off Nash.

He stated there was a "certain type of dope dealer you don't rob, and that was Mr. Nasrallah." Whether Nash took some sort of pride in that statement or not was unknown; however, Lange imagined he didn't want to be referred to as a "certain type of dope dealer."

Ed Rucker was the first to cross-examine Lind and wasted no time. He led off with "Isn't it true that you called yourself a robber when asked your profession at the trial of John Holmes in 1982?" Lind responded without hesitation. "We've established that I'm not a very nice guy, and I lie sometimes. But no matter what I've done, I never killed anybody. They did!" Lind pointed at Diles and Nash.

The defense lawyers were on their feet screaming their objections as Judge Rappe instructed the jury to disregard Lind's last remark. Things didn't get any easier for the defense as Lind brooked no nonsense from the lawyers throughout his testimony, which went on for several hours. As experienced as the attorneys were, if this had been a boxing match, it would have been David Lind by a knockout.

As most criminal trials progressed, both the prosecution and the defense, gave increased attention to the members of the jury. This was certainly true in the Nash/Diles trial. Lange, McClain, Fairbanks, and the prosecutors were constantly observing the jurors throughout the trial in an attempt to pick up any signs of possible inattention, bias, nervousness, or anything else that might portend what a juror was thinking or if he or she had an agenda.

For some time, they had all noticed that eighteen-year-old juror Shaunte Taylor from South Central Los Angeles seldom took notes or interacted in any fashion with other jury members. While the jurors were not permitted to converse personally when seated in the jury box during the trial, it was fairly easy to see during breaks and when they were entering and exiting the courtroom who was relating to other jurors and who was not. Clearly, Taylor was not. This was concerning. She might have had a bias, might not have wanted to be there, or might simply not have been very personable.

During a lunch break, McClain and Lange decided to grab a bite in the courthouse cafeteria. They had the time, which was rare, and the food wasn't bad. As they exited the lunch line after paying, they narrowly missed physically running into Ms. Taylor. Lange had to do a sudden side step, and Mac followed. She looked at both of them, and since it was a no-no to speak with any juror, Lange gave a slight nod, and Mac smiled at her. She responded with an angry glare that the detectives wouldn't have given Charles Manson. It was pretty clear she didn't like them. That was not a good sign.

During the second week of the trial, Scott Thorson was called to the stand by Carol Najera. Thorson recounted his previous testimony as Carol walked him through the entire scenario of Diles forcing John Holmes into Nash's house for a little "up close and personal" discussion with Nash. Najera also delved into Thorson's history, his life with Liberace, and the palimony suit that followed, a tit-for-tat for Abramson's preliminary hearing cross-examination, should the subject be brought up again by the defense.

In keeping with the court's two-jury edict, Dale Davidson picked up the questioning and asked Thorson to describe what he had heard from behind the closed door of Nash's bedroom when Diles and Nash had Holmes out in the living room. Thorson stated Diles and Nash were "beating Mr. Holmes up…I heard Mr. Nash telling Mr. Holmes that if he didn't take him to where those people were who robbed him, he would have every member of his family killed." Just after that statement, the trial was adjourned for the weekend.

Throughout the trial detectives kept Thorson housed in a Little Tokyo hotel in downtown Los Angeles close to the courthouse. He was under constant security as a protected witness. Keeping him on a leash would be an interesting challenge since Scott still had a raging cocaine addiction problem. The coke was his problem; keeping him off the streets was Lange and McClain's problem.

Thorson attempted on more than a couple of occasions to slip out in the middle of the night to score drugs. Thankfully, his security detail stayed on top of things, at least most of the time. Lange got a call very late one night. The security detail officer who phoned said Scott had slipped out and was apparently on the streets, looking for something to suck up into his nose.

The search was on for a couple of hours until he finally made an appearance at the hotel pretty close to sunrise. He had ventured south into the Skid Row area of the city. It was a minor miracle that he returned at all and didn't end up in the ER or worse. All the while, the detectives were thinking, "Wouldn't the defense lawyers love to know about the prosecution's star witness and his midnight meanderings?"

Monday morning, March 26, 1990, Thorson was back on the witness stand. Deputy DA Davidson was delving more deeply into what Scott had overheard at the Nash residence. Thorson stated, "He [Nash] said he'd have them all on their knees, teach them a lesson, and that they'd never steal from him again."

Later, Thorson was questioned about conversations he'd had with Nash subsequent to the murders while they were freebasing cocaine together. Thorson said Nash would become upset while under the influence of the drug and once stated to Scott, "Things had gone too far…It had turned into a bloody mess." Thorson also related how Nash threatened him with "People have a habit of disappearing in the canyon. By the time they find you, Scott, I'll have every tooth in your head pulled so they can't even identify you."

Nash lawyer Jeff Brody cross-examined Thorson and went for his throat. Brody first drove at Thorson for a deal he had supposedly made with the district attorney's office to avoid prosecution on pending charges. Brody pounded away at that with no evidence to back it up, which would certainly not have stopped him anyway. Brody then flatly asked Thorson if he concocted lies and made his statements up. Scott denied it. That was followed by accusations that Thorson read these revelations in the newspaper, and Brody leaned in even harder: "You made all this up over the last three days, didn't you?" A bit shaken, Thorson denied this but didn't challenge it.

Following Scott Thorson, several other witnesses were called to testify and were likewise attacked from every conceivable angle. However, when Susan Launius was called to the stand, the defense backed off considerably. It would not have been wise for them to go after a victim who had been beaten to within a whisker of her life by their clients in front of the jury.

Regardless, much of her testimony was vague anyway, essentially the same as during the Holmes trial. Among the prosecutors there was a belief that Launius was holding back somewhat about recollections. If true, this certainly could have been due to her fear of Nash, which would be understandable.

On May 10, 1990, the case against Ed Nash concluded and was sent to the jury. The case against Greg Diles continued. On May 15, 1990, the Nash jury foreman notified Judge Rappe that one of the jurors, Shaunte Taylor, was refusing to deliberate. The foreman stated Ms. Taylor would not discuss the evidence that had been presented. Additionally, Taylor believed the prosecution's witnesses were liars who had given testimony for favorable treatment in their own cases.

The jury was hung eleven to one for conviction. The foreman saw a hopeless deadlock. While Judge Rappe had the judicial authority to recuse the juror for refusing to deliberate and appoint one of the six alternate jurors to replace her, he instead declared a mistrial.

Note: While the action by the judge was disturbing since he could have recused the juror for refusing to deliberate instead, he may have been concerned about an appeal if there had been a conviction. Later, the six alternate jurors were polled. All six stated they would have voted to convict Ed Nash of murder.

On May 29, 1990, the Diles jury foreman reported to Judge Rappe that they, too, were hopelessly deadlocked. They were sent back to deliberate further and eventually hung up the verdict, ten to two for acquittal. Once again, the judge declared a mistrial. Both Ed Nash and Greg Diles would be retried for the Wonderland murders.

Note: When a criminal trial concluded, regardless of the outcome, detectives always believed it was incumbent on the prosecution to interview the jurors about their decision if the jurors were willing. For all the obvious reasons, the prosecution in this case needed to know how the jurors' decision came about. If there were strong points or weak points that had impressed the jury, the prosecutors would want to know what they were for consideration in the next trial. While some of this did occur informally, because of the eleven-to-one finding of guilt and the obvious refusal of juror Taylor to deliberate, this was not pressed.

Some ten years after the Nash trial was hung eleven to one for conviction, a juror in that matter, Yvonne Maxwell, was interviewed by reporter Susan Goldsmith of the *New Times LA*. Ms. Maxwell believed much more had been going on with fellow juror Shaunte Taylor during their deliberations than just Taylor's stated belief that Ed Nash was innocent of participating in the murders.

Maxwell stated, "If it hadn't been for her [Taylor], he [Nash] would have been convicted. She kept saying over and over again, 'You can't trust the cops. They lie and plant evidence.' She would not consider the evidence in the case. It seemed like what she was saying was something that had been rehearsed." She went on to say, "Those people were killed in such a brutal way, and the thought that Nash could get away with it really bothered me and a lot of the jurors. That's why we stuck our necks out and complained to the judge."

Twenty-Four

ONE MORE TIME

Ever since the hung jury in the first trial, considering what the lone juror holdout stated to the other jurors, the detectives and the prosecution team had been concerned about jury tampering. If the hierarchy of the district attorney's office pushed the issue, this possibility would have to be investigated by some outside agency without any hint of conflict. Making this allegation would also make things even more perplexing than they already were. At that particular time, there was no evidence of collusion or tampering in the trial. The DA decided to let it lie for the time being.

Late in 1990, the prosecution was once again ready to go after Adel Nasrallah and Gregory Diles for the Wonderland murders and the attempted murder of Susan Launius. Reflecting back on the eleven-to-one vote for conviction following the previous trial, Lange and the Wonderland team were confident that this time around, they would nail Nash. Now, there would not be the confusion brought on by a second jury for the second suspect. If everything went the way the prosecution planned, Diles would be pulled in right along with Nash evidence-wise. Again, there had been a shake-up of defense lawyers. This was becoming routine. Nash's attorney, Jeffrey Brody, had been replaced by another well-known and highly regarded Los Angeles lawyer, Bradley Brunon. Additionally, local attorney Michael M. Crain joined

Richard Lasting representing Diles. By now, Greg Diles had lost some one hundred pounds while in custody. Depending on how one viewed this, it could be good or bad, clearly though, a testament to what incarceration does to a murder suspect and his diet.

Carol Najera and Dale Davidson put on essentially the same case they had previously. They brought in the same witnesses and evidence. The defense, however, intended to call the jailed Paul Kelly and his girlfriend, Maggie Gifford. In order to preempt the defense, the prosecutors would call Kelly and Gifford first as hostile witnesses. Here, the presumption was that the witnesses would be antagonistic to the prosecution's efforts as a whole. This allowed the prosecutors a bit more latitude when examining this type of witness.

The defense maintained that Paul Kelly was the real killer, motivated by a hatred for victim Ron Launius and a soured drug deal or two with the Wonderland gang. It was going to be interesting to see the defense describe just how Kelly gained entrance to the murder scene and how he went about pulverizing five people at the same time in a closed environment in the early morning hours of July 1, 1981. It would also be of interest to see just who the defense would claim had assisted Kelly and why. Presumably, any thinking juror would understand that one person would not attempt to take on a house full of badass, drug-addled robbers by himself.

This time, in their opening statements, Davidson and Najera tied Nash and Diles to an organized narcotics ring responsible for distributing dope throughout Los Angeles County. They brought the involvement of John Holmes in early and told the jury he was responsible for a robbery at Nash's home that was the genesis of the brutal murders on Wonderland Avenue.

In the minds of attorneys Ed Rucker and Bradley Brunon, their client was a businessman who had, unfortunately, gotten himself involved with drugs and had a bad habit of dealing with unsavory characters from time to time. They were out to prove that Nash was in no way involved in this horrendous crime. As for the Diles's attorneys, Lasting and Crane, they told the jury their guy was just a parking lot attendant who had been pulled into this mess merely because he worked for Nash.

It was more than clear that both defense teams would target Paul Kelly as being responsible for the killings…and they said they were going to prove it. Dale Davidson argued successfully that Paul Kelly was only a prosecution witness initially, was in custody, and would no doubt plead the Fifth Amendment when called as a witness. Kelly's testimony would be heard in- camera first, which meant in the judge's chambers, with the attorneys on the record but outside the presence of the jury.

If Kelly was called to testify in front of the jury straight out of the state prison system and invoked his Fifth Amendment right against self-incrimination, it could sway one or more jurors in a direction the prosecution didn't want them to go. His long involvement with drug dealing would come out as well as his association with one Fat Howard Cook. Going in-camera first was a win for the prosecution. The judge would then rule on whether or not Kelly would be heard by the jury.

As in the past trials, Lange introduced the crime scene videotape, and once again it elicited gasps from the jurors and others in the courtroom. Clearly, no human being could come close to accurately describing the viciousness of the crime scene like the video did. The media devoured it.

Note: The videotape also ignited an LAPD internal affairs investigation some years later when it became part of the introduction to a newly released motion picture about the case. As the one who narrated the tape, Lange guessed someone thought he or Souza might have had something to do with this. They didn't. Of interest, however, was the fact that the tape had not only been shown in open court on at least three separate occasions for all to see, but had also been turned over to defense attorneys per the discovery process. There were at a minimum a dozen lawyers who had access to the tape at one time or another.

Although Lange and Souza had been approached by the production company to serve as technical advisers, they had turned down the offer because the script was wholly inaccurate and more of a story about John Holmes than the actual murder investigation.

Shortly after the murders, Maggie Gifford, girlfriend of Paul Kelly, had been contacted and interviewed by Lange and Souza. The interview was recorded. Gifford said she was familiar with the victims and had visited the

Wonderland house on various occasions. She apparently was attracted to Ron Launius, and this was known to Kelly. On the tape Gifford said Kelly had told her he was going to "eliminate a few people she cared about." It was apparent Kelly made the threats to keep Gifford away from Launius. There were also references to the relationship between Paul Kelly and Fat Howard Cook.

The court's ruling was that Kelly would testify in open court in front of the jury. Although Lange later testified they could never actually put Paul Kelly at the crime scene, this was a solid score for the defense. Shortly thereafter, Kelly was escorted into the courtroom and sworn in. He was attired in his prison garb and in chains, looking every bit the thug he was. He invoked his rights under the Fifth Amendment and was quickly shunted back into the court's lockup section. Nash's defense had had its day in court, as had their suspect. It was all show and tell.

Closing out for the prosecution, Deputy District Attorney Dale Davidson conceded the possibility that Kelly might be one of the murder suspects, but said that he did not set the killings up. That was done by Ed Nash. To the detectives, while that could have been a reasonable argument on its face, there was never any substantive evidence to inculpate Kelly. In summing up the defense case, Ed Rucker said it was Paul Kelly, Paul Kelly, and Paul Kelly. He did it. The tape with Maggie Gifford said it all. Unfortunately, the jury said it too.

Note: In alluding to the possibility that Paul Kelly might have been a suspect in the actual killings, the prosecution had opened the door for the defense to walk in with Kelly, much to their dismay.

On January 17, 1991, Ed Nash and Gregory Diles were acquitted of the Laurel Canyon murders.

Two jurors later came forward and stated publicly that Paul Kelly should have been on trial for the murders instead of Nash and Diles. They believed the defense showed this beyond any reasonable doubt. Two trials, two different juries, same suspects, same witnesses, same evidence, same prosecutors, same judge, but one came back eleven to one for conviction and the other twelve to zero for acquittal. Lange and McClain knew they should never put their money down on what a jury might or might not do. Different people see things differently. Or was it something else?

Subsequently, the detectives pondered the possibility of an alternate being appointed to the jury in the first trial. If that had occurred, Nash would no doubt stand convicted. There would not have been a second trial. It also stood to reason the judge would have been concerned that if there were a conviction, the defense might have won on appeal. There was then the possibility that the judge would be criticized because he had recused a hold-out juror in the case.

Knowing Ed Nash had been acquitted of orchestrating a massacre that resulted in five people getting their heads beaten in was one thing; realizing all the other lives he had ruined and gotten away with was another. For years, Nash had lured young girls into his den of depravity with the promise of drugs. Once they were hooked, he had them at his mercy and took full advantage to denigrate and humiliate them with impunity.

On more than a few occasions, reliable sources close to Nash related to detectives that one of Nash's more disgusting and perverse practices had to do with him refusing to give his addicted female victims the drugs they were craving unless, and until, they licked his anus clean after a bowel movement! The detectives made inquiries about this and other depraved revelations concerning Nash, but they were never substantiated. However, these sources were in a position to be aware of Nash's sexual proclivities and found these repulsive accusations to be believable.

Twenty-Five

A New Day...Kind Of!

In September of 1996, eight years after Bob Souza retired, Tom Lange pulled the pin as well. He left the Los Angeles Police Department with slightly under twenty-nine years of service. While Lange had always respected and enjoyed what he did for a living, he had simply had enough. Between the Laurel Canyon murders, O. J. Simpson, and a couple hundred other cases, his wife had also had enough. Still wanting to stay busy, Lange assisted in the writing of *Evidence Dismissed*, his book on the Simpson case. Lange also busied himself as a licensed private investigator in California and did some consulting on a few murder cases and television productions. However, unknown to Lange at the time, he was not yet through with the Wonderland murders or with another old case that had dogged him for years.

Every now and again, there was a blurb on television or in the newspapers about Nash, the Wonderland murders, or some television production or feature film using the case as a backdrop. Lange, Souza, and McClain were all somewhat amused when they read that Ed Nash had sued his attorney, Ed Rucker, for an undisclosed amount of money, claiming something to the effect that Rucker had overcharged for his services. A settlement was apparently reached, but the terms were not disclosed. Incredibly, the man had kept Nash from going to prison for the rest of his life. Lange actually ran across Rucker at a law office in Santa Monica while doing an interview on a case. He was very pleasant, as usual. He didn't mention the settlement or anything else regarding his erstwhile client or the Wonderland case in general, and Lange didn't ask.

On July 7, 1999, Detective Jeff Redmond, who was assigned to the LAPD's Organized Crime Intelligence Division, phoned Lange. One of Redmond's supervisors happened to be a well-known figure in the Wonderland murder case, Lange's old partner and good friend Mac McClain. Redmond said he would like to have a sit-down with Lange regarding the Wonderland murders. He wanted their chat to be sooner rather than later. It was not a problem for Lange.

Redmond and his partner were knocking on Lange's front door early the following morning. The introductions were light. Lange had seen Redmond and his partner around before, and they were both very familiar with McClain. Mac had become more of an administrative supervisor at the Organized Crime Intelligence Division. He was not working in the field and not a part of what Redmond was bringing to Lange's home.

Redmond told Lange he and his partner were working with the US Organized Crime Strike Force and US Attorney Steve Larson, as well as federal agents of the FBI and the IRS. They were in the process of once again targeting Ed Nash for numerous federal violations of law. Other Nash associates were also involved.

Redmond went on to state that a federal grand jury had once again indicted Ed Nash for organized crime activities and corruption under the Racketeering Influence and Corrupt Organization (RICO) Act. It was a sixteen-count indictment including several federal crimes such as money laundering and conspiracy to defraud the US government to commit offenses against the United States. Lange would be called as a witness for the Feds.

The federal counts also included conspiracy to distribute and possession with intent to distribute a controlled substance and what was referred to as

Racketeering Act Two: Murder of Ronald Launius, William Deverell, Barbara Richardson, and Joy Audrey Miller! Lange had a hard time controlling his joy at the news, but he also had a concern about the murder charge. Nash had already been tried and acquitted of the murders. There would be a double jeopardy problem.

"No," said Redmond. The indictment read, "Defendant Nash, unindicted co-racketeers Gregory DeWitt Diles and John Holmes, and others known and unknown to the Grand Jury, did commit and aid and abet the following violations of state law involving murder, either one of which constituted Racketeering Act Two."

Nash would not be re-tried for the murders; he would be tried for conspiracy and aiding and abetting in furtherance of the murders. This was not double jeopardy but a well-thought-out tactic by the Strike Force.

There were a couple of other counts in the indictment of great interest. Racketeering Act Four: Bribery of a Juror in a State of California Murder Trial. The chickens had come home to roost for former Nash juror Shaunte Taylor. Things did not end well for her. An additional count described Bribery of a Witness in a State of California Murder Investigation. (Truth be told, there were no doubt more than one!)

Redmond told Lange that after his arrest earlier for the murders and prior to the first trial, Greg Diles had been put into the general population at the Men's Central Jail in Los Angeles. This proved to be a huge mistake, as alluded to earlier. While in the lockup, Diles hooked up with a Rollin' 30s South Central gang-banger by the name of Teag Byers. Byers had been sentenced to life imprisonment on an unrelated matter. He was also a gang associate of the brother of juror Shaunte Taylor. The brother had had his own brushes with the LAPD as a gang member. One apparently involved a barricaded standoff situation.

According to Redmond, Diles and Byers put their heads together and realized that Shaunte's brother might be amenable to a business arrangement between the Nash forces and Ms. Taylor, who they had recently discovered had been selected as a jury member in Nash's murder trial. Later, stepping into the middle of all this was Nash associate Joe Mikaelian, a purported Armenian organized crime figure. Mikaelian figured prominently in the US Organized Crime Strike Force investigation, not just as a potential defendant, but also as a witness.

Mikaelian delivered $70,000 in cash to Taylor's brother, who distributed the money to his sister (for services rendered), his mother, and, of course, himself. He forgot to deliver some of the dough to his old pal Teag through an intermediary. That was a big mistake on his part. Shaunte's brother wound up getting "dumped" in a drive-by shooting. The situation did not sit well with Ms. Taylor, who was then more than happy to deal with the Feds and their investigation. For immunity from any prosecution, she would testify at the federal RICO trial about her role in accepting a bribe as a juror in the Nash trial, but with one caveat. Shaunte would only allow it to happen if she and her family were granted entry into the federal witness protection program. She would not be charged with a crime herself since the statute of limitations had expired.

Enlightening Lange further, Redmond went on to state that as part of their investigation, some two years prior, they had to locate and interview Greg Diles. Diles was also on the chopping block to be indicted by the Feds. He was apparently still living with his mother and brother Sam in South Central Los Angeles.

When Redmond and his partner knocked on Mrs. Diles's front door, they were met by her other son, Sam. They identified themselves, even though Sam already knew who they were, and they knew Sam. They asked if they could speak with Greg. Sam said, "That's no problem" and invited them in. He led the detectives into the living room and stated something to the effect of "OK. There he is." Sam was gesturing toward a small urn prominently displayed on the mantel above the fireplace. The urn contained the ashes of Greg Diles. The good news…Sam Diles had a sense of humor. The bad news…Greg Diles was dead. He'd succumbed to liver disease on January 16, 1997. At least now he wouldn't be indicted for aiding and abetting murder.

Later, Lange shared the good news with his former partner Bob Souza, immersed in his South Orange County life style. Souza happened to be in La Jolla, his favorite beach city, scouting out properties when he got the call from Lange. Lange was elated, and the two detectives reveled in the news that Nash would be going back to prison. Souza said, "So Eddie is in handcuffs again. Couldn't happen to a sweeter guy."

Lange and Souza briefly discussed their old federal nemesis, Henry Hoskins. The two close friends and former partners agreed to get together in the near future.

Ed Nash was once again arrested on May 19, 2000, on the RICO indictment and booked into a federal lockup east of Los Angeles.

Note: As a somewhat humorous side note, a very well-placed and close friend of Lange's shared a story about Nash just after his arrest on the indictment. Apparently, Nash had initially been housed with a number of inebriated, foul-smelling and belligerent members of the Mongols motorcycle gang, who had just been rounded up, arrested, and also charged with several RICO counts in an unrelated matter.

As the story goes, Nash was wearing a protective face mask for medical reasons that the bikers took issue with. One thing led to another, and it wasn't long before the gang opened up on Nash, cursing him in a threatening manner, which had him screaming for help. It did take a few minutes for the deputies to respond. Lange imagined Ed hadn't been that shook up since Ron Launius shoved the barrel of his gun down his throat.

Not long after his arrest in 2000, Ed Nash made the $1.5 million bail that was set and was released pending trial. In January of 2001, however, he was picked up and tossed back into jail for violating the terms of his release. The terms had clearly stated that Nash surrender his passport, wear a monitoring device, and not telephone, write to, speak with, or in any other fashion attempt to communicate with any and all known criminal elements or their representatives.

Somehow realizing the Feds were tapping his home phone in Tarzana, Nash was overheard instructing associates to call him back on another phone line that was not tapped to discuss whatever they wanted to discuss. Additionally, he was caught on two occasions associating with a lawyer acquaintance who was also a witness in his RICO case. Nash's flaunting of his terms of release and his unbridled arrogance would once again cost him his freedom.

———◆———

I n the spring of 2001, US Attorney Terri Law was approached by *New Times LA* reporter Susan Goldsmith, who was following up on the entire Nash saga for a major news story. Law had been looking into various business relationships among the ex-federal agent Henry Hoskins, Nash, and Hal Glickman. The fact that the federal prosecutors had one of their own former agents in their crosshairs might have inspired the attorney to comment, "It's an ongoing investigation." Sometimes boiler plate was the only way to go for the Feds.

Note: Subsequently interviewed by the same New Times *reporter, Hal Glickman stated he "just happened to put up the money for Henry" when Hoskins wanted to start a private investigator business. Glickman said it was merely "one friend helping another." Of course Hoskins "just happened" to run his private investigative business out of Club Hollywood, which was owned by Ed Nash and managed by Hal Glickman.*

———◆———

S eptember 11, 2001, was, for many thousands of Americans, the single worst day of their entire lives. For Ed Nash, the day before, September 10, 2001, was also momentous, but in a different way. On that day he appeared in a federal courthouse in downtown Los Angeles following several months of incarceration. It was eight days before he was to begin his latest federal trial.

Nash had been joined by yet another new attorney, Donald Re. Nash pled guilty to all counts as outlined in the federal RICO indictment handed up in June of 1999 to US District Court Judge Carlos R. Moreno. There would be no trial.

After the plea, Nash attorney Re gave an impromptu news conference regarding his client's admissions. At the time there was still significant interest, and the news folks were gearing up for the trial. Under the heading "What did he just say?" Re stated that Nash had "sent some people to get his property back. That's it." Yet Nash had just pled guilty to conspiracy to commit the Wonderland murders, aiding and abetting the murders, and bribing one of the jurors in his murder trial. The biggest surprise of all was the fact that Donald Re could say all these things with a straight face.

The Feds had once again successfully played *Let's Make a Deal* with Nash's people. He was eventually sentenced to thirty-seven months of confinement. This would not be what most folks in the know called hard time. Nash would get one year off his sentence as time served and was ordered to pay a $250,000 fine. After a certain amount of pleading by Nash's lawyers, there was probably also consideration for a purported myriad of medical maladies attributed to Nash. (The now-familiar and "serious" nasal condition was also back in play.) He would not serve anything near his thirty-seven-month sentence.

On the evening following Nash's plea, Lange was contacted at home by *Los Angeles Times* writer Josh Meyer seeking Lange's opinion on the day's court proceedings and plea. He wanted the story for the morning paper…on Tuesday, September 11, 2001.

In the article Meyer, who had also been present at Donald Re's impromptu press gaggle the morning before, quoted him as stating, "The record should be clear that the defendant is not admitting, and in fact denies, involvement in committing those murders." It was a final half-hearted attempt to save what little legitimate reputation Ed Nash had left.

Note: It was always amusing to listen to a murder suspect plead guilty to a horrendous crime and then have his attorney deny he had anything to do with it later.

When Meyer asked for Lange's opinion, looking at the plea from a strictly pragmatic point of view, Lange stated, "There were a lot of negatives for the prosecutors going into this. So I believe it's a righteous plea. How much more do they want to be perceived as beating up on an old man? So it works out well for all of them." Thinking back, Lange believed he probably should have added, "Except for Lady Justice."

Souza and McClain were never contacted by the Feds or the news media. Both had kept a low profile throughout. After retiring, knowing that Lange had a solid handle on the Wonderland case, Souza had asked Lange to keep him out of the mix as he had had his fill of everything. Lange respected his wishes and never mentioned Souza's name to anyone involved in the affair again.

The *LA Times* headline for the article in the September 11, 2001, morning edition more or less put a ribbon and bow on the entire Wonderland affair: "Surprise Plea Ends Lurid Case." However, headlines the following morning, September 12, 2001, in the *Los Angeles Times* as well as newspapers around the world, were a bit more ominous—"America Attacked!"

Postscript

The writers of this book felt as though they could have gone on for another sixty or seventy pages, explaining to the reader all about the many other characters they encountered while investigating the Wonderland murders… but why? To be honest and hopefully not too judgmental, most were simply ne'er-do-wells looking for a shot at life at someone else's expense. There's no other way to put it. It would be a colossal waste of time for the reader and the writers as well. There are always many wannabes, people looking for exposure for one reason or another, and a whole host of folks who are fascinated with high-profile "cop stuff." The Laurel Canyon murder investigation was no different. Their relevance to this case was either negligible or nonexistent.

The months and years turned to decades, and suddenly it was 2017. There had been incredible changes, and advanced technologies had revolutionized police work. This certainly included the incredible DNA revolution in science, greatly improved computer capabilities, and mind-blowing communications advances, to name just a few. In a way this was very good news; in another way it was not. This bears repeating: a lack of communication is the bane of all police work.

It seems most people no longer talk…they text. People no longer write… they e-mail. People look to small hand-held electronic devices to dictate their daily lives through something called the Internet. People no longer sit down and read books…they listen to someone else read audio-books to them. Personal contact seems to be a thing of the past, and in most segments of society, this means that assumptions will be made, and that is not necessarily a good thing.

This does not bode well for police work as a whole, a profession that to a large extent depends on instinct and one's ability to relate to others. Unfortunately for law enforcement today, police work is bent more on attempting to solve the sociological ills of the community than it is on solving crimes and putting bad guys where they belong—in the can. Police agencies cannot have it both ways with a feather duster in one hand and a gun in the other.

———

Aside from various business interests in a few Westside eating establishments and an investment here and there, Ed Nash had more or less slipped off law enforcement's radar. Gone were the days of brutal killing, dope peddling, intimidation tactics, search warrants, informants, narcotics rip-offs, conspiracies, and tantalizing headlines, at least as far as Adel Nasrallah was concerned. Was it age, health concerns, or fear of being caged up in prison for the rest of his life that had mellowed Ed Nash? No one knew. Perhaps he didn't know either.

By 2003 Nash was a free man, his incarceration on the RICO charges complete, although this didn't mean he had served his full thirty-seven-months. Once again, it was something about a nasal malady that just couldn't be treated while he was serving time at Club Fed. The cops thought they had a pretty good understanding of the reasoning behind the soft sentencing on his plea bargain. In order to settle things for good, the Feds probably could not have gotten anything better. The plea certainly saved money, time, and effort. And, of course, the Feds would have also had to figure on the possibility of hanky-panky with a jury of Ed Nash's so-called peers. Regardless, he had taken up residence in a condominium on Etiwanda Avenue in the Tarzana area of the San Fernando Valley.

Nash was purportedly living with a woman described as his common-law wife. Her name was Estee and she was many years younger than he. Although not legally married, she had apparently taken his last name as her own. That would be Nash, not Nasrallah. The rumors were that Ed was in poor health, but no one was talking.

———

Meanwhile, Scott Thorson continued his journey into oblivion. In 1982, he had sued his former show biz lover, Liberace, for palimony, to the tune of $113 million! In 1986, he settled for $95,000. That would appear to be a bit of a letdown and a big disappointment for Scott. In spite of his somewhat effeminate life style, Liberace was no push over. Thorson had been kicked right back out into the street he had crawled in from.

In November of 1991, Thorson found himself in Jacksonville, Florida. He was in a hotel room in the company of one Melvin Jerome Owen. The two men were allegedly smoking crack cocaine when, for reasons unknown, things went sideways. Scott was shot in the chest three times by Mr. Owen. He was rushed to a local hospital where he underwent emergency surgery and actually survived, recovering fully. The cops handling the case seemed to allude to what could be described as a "muddled motive" for the shooting…this writer's words, not theirs.

By 2012, Thorson had made his way out west once again. His struggles with addiction continued, if they were even really "struggles" in any sense of the word. That same year, Scott was diagnosed with hepatitis C, a deadly viral infection of the liver, and later was found to have cancer. In spite of all this, he still managed to stay on the wrong side of the law.

In February of 2013, Thorson was busted once again in Reno, Nevada. The charges included burglary with the use of a credit card without the owner's consent. He later received a suspended sentence and five years' probation. It took him little time to violate the terms of that probation. Perhaps he had forgotten that he was in Nevada, not California.

On January 23, 2014, Scott Thorson's probation was revoked, and he was summarily sentenced to eight to twenty years in a Nevada prison cell. He was ensconced at the Northern Nevada Correctional Facility, reportedly under the name Jess Marlow

Note: Over the past several years Thorson had used the alias Jess Marlow for reasons unknown. For many years there was a well-known Los Angeles news anchor at NBC News by the name of Jess Marlow. He was well liked and highly respected in his profession and private life. He was also greatly dismayed when he heard that Scott had begun to use his name. He made it known that he was considering legal action against Thorson. That didn't affect Scott in the least. The real Jess Marlow died in 2014.

In December of 2017, Tom Lange spoke with former LAPD Robbery/ Homicide Division detective Rick Jackson. Jackson had been the first LA detective to arrive at the Wonderland crime scene in 1981. He was also the investigator on a robbery case in Los Angeles where Thorson had been convicted. Earlier in 2017 he was subpoenaed to testify at a sentence reduction hearing for Thorson in Reno, Nevada. Jackson stated that at the time Thorson appeared healthy, clean, sober, and alert. Thorson had also been lauded for his work with other inmates during his incarceration, but still remained in prison as 2017 came to a close.

The cops' old reporter pal Adam Dawson left the news business and became a licensed private investigator in California. He also became a good friend to Lange and Souza. Upon Lange's retirement in 1996, he went to work with Dawson as a licensed private investigator. Lange and Souza had received their private investigator's licenses sometime back in 1979 with the intention of working in the private sector upon retirement.

As a private investigator, there was some criminal defense work Lange was not comfortable doing, so his role in defense work was usually limited to consulting on homicide cases. After a relatively short period with Dawson, Lange went to work as a fraud investigator for a major insurance company. He also continued consulting and became involved with the California Department of Justice and law enforcement training seminars.

As for Adam Dawson, he was a highly sought-after and successful private investigator. He certainly didn't have to advertise. It was word of mouth only. Tom Lange had been working around cops, lawyers, and private eyes for nearly fifty years. In terms of ability and common sense, Dawson ranked at the very top of the list of honest and competent private investigators.

J erry Van Hoorelbeke, also known as Jerry Van and convicted on two counts of assault with a deadly weapon on a peace officer in June of 1979, was not content sitting out his time in jail keeping his mouth shut. He would talk about anything to anyone who would listen. He wrote page after page about people he knew and had dealings with, as well as people he thought he had known and had dealings with…like Jimmy Hoffa.

On June 3, 1985, *Los Angeles Times* reporter Bill Farr wrote that Jerry Van Hoorelbeke had his sights set on Attorney James Henderson, the head of the Los Angeles US Organized Crime Strike Force, and an assistant by the name of Richard Crane. His claims of corruption included his incredibly weak argument that Henderson had been arranging favorable treatment for various organized crime figures, including one Ed Nash.

This, of course, ignited an inquiry by the US Department of Justice. After wasting a considerable amount of time and effort, they released their finding: unfounded. That means that there was not even a hint of malfeasance.

Was Hoorelbeke perhaps miffed that Henderson hadn't done more for him during his life as a federal snitch? It seemed plausible. This scenario was also beginning to sound suspiciously familiar to the detectives. Henderson eventually retired from government service and enjoyed a successful career as a private attorney in the Los Angeles area.

Jerry Van didn't retire but instead published a book through Amazon that was released in January of 2006. The book aligned him with a bunch of questionable characters associated with organized crime and attacked anyone who didn't have nice things to say about him.

Van Hoorelbeke's book, *Underworld Secrets*, didn't quite make the *New York Times* best seller list. In fact, it made no lists of any consequence at all. It was incredibly long, boring, and self-serving. Amazon released only two reviews of the book. They both aptly pointed out the author's self-aggrandizement in the book and suggested that any potential reader should not waste his or her money or time.

After his release from prison, Jerry Van ventured north and spent time in the Los Angeles area, settling for a while in the San Fernando Valley. In 2006 he ended up in Las Vegas where he still remains to this day. What he is currently doing in Vegas is anyone's guess.

W ith very few exceptions, most of the Wonderland players did not end up in a happy place. The star witness, David Lind, appeared to have cleaned up his act, at least temporarily, following his many appearances in court on behalf of the prosecution in the Nash case. He had proved to be a nightmare for the defense when testifying in hearings and at the various trials.

Patti Jo Fairbanks from the LA District Attorney's Office, once again displaying her mastery as a witness coordinator and confidant, had kept close tabs on Lind as well as many others. It appeared David had settled down after spending the majority of his life behind bars. But it did not last. It all came to an end with a heroin overdose on November 16, 1995. David Lind was buried at Santa Rosa Memorial Park in Santa Rosa, California.

T racy Ray McCourt apparently wore out his welcome in the state of California and ended up for a time in Kentucky, where he was reported to have actually picked up a few college credits at a state institution. He then purportedly headed to Colorado in the late 1990s. However, he was back in California around the time that his mother passed away in 2001. Throughout the Wonderland investigation, Tracy had only two known residences in Los Angeles: his mother's home in North Hollywood and the Los Angeles County jail.

McCourt eventually returned to Colorado, and it took little time before he was once again experiencing his life in prison. That time, it was for assault with a deadly weapon and distribution of a controlled substance. After serving his time, he was released and apparently became involved in the legitimate side of a business in telephonic communications of some sort. Unfortunately for

Tracy, that was short lived. He died on October 18, 2006, apparently from the ravages of hepatitis C. He was buried in Denver, Colorado.

———

Paul Kelly, better known as the Red Herring (as opposed to the defense's Red Baron of the Laurel Canyon murder case), died of unknown causes several years after the trial. It was easy for some, including the cops, to dismiss him as a suspect in the killings. However, once the prosecution alluded to the possibility of his participation in the murders during the trial, it was all Nash's attorneys needed. To be fair, the prosecutors had been forced into a corner and really left with no good option regarding Kelly as the defense's foil.

While Nash's defense lawyers impressed the twelve jurors with Kelly as a killer, they actually had gotten away with leaving out one important factor: evidence of his guilt. Supposition and innuendo were never meant to be evidence. There never really was any, but apparently, it never mattered anyway.

According to Ed Nash's lawyers, Fat Howard Cook had colluded with Paul Kelly and sent him and others to the Wonderland home to commit the murders. Kelly was supposedly a willing participant. The defense reasoned that the Wonderland bunch owed money to Cook for services rendered that was long overdue. Clearly, no evidence was ever offered up to show this either; besides, if money was owed to Cook, he certainly would never get it back from dead people. And who were the others who went to Wonderland with Kelly and beat on people with pipes? No one ever said; no one ever asked; no one ever cared. Perhaps, no one ever existed.

After the Wonderland trials ended, Howard Cook seemed to fade into obscurity. It was perhaps a very good thing for him—something about sticking around too long after the party's over. The cops wondered if he ever recovered his fur coats.

———

After the death of Greg Diles in early 1997, his younger brother Sam still lived with his mother in South LA and managed to stay out of jail. Sam had appeared to be a viable suspect in the killings early on in the investigation, due in large part to his relationship with Greg, not to mention a violent criminal background of robbery and assault. The old familiar problem of no evidence precluded a criminal filing.

Sam Diles had picked up an occasional security gig at a couple of Nash's places subsequent to the murders. On May 9, 1983, while working as a security guard at the Kit Kat Club on Santa Monica Boulevard, Diles approached a patron who had apparently had too much to drink. He told him to leave the club or be thrown out. When the guy balked, Sam answered by cracking him upside the head with the barrel of a six-inch chrome revolver. He then forced the customer out the front door and onto the sidewalk, where he again struck him in the head with the revolver. As the now-victim/patron raised his arms over his head, attempting to defend himself, Sam shot him in the right wrist. The incident became another line or two on the log of a very long rap sheet for Sam.

In 2002, Sam Diles joined his brother Greg in an urn on the mantel above the fireplace in his mother's home on Crenshaw Boulevard in South Los Angeles.

———

In October of 2003, the motion picture *Wonderland* was released. John Holmes's former wife Sharon and his former girlfriend Dawn Schiller had gotten together and collaborated with Hollywood to deliver their stories about their respective lives with John. The two women had remained friends throughout the years, irrespective of their relationships with the King of Porn. Instead of *Wonderland*, the movie could have been aptly titled *Misery Loves Company* or even *Survival of the Fittest*.

There was really no talk of an Oscar after the movie review website *Rotten Tomatoes* opined, "A sordid and pointless movie with some good performances." Things got no better for the producers of the picture when the late and highly respected movie critic Roger Ebert harpooned them with "True crime procedurals can have a certain fascination, but not when they're jumbled glimpses of what might or might not have happened involving a lot of empty people whose main claim to fame is that they're dead." These less-than-stellar reviews ended with what Stephen Hunter of the *Washington Post* had in mind: "Overblown, overheated, over-directed, overacted, overlong, and over here, in the local bijoux." He might have added, "also, *not* overly factual."

———•———

Meanwhile, Lange's old partner Bob Souza worked himself into that second career in Hollywood. As a member of the Writers Guild, he co-wrote the tongue-in-cheek cop flick *Hollywood Homicide*, which starred Harrison Ford and Josh Hartnett. The script was based on Bob's occupation as a homicide cop and part-time real estate broker. As mentioned earlier, Souza went on to be a script consultant and technical adviser for the entire run of the hit television series *Cold Case*. Not one to leave his old partner behind, he took Lange on as a backup technical adviser when needed. Souza also stayed busy after affiliating himself with a security consulting firm in Los Angeles, specializing in high-profile clients. After nearly fifty years of cop stuff, the security business and Hollywood nonsense, Bob and his wife packed it in for the Great Northwest to join his younger son Ron and his family. The partners have remained in constant communication over the years, and it was that very close relationship that led to the writing of *Malice in Wonderland*.

———•———

Frank Tomlinson retired with twenty years of service and went on to become a counselor for young people, working through his church. He was, no doubt, very good at that particular endeavor. He clearly demonstrated those types of communication skills throughout his police career. Frank also became a writer, involving his literary talents with mostly law enforcement–type stories, some of which he had been personally involved with. He still resides in California, north of Los Angeles.

———•———

Robbery/Homicide detective John Helvin lost his battle with cancer, and his partner, Jack Holder, suffered a fatal heart attack. Both men were solid, honorable, and just trying to do their jobs, irrespective of their personal feelings. They joined Lieutenant Ron Lewis, Lieutenant Jeff Rogers (SWAT), Captain Bill Cobb, Captain Jim Docherty, and Detectives John St. John, Glenn Souza, and Al Gastaldo in death.

———•———

As previously related Enoch "Mac" McClain was promoted to Detective III and closed out a very productive police career as a supervisor in the Organized Crime Intelligence Division. The LAPD had lost one of their very finest.

Mac retired to a rural community well east of Los Angeles and took up some ranching on a small scale with a few horses, chickens, and some crops (including grapes for his wine-bottling interests) and also maintained a good-size koi fish pond. He actually became the president of the Southern California Koi Fish Society.

However, what Mac was most proud of was his service as a US Marine. He served six years of active duty, attaining the rank of sergeant. His service included one year in an infantry unit in Vietnam. While in country, he distinguished himself in combat. As an element of the Third Marine Division, his unit, and the units of Tom Lange and Hollywood homicide detective John Miller, were awarded the Presidential Unit Citation ".... for extraordinary heroism and outstanding performance of duty in action."

Mac McClain never left the Marine Corps. While it is true that there were no ex-Marines, only former Marines, Mac took this a bit further. He became the president of the Semper Fi 1 Honor Burial Detail located at the Riverside National Cemetery in Riverside, California. His unit included some eighty retired and former US Marines who conducted full military honors for veterans of all branches of the service at the cemetery. The unit had received national honors from the US military at Arlington National Cemetery outside of Washington, DC, and in nearly twenty years of service, Mac's unit had conducted thousands of US military veterans' funerals. He remains extended family with Lange, and the two stay in close touch.

Dorothy "Dottie" Glickman died much too young in 1999. She supposedly lost her battle with addiction, but details were sketchy. Apparently, questionable choices in her life had led to destructive results and an early demise.

Henry Lee Hoskins apparently had his ups and downs with Hal Glickman and Club Hollywood. After some running around between Vegas and LA and with his private investigator business more or less on the rocks, Hoskins settled in Gardena, a small gambling mecca a few miles southeast of downtown Los Angeles. It was here that he set up a bail bond business à la Hal Glickman, his longtime friend and confidant.

In the spring of 2001, Hoskins was interviewed by *New Times LA* reporter Susan Goldsmith in his Gardena office about the ongoing federal investigation of Ed Nash. When asked about any business relationship with Hal Glickman, he retorted in a huff, "Basically, it's no one's business."

When pressed by the same reporter about any favors bestowed on him by Nash, Hoskins became somewhat agitated and replied, "I never received anything…As far as any relationship with Ed, basically none. I didn't work for the government then, and I don't think I did anything inappropriate." Of some interest here was Hoskins referring to "Ed," a man he supposedly investigated for numerous RICO violations including murder over the years, and then replying about possible "favors bestowed" with "I didn't work for the government then."

Hoskins also got involved in local politics. He was appointed to the Gardena Valley Chamber of Commerce and soon became its president after seeing to it that one of the board members was removed following an investigation of the embezzlement of $35,000. The woman involved was arrested and eventually convicted of the crime.

By 2006, Hoskins had befriended one Sonia Rios Risken of Lomita, California. It seemed Ms. Risken had been accused of having her first husband, Dennis Risken, murdered in the Philippine Islands in 1987. This charge was somewhat exacerbated in 2007 when she was also accused of having her second husband, Larry, murdered in the Philippines. Both had been shot under similar and mysterious circumstances. Perhaps that is why the local press dubbed Ms. Risken the Lomita Black Widow.

The case became a minor sensation in the media, and it was featured on the CBS television crime show *48 Hours*. In the broadcast, Hoskins defended Risken and was later rumored to have had some type of unspecified "relationship" with her. In 2007 Sonia Risken, age sixty, was shot and killed by her nephew in her Lomita home.

Note: Henry made himself scarce.

The nephew and an accomplice were later arrested and convicted of her murder in 2011.

In late July of 2009, Henry Hoskins was in his small apartment above his bail bond business on Western Avenue in Gardena with his twenty-two-year-old girlfriend. Very late that evening, the girlfriend was in another room when she heard what sounded to her like a gunshot. She rushed into the bedroom only to find Henry dead on the floor from a bullet wound to the head.

A panicked call to 911 brought an ambulance and the local cops. The Gardena police investigated the matter as a murder; however, the mode of death was eventually determined to be suicide, per the Los Angeles County Coroner's Office.

Linda Call, a real estate broker and friend of Hoskins who first met him when the two served together on the Gardena Valley Chamber of Commerce, didn't buy into the coroner's finding. "I'm not accepting it. I just can't. How can they label that so quickly? I'm hoping it's just a ploy to draw out the killer. I just can't believe it." Henry Hoskins was seventy years old.

The detectives would later reminisce about Hoskins and wonder just what he was thinking as he placed the barrel of the gun to his head. Had his past finally caught up to him? Can a sociopath really experience guilt?

Harold "Hal" Glickman went on to manage a number of enterprises for himself as well as Ed Nash. Of course, the more interesting relationship was always with Henry Hoskins. In February of 2001, Glickman was also interviewed by the same news magazine that Hoskins had been. Regarding any personal relationship with Hoskins, Glickman stated, "[Hoskins] came to talk to me and said he wanted to be a private investigator, and I just happened to put up the money for Henry…He had no dealings with Nash."

That was followed by an additional interview some weeks later when Glickman apparently had a lapse in memory and stated, "Henry never worked for me. We were partners in business…I didn't put up no money for him. I helped him get work for his private investigation firm. I got him clients."

Apparently, it was a good day in February 2001 for the reporter to catch Glickman with his pants down around his ankles. When questioned as to the possibility that Judge Ricks had been bought off to reduce Nash's prison sentence, Hal stated that Nash did, in fact, have Ricks bought off with his help. "I got hold of people…Ricks was vulnerable at the time."

Incredibly, closing out this interview with the *New Times LA*, Glickman stated to the reporter, "You're not going to put all this in the newspaper, are you? I'll deny it." It's doubtful whether anyone would have known where to go with any of that. This all spoke for itself. Where is Hal Glickman today? No one asks, and apparently, no one cares.

———•———

Larry Martin Hershman, or, as the cops and the Wonderland bunch called him, Cherokee, finally put his legal problems in the Los Angeles area behind him. Throughout the murder investigation, he had been more of an intelligence source than a witness in the murder case. But for the good fortune of getting popped for auto theft in Kingman, Arizona, on June 30, 1981, he most certainly would have been victim number six at Wonderland.

Later, Lange and Souza also found out Cherokee may well have been responsible for talking Ron Launius out of killing the housekeeper during the Alligator Arnie robbery in the San Fernando Valley, which had been orchestrated by Tracy McCourt.

With nothing breaking for Hershman in LA, he headed north to his old haunts in the Sacramento area, where he ended up taking a job as a long-haul truck driver. Apparently, he liked the work because he ended up making a career out of it. He also raised a fair-size family and began what most people would consider a normal life.

In 2016 Cherokee was diagnosed with cancer and succumbed to the disease in October of that year at age seventy-one. He had left his checkered past behind years ago and now a large family as well. He was laid to rest in Fair Oaks, California. Souza and Lange sometimes wondered if he ever got his buckskins back.

———•———

In early 2017 Tom Lange was contacted by a producer from NBC Universal Los Angeles. He told Lange that the network would begin shooting a new true crime series to debut on the Oxygen Network in January of 2018. *Mysteries and Scandals* would be a thirteen-part series with hopes of adding on more cases later. It would feature high-profile murder cases, one of which would be the Laurel Canyon murders. It would be the first segment of the crime series to be filmed. Would Lange be interested in giving an interview?

Lange got together with the production company a week later and sat for a three and half-hour interview. That didn't even seem to scratch the surface of everything that had transpired over the many years of the case. It was only going to be a one-hour show, which translated to about forty-four minutes of air time. There's much that will never get in, but the production company was pleased with what they got.

Lange was also told by the production people that Sharon Holmes had passed away some two years earlier. It is believed that she had suffered from dementia for an extended period of time.

A couple of weeks later, Lange was contacted by the same producer, who told him that one of the other guests to appear, Holmes's old girl-friend Dawn Schiller, wanted to e-mail Lange. She did so, and the two ended up communicating. Lange was heartened to hear that Dawn had completely turned her life around after leaving Holmes. She had for some time been mentoring young people at risk, using her own life experiences as the example.

She was also working with law enforcement to any extent she could in her quest to get to young folks before the law did. She didn't do these things from a soapbox to entertain herself. She actually went into juvenile hall in order to get to kids with personal problems. If there was ever anything positive to come out of the Wonderland murder maelstrom, this would be it.

In their attempts to put together the best documentary they could, the NBC folks wanted to contact Ed Nash to facilitate an interview with him. It had been years since Nash had paid any attention to the media, and vice versa. All they had was a phone number for Nash's former wife Jeanna. While they were successful in contacting Ms. Nash, she was not pleased to speak with them. The conversation was brief but constructive. Ed Nash was dead.

According to Jeanna, Nash passed away on August 9, 2014, at his home in the San Fernando Valley from natural causes, also known as old age. The family did not want the entire Wonderland affair to be relived through the media, so they apparently went through somewhat complicated and no doubt expensive measures to conceal the death.

What may have facilitated the family's plan and added to their quest for privacy was the fact that if a person had been under the care of a doctor consistently and a particular physician had signed off on the death certificate, the county coroner would not even be consulted, as long as the death was considered natural. And, of course, there was always the possibility that the death certificate had been "misfiled" or somehow "misplaced" for a period of time.

Adel Nasrallah was interred at the Holy Cross Cemetery in Culver City, California. Block number 23 in the Risen Christ Mausoleum reads as follows:

Adel Gharid Nasrallah
1929–2014
"Beloved Father
You Will Always Be In Our Hearts"

Ed Nash was gone, much like the entire Wonderland affair, blown away by the winds of apathy and time.

Acknowledgments

Any high-profile multiple murder investigation that encompasses some twenty-plus years of police work has got to incorporate literally hundreds of people. It is those men and women of law enforcement whom we truly thank for all their commitment, involvement, and assistance over the many years of attempting to bring the very worst of society to justice.

Although it would be impossible to name all these people, there must be an acknowledgment of the LAPD Robbery/Homicide Division and commanding officer Captain William O. Gartland (WOG) and the late Chief of Police Daryl F. Gates, Scientific Investigation Division, Organized Crime Intelligence Division, Administrative Vice Division, and Administrative Narcotics Division. Also, our gratitude goes out to the Los Angeles Police Protective League and its dedicated staff.

From Tom Lange: To my very special wife, Linda Lange, who has had to put up with my nonsense for all these many months of seclusion while writing about "another case," yet she's always been there.

For my daughter, Melissa, her husband Mike Gazzola (and his super marketing skills), and the kids, Ashton and Kailey, for their continued strong support.

For my other daughter, Megan, and her assistance on the book, her husband Nick Owens (LAPD) and his assistance, and their daughter Brooklyn for their longtime strong support.

In loving memory of my sister, Sharon Taylor, of Plantation, Florida.

To my sister, Gail Smith, of Jupiter, Florida, and her "kids" Dawn and Walter, for their great interest and support.

In addition to my sister Gail, my other New England/Canada traveling companions—our own Aussie "alien" Bruce Crighton, as well as "Rocket" Stan and Lutie Smith of Atlanta, Georgia. Also joining our little group were former Nassau County, New York, "old-school" homicide cops and Vietnam veterans Joe Carbone and wife Denise as well as Walt Swenson and his wife Kathy. Thank you all for your interest and support.

To my good friend of over fifty years and Vietnam Marine vet John Miller, one of the finest LAPD homicide cops who ever hit the streets. Also, to his wonderful wife Kathi and daughter Eleni for their tremendous support

To another great friend of over fifty years, my former LAPD partner Dick Rudell and his wife, Linda. Dick, too, distinguished himself as one of the LAPD's finest for over thirty years.

To another of the old Hollywood Division bunch, Paul Barron, otherwise known as the LAPD's public relations ambassador of the 60s and 70s.

To former classmate, boss, and good friend Lieutenant John Rogers and his wife Barb for their support and John's leadership at Homicide Special.

To former Homicide Special detectives Leroy Orozco and Paul Tippin for their assistance throughout much of this case and others.

To former Major Crimes homicide cop Mike Thies, who helps hold the retired LAPD family together with *The Rotator,* and exceptional former SID criminalist Peggy (Fiderio) Thies, both for their longtime friendship and support.

To my former "roommate" Norm (former LAPD detective) and wife Sandy Jackson, longtime close friends and supporters.

To friends Crissie and Chuck Lovold (LAPD).

To more of the "old-timers" at RHD: Jerry "Frog" LeFrois, Bud and Chris Arce, Jerry and Norma Jean Stephens, Norm and Eileen Roberge, Mike Watson, Jack Giroud, Frank and Paula Garcia, Jimmy "Greydog" Grayson, Joe Getherall, Denis Cremins, Larry DeLosh, Brad McGrath, Danny Lang, John and Gloria Martin, Fred Miller, Bud Watts, Otis Marlow, Ted Ball, Mike Berchem, Ron Ito, J.R. Kwock, Buck Henry, Al Moen, Joe Najera, Jim and Suzie Barry, Hank Petroski, Bob Grogan, Rich Aldahl, Brian Carr, Jimmy Harper, Vic Pietrantoni, Rick Jackson, Dennis Kilcoyne, Paula Donahey, Nancy Claiborne and all of RHD.

To friends Manny and Deb Dickerson, LAPD Air Support Division chopper pilots.

To the memory of Phil Vannatter, my old homicide partner.

To the memory of good friend, RHD detective and patriot Ralph Waddy. *Semper Fi.*

To friend and well-known character actor Ron Masak (*Murder, She Wrote!*) and his wife, Kay, for their longtime support of law enforcement.

To good friend Tim Lewis, former California Highway Patrol and president of LCI Services. Thanks for all your considerable support over the years and for allowing me to be a part of your outstanding law enforcement seminars.

To Clay Young (Podcast225.com) of Baton Rouge, Louisiana, for his interest in and support of this book and other projects, as well as his unwavering support of law enforcement.

For Ed Nicklaus and his wife, Lori, of Sterling, Illinois. Thanks for always being there for over fifty years, from boot camp to Pendleton, to the Rock, to Vietnam, to all the reunions, and way beyond.

Also, for Charlie Lerma and his wife, Irma, of Burnet, Texas. Another Nam brother who, although he lived far away, was always close.

To the rest of the First Platoon who are still kicking around…Charlie Duncan, Kenny Majors, Paul Jones, and Neil McCaffrey.

To the memory of our most recently departed 1/9 brothers Danny Enriquez of Midland, Texas, and Ray Saffell of Des Moines, Iowa. *Semper Fidelis!*

To former Alameda County Deputy District Attorney Rock Harmon, my friend and world-renowned DNA expert with no mush in his mouth.

To the memory of former San Diego County Deputy District Attorney and judge, George "Woody" Clarke.

To Rod Englert, friend and universally recognized crime scene expert and author of *Blood Secrets*, for your longtime support.

To the Los Angeles County District Attorney's Office and former DDA, Judge Ron Coen, former DDA, Judge Carol Najera, former DDA Dale Davidson and the late former DDA Sterling "Ernie" Norris. A special acknowledgment to Patti Jo Fairbanks of rural Indiana, who kept it all together for the rest of us.

To the Los Angeles County Sheriff's Office and current Sheriff Jim McDonald, as well as the Los Angeles County Coroner's Office and former longtime friend to cops everywhere, Scott Carrier. To all the field agents at the Federal Bureau of Investigation who rendered assistance on this and so many other cases as well as the US Department of Justice, in particular the DOJ's Organized Crime Strike Force.

To Los Angeles Sheriff's homicide legend Lieutenant Gil Carillo, a friend and incredible law enforcement lecturer.

To Dan E. Moldea of Washington, DC, a good friend and one of the finest true-crime authors of this generation. Thanks for your support and all the advice, especially "Just write!"

To authors Gus Russo of Baltimore, Maryland, and Mark Olshaker of Washington, DC, two more talented true-crime writers. Thanks for your interest and support.

To friend and former LAPD officer Jim Bultema, insightful, dedicated and historical author of the Los Angeles Police Department and his May, 2018 release of *Unsolved: Cold-Case Homicides of Law Enforcement Officers*.

To longtime friends Jim and Ellie Kokotos of Simi Valley, California, for their continued longtime support.

To Ken Richardson of Auckland, New Zealand, former private secretary to five of New Zealand's prime ministers, for his longtime support and interest.

To Ginger and Don Henthorne of Simi Valley, California, for their friendship and longtime strong support of law enforcement.

To Bob Martinez of Simi Valley, friend and former Marine and Marine Corps League bugler for all things patriotic.

To the memory of Ann Gartland (WOG's wife) for her steadfast support of the LAPD and law enforcement everywhere.

For all the "boys" down at the old Oakridge gym for the many years of "sea stories" and support: Dennis Purcell and Ray Lloyd (former Inglewood Police sergeants); Mike Purcell (Ventura County Sheriffs crime lab); Jay Broyles (former Beverly Hills Police); Randy Fredrickson and Jesse Castillo (former LAPD); Dave Ross (Detective/Sergeant, LAPD Homicide and USMC); Sergeants Terry Ruppel and Brian Lafferty (LAPD); "The Boss" Ines Mossbacher and husband John (LAPD); Dr. Felix Negron (resident philosopher); Denis Flood (writer and former USMC, USN and DOD); Dave Tankenson (former Captain, Culver City Police); John Garner (former Ventura County Sheriffs); Lieutenant Ryan Rabbett, Brandon Lyman

(LAPD) and wife Vicki Lyman; Greg Kapp (Santa Monica Police); Robert Harrington (resident Democrat); Steve Doukas, Bob Nate (ninety-three year old US Navy veteran severely injured when his ship was struck and went down during the Battle of Okinawa in the spring of 1945); Tom Pridipun and wife Wanapau, Dave Molina, Al Horwitz, Perry Himber, Joe Gondrez, Jim Lowry (former LAPD) and everyone else at the gym who make working out such a pleasure for old folks!

To Mac and Jill McClain and their daughters, Kelly and Sabrina, great friends for life and forever.

To Adam Dawson, for decades of friendship and support.

Thanks to globe-hopping longtime great friends Terry and Ginger Smith of, among other places, Del Mar, California, and, of course, for introducing me to my wife so long ago.

To Teresa Pratt for a nothing less than incredible graphic cover design for our book.

———

From Robert Souza: To my devoted wife of fifty-three years, Sharon Souza, my best critic who has endured a lifetime of my independent pursuits and absences, and for her unwavering support throughout.

To my incredible sons, Sean and Ronald Souza, for being the solid, responsible citizens and family men I dreamed they would be and for all their help and support over the years.

To my daughters-in-law, Debbie and Michelle Souza, for their love, support, and devotion to their families.

To my six dynamic grandchildren, Danielle, Leeann, Jordan, Chadler, Perri, and Aaron for their love, encouragement, and incentive for me to write.

To my older brother Glenn (rest his soul) for his inspiration and guidance that kept me out of the California Youth Authority as a rowdy teenager and for his mentoring me as a young police officer, helping me shape my career.

To my loving big sister Joan Clark, for always being there for me. For pushing me to excel in high school English and to take four years of typing that has paid off many times over.

To my loving sister-in-law Teri Lee Bradley and brother-in-law Michael Johnson, for their interest in and unwavering support for my projects over the years.

To my Colorado cousin, Marny Pearson, although my elder, she remains my wittiest fan and critic.

To a few of my LAPD brothers, former partners, and lifelong friends: Gerald (Frog) LeFrois, Bob Grogan, Rich Aldahl, Buck Pearse, Ed Peters, Ken Staggs, Ron Code, Dan Jones, Jerry Darr, Jim Halloran, Jimmy "Greydog" Grayson, Jack Giroud, Tim Tyree, Ed Hoffman Mike Hillman and Jack Jones.

In memoriam: Tom Thompson, Rich Fox, Al Gastaldo, Russ Kuster, Rich Rockhold, John Calderwood, Chet Turner, Ed Elliott, Ralph Waddy, and Vinnie Barrett.

To my dear friends and poker pals for their love and encouragement: Judy Juranek and Vernon Juranek (rest his soul), Jack and Pat Pierini, Patty Blaine and Jerry Blaine (rest his soul), and Roger Juranek.

To Rick and Teresa Pratt for over fifty years of friendship, and Teresa's beautiful contribution to this book and her awesome graphic cover design.

To my dear friends Kathy and Andy Shaker for their super hospitality and lifelong friendship.

To a few showbiz folks who were instrumental in my desire to write:

To the cast and crew of the *Cold Case* television series where I spent seven years of my life with some of the most talented people in the business. John Finn, a fine actor, loyal friend and co-conspirator; the other fine thespians, Kathryn Morris, Danny Pino, Thom Barry, Jeremy Ratchford and Tracie Thoms; good friends Anthony D'Esposito, best A.D. in the business and Jimmy Romano, highly regarded stunt coordinator.

William Shatner for encouraging me to write and securing my first professional writing assignment qualifying me for membership in the Writers Guild of America West.

David Charnay (rest in peace) for believing in me early on and providing the facility and funds to further my creative projects.

Ron Shelton for giving me the opportunity to write screenplays and for giving me a full hands-on film-school education.

To Lou Pitt for his investment of time and management and believing in my creative projects.

To Bernie Pollack, a true friend and wardrobe extraordinaire and to his son Chris for all the good times and hosted poker games.

In loving memory of my nephew Scott Clark, a good man taken from us too soon.

In loving memory of Shelly Juranek Smith, a dear friend taken from us too soon.

To Johanna Payne, my friend and favorite Idaho crime story fan.

To Ed Sperry, my friend and fellow Idaho broker. Thank you for your service.

About the Authors

Tom Lange joined the Los Angeles Police Department in 1967 after serving as a (sergeant) squad leader in Vietnam with the US Marines. In nearly twenty-nine years with the LAPD, including over twenty-one years as a homicide detective, he received more than sixty commendations from various law enforcement agencies. He qualified in both state and federal court as an expert in homicide investigation and blood-spatter examination. He has lectured and been involved in numerous police training seminars in the United States and Canada. He has appeared on several television and radio broadcasts and has been involved in numerous police-related documentaries. He has also been a technical adviser on a number of television productions. He was involved in more than 250 homicide investigations during his police career and assisted in many more as a licensed private investigator. He retired from the LAPD in 1996 and is the coauthor of *Evidence Dismissed: The Inside Story of the Police Investigation of O. J. Simpson.*

    Robert Souza joined the Los Angeles Police Department in 1966 after serving a three-year enlistment in the US Army. His military assignments included Seoul, South Korea; Fort Carson, Colorado; and Fort Devens, Massachusetts as a supply sergeant. In twenty-two years with the LAPD, he worked all front-line specialized units, including seventeen years of homicide investigation involving hundreds of cases. He attended night college classes and earned a bachelor's degree in English. He received several commendations for exemplary police work, including the distinguished Meritorious Service Award for his contributions to serial killer investigations. He qualified as an expert in homicide investigation and lectured to various police agencies. As a private investigator, he handled the gamut of cases including homicide, robbery, cargo theft, mortgage fraud, and embezzlement. He retired from the LAPD in 1988 and pursued his interests in real estate development and filmmaking. He worked on two feature films and co-wrote *Hollywood Homicide* starring Harrison Ford. He was also script consultant and technical adviser for seven seasons on *Cold Case*, a hit television series.

Tom Lange

Robert Souza

Made in the USA
Middletown, DE
24 June 2020